The Access Principle

Digital Libraries and Electronic Publishing
William Y. Arms, series editor

Gateways to Knowledge: The Role of Academic Libraries in Teaching, Learning, and Research, edited by Lawrence Dowler, 1997

Civic Space/Cyberspace: The American Public Library in the Information Age, Redmond Kathleen Molz and Phyllis Dain, 1999

Digital Libraries, William Y. Arms, 1999

From Gutenberg to the Global Information Infrastructure: Access to Information in the Networked World, Christine L. Borgman, 2000

The Intellectual Foundation of Information, Elaine Svenonius, 2000

Digital Library Use: Social Practice in Design and Evaluation, edited by Ann Peterson Bishop, Nancy A. Van House, and Barbara P. Buttenfield, 2003

TREC: Experiment and Evaluation in Information Retrieval, edited by Ellen M. Voorhees and Donna K. Harman, 2005

The Access Principle: The Case for Open Access to Research and Scholarship, John Willinsky, 2005

The Access Principle

The Case for Open Access to Research and Scholarship

John Willinsky

The MIT Press
Cambridge, Massachusetts
London, England

MIT Press books may be purchased at special quantity discounts for business or sales promotional use. For information, please e-mail ⟨special_sales@mitpress.mit.edu⟩ or write to Special Sales Department, The MIT Press, 55 Hayward Street, Cambridge, MA 02142.

This book was set in Sabon on 3B2 by Asco Typesetters, Hong Kong, and printed and bound in the United States of America.

Library of Congress Cataloging-in-Publication Data

Willinsky, John, 1950–
The access principle : the case for open access to research and scholarship / John Willinsky.
    p. cm. — (Digital libraries and electronic publishing)
Includes bibliographical references and index.
ISBN 0-262-23242-1 (hc: alk. paper)
1. Open access publishing. 2. Scholarly electronic publishing. 3. Science publishing. 4. Libraries and electronic publishing. 5. Communication in learning and scholarship. 6. Communication in science. I. Title. II. Series.
Z286.O63W55   2006
070.5'797—dc22   2005047471

10 9 8 7 6 5 4 3 2 1

To JMH and ARH

Contents

Introduction   ix

Acknowledgments   xvii

1   Opening   1

2   Access   13

3   Copyright   39

4   Associations   55

5   Economics   69

6   Cooperative   81

7   Development   93

8   Public   111

9   Politics   127

10 Rights   143

11 Reading   155

12 Indexing   173

13 History   189

Appendixes

A   Ten Flavors of Open Access   211

B   Scholarly Association Budgets   217

C   Journal Management Economies   221

D   An Open Access Cooperative   227

E   Indexing of the Serial Literature   233

F   Metadata for Journal Publishing   241

References   245

Index   271

Introduction

By the dawn of the twenty-first century, the tidy but modest library that looks out on the gardens at the Kenya Medical Research Institute (KEMRI) in Nairobi was able to subscribe to only five medical journals. As Nancy Kamau, the institute's librarian, explained to me, since KEMRI had opened in 1979, it had been forced to cut one journal title after another from its list of subscriptions, as prices kept jumping ahead of the budget allocation and the Kenyan currency fluctuated. The real shame of it, Kamau pointed out, was that the final five subscriptions, which they could barely afford, did not include the leading journals on the institute's principal research interest, tropical diseases. How could KEMRI properly support its current projects in biotechnology, leprosy, malaria, public health, and other areas with an inordinately small sample of the relevant literature? Funding for these projects, which came from collaborations with developed nations (ranging from the Wellcome Trust in the United Kingdom to the Walter Reed Army Institute of Research in the United States) went into salaries, support for students, and keeping the institute running. And although the institute's faculty found ways to get their hands on a specific article, whether by requesting a copy from a colleague they knew in the West or by picking it up when they had an opportunity to travel abroad, the leading medical research center in East Africa was itself operating more and more in a research literature vacuum.

Then in July 2001 came a turning point. As Kamau went on to explain, the World Health Organization managed to convince six of the leading corporate journal publishers to provide developing nations with open access to the electronic editions of their medical journals. This meant that the online contents of a sizable number of medical journals were suddenly available at no charge to the faculty and students at KEMRI and elsewhere. The program, known as HINARI (the Health InterNetwork Access to Research Initiative), had grown since then to encompass over 2,000 journals in the health field, and it had not been long before the initiative had registered over 1,000 institutions from 101 of the world's less fortunate countries.

When I visited in June 2003, the KEMRI library had but one computer for its patrons to use with the Internet, and there was a signup sheet on a clipboard for faculty and students to place their names on to secure some time examining the wealth of literature newly available as a result of the initiative. A local university had recently sent over another six computers, which were still sitting in boxes, in an effort to help KEMRI take advantage of this boon to access the journals it needed. The sudden and radical turning point in the intellectual fortunes of KEMRI's faculty and students spoke to how the Internet was being used in innovative ways to increase access to research. HINARI offered a particular model of open access to medical literature, and it greatly strengthened KEMRI's ability to fulfill its promise as a research and training center. But the introduction of this open access approach to scholarly publishing is also having a public impact that extends well beyond the academic community.

Under very different circumstances, the lead piece in the *New Yorker*'s "Talk of the Town" for September 15, 2003, took issue with the educational emphasis that the U.S. government was placing on student test scores, with the scores serving as the entire measure of a school's success or failure (Gladwell 2003, 34). In driving this critique home, the item's author, staff writer Malcolm Gladwell, reached out to a study by Robert L. Linn (2003) that challenged the very reliability of the achievement tests the government was relying on. Linn's study had been published two weeks earlier in *Educational Policy Analysis Archives*, an open access journal from Arizona State University. The journal had not issued a press release for Linn's study, as medical journals do on occasion with breakthrough discoveries, nor had a research summary been issued. Gladwell found the study with Google, in all likelihood, and was able to read it with a subscription because Linn's work was published in an open access journal.

Public access to research has become all the more important in recent years with the increased emphasis on political accountability and the corresponding call for "evidence-based policymaking" in government. Nowhere is that more apparent than with the recent U.S. Education Act, otherwise known as the No Child Left Behind Act of 2001. The act states, for example, that government funding will be provided to "implement promising educational reform programs and school improvement programs based on scientifically based research." The chances of "state educational agencies and local educational agencies," as they are identified in the act, finding such research hinges on these bodies' having open access to scholarly literature, much as such access helped Gladwell make his case against the act. Such are the public and democratic prospects of open access publishing models.

Now, a few years earlier, Gladwell (2000) had published a book on what he called the "tipping point," which describes how an idea or product can go from relative obscurity to that moment of recognition when "little things can make a big difference," tipping the idea into general acceptance. The Kenya Medical Research Institute's sudden ability to access the literature it needs to carry out its important work in health or the *New Yorker*'s citing a freely available research study is unlikely to prove the tipping point for the open access approach to scholarly publishing. However, as I go on in this book to describe, the occurrence of a significant number of such moments and instances suggests that the tip is on, if by no means over. What is clear at this point is that open access to research archives and journals has the potential to change the public presence of science and scholarship and increase the circulation of this particular form of knowledge. What is also clear is that the role that open access will play in the future of scholarly publishing depends on decisions that will be made over the new few years by researchers, editors, scholarly societies, publishers, and research-funding agencies.

This is a book that lays out the case for open access and why it should be a part of that future. It demonstrates the vital and viable role it can play, from both the perspective of a researcher working in the best-equipped lab at a leading research university and that of a history teacher struggling to find resources in an impoverished high school. This book presents my take on the case for open access as a focused effort, if not a wholesale movement. It is driven, however, by something broader which I term *the access principle.*

In reviewing the case for open access, it makes more sense to focus readers' attention on ways of increasing access, rather than holding to a strict line on whether a journal article, a journal, or a publisher, for that matter, is open or closed. This may set me off somewhat to the margins of the open access movement. But I believe that access to the scholarly literature has never been an open-and-shut case. Scholars have always sought better ways of finding and sharing the knowledge embodied in this literature. So my approach to open access is to hold to an access principle that could be put this way: *A commitment to the value and quality of research carries with it a responsibility to extend the circulation of such work as far as possible and ideally to all who are interested in it and all who might profit by it.* What follows on this principle, given the current transformation of journals from print to online formats, is that researchers, scholarly societies, publishers, and research libraries have now to ask themselves whether or not they are using this new technology to do as much as can be done to advance and improve access to research and scholarship.

It should be said at the outset that this is not about making the research article absolutely and unequivocally free. Information may want somehow to be free, but open access is not free access. The open access article cannot be read without a substantial investment in hardware, software, and networking, even if that investment has been made by the local public library, supported by the taxes paid in some small part by those who would read open access articles there. This is another way of saying that the open access movement is not operating in denial of economic realities. Rather, it is concerned with increasing access to more of the research literature for more people, with that increase measured over what is currently available in print and electronic formats. The open access movement is acting on a scholarly tradition that has long been concerned with extending the circulation of knowledge. Yet it is a response, as well, to the conjunction of two conflicting current events in the history of scholarship, one impeding and one accelerating that circulation. This conflict is what has brought the access question to the point of a movement. The first of these events is a steady escalation in journal prices, with the rate neatly summarized by Peter Suber (2004a), both analyst and advocate of open access developments, as "four times faster than inflation for nearly two decades." The second event is the advent of the Internet and digital publishing, which in a decade has transformed how readers access journals and created a viable alternative to a publishing model that, as a result of the first event, was otherwise rendering more and more of the literature affordable to fewer and fewer institutions. That viable alternative is now known as open access.

This book develops the case for this principled approach to open access in two ways. It deals with the practical matters of digitizing scholarly journals, from the perspective of scholarly associations, copyright law, publishing economics, journal design, and journal indexing. In addition to such practicalities, the book also considers some of scholarly publishing's more expansive themes, as open access speaks to extending the research capacities of developing nations, increasing public rights of access to knowledge, and furthering the policy and political contributions of research, as well as drawing attention to interesting parallels in publishing history.

I have gone with this breadth of argument in this book to try to make clear just how much is at stake with open access, when it comes to a simple matter like who has the right to read research. I have also done so in the hope that, taken together, the many strands of this case, from Internal Revenue Service filings to Newton's first and only article, will have the strength to move those in the academy and outside of it who have yet to be moved from those complacent and comfortable habits of scholarly publishing, habits that are preventing many, amid this shift in media, from seeing the new possibilities for furthering the access principle.

In pursuit of this principle, I should also disclose at the outset, I have become involved in developing publishing software that would contribute to, as well as test, the prospects of open access. All of the software (for journals, conferences, and indexing) is open source and freely distributed. Yet the lack of a financial stake in it on my part doesn't prevent my deep investment in it from showing at times in this book. It is the product of a highly talented team of undergraduates and graduate students who have come together in the Public Knowledge Project at the University of British Columbia. The principal piece of software, known as Open Journal Systems, has contributed much to my understanding of online journal processes, economics, indexing, and reading, and figures as such in this book. Additionally, this effort to build robust software that improves the quality of access to journals proved an excellent focal point for discussing the possibilities of open access publishing with researchers, editors, librarians, and publishers in many parts of the world.

Open Journal Systems has turned out to be more than a talking point and a test bed for the ideas discussed in this book. It has moved beyond the proof-of-concept stage, with the assistance and encouragement of an international open source community, and is now being used to publish open access journals, as well as some subscription journals around the world, with versions now available in seven languages. Given the interest shown in this open source software, a partnership was formed in early 2005 among the Public Knowledge Project, the Canadian Center for Studies in Publishing at Simon Fraser University, and Simon Fraser University Library to oversee the long-term development of Open Journal Systems, Open Conference Systems, and the PKP Harvester.

This book, however, is not about the development of publishing software; it is about the age-old question of access to knowledge. In considering what open access has to offer on that question in this book, this is a work of inquiry and advocacy. Its goal is to inform and inspire a larger debate over the political and moral economy of knowledge that will constitute the future of research. It seeks to elevate the questions currently being raised about how research is published, so that they are seen to shine a greater light on our work as scholars and as citizens of a larger world. And at this historic moment, in this transition in journal publishing from print to digital formats, the model of open access publishing challenges not only traditional methods of publishing scholarly work, but the very presence and place of this knowledge in the world.

What, then, of the all-too-obvious irony of publishing a book in print and on sale in bookstores about making online research free for the world? I have published and circulated earlier versions of most of these chapters in open access journals and as e-prints on my Web site. And I have now chosen to thoroughly revise the body of this work in book form. This represents an effort to reach a wider audience of the yet-to-be-convinced-of-the-possibilities-of-open-access (let alone the yet-to-find-things-online) and out of my admitted attachment to the book's becoming look and familiar feel. Just as importantly, I have chosen to go with this form because the book remains the medium that best serves the development of a wide-ranging and thoroughgoing treatment of an issue in a single sustained piece of writing. The printed book remains part of the future of how we come to know and how we come to share that knowing. But it is not the only form of knowing, as the inventors of a periodical press discovered more than three centuries ago. There are now still other possibilities to consider.

Acknowledgments

I wish to thank to Janice Kreider, Pia Christensen, and Anne White, who provided helpful assistance and thoughtful comments that furthered the work that has gone into this book. Many lessons about online publishing were learned from the Public Knowledge Project software team that worked on Open Journal Systems, led by Kevin Jamieson and including Chia-Ning Chiang, Jason Chu, Rory Hansen, Vikram Goghari, Patrick Inglis, Henry Kang, Daniel McLaren, Alec Smecher, Robert Wickert, and Eunice Yung. I also want to acknowledge the assistance and counsel of Mary Barton, Hillel Goelman, Alnoor Gova, Randall Jonas, Ranjini Mendis, Florence Muinde, Sal Muthayan, Miriam Orkar, Faith Shields, Pippa Smart, and Larry Wolfson, as well as to express my gratitude for the support that this work received from the Social Science and Humanities Research Council of Canada, Max Bell Foundation, John and Catherine D. MacArthur Foundation, and Pacific Press Endowment at the University of British Columbia. Doug Sery, Deborah Cantor-Adams, and Michael Harrup at MIT Press never failed to remind me of what publishers bring to the making of books. Much of the work presented in the chapters of this book originally appeared in open access journals and archives, where it received a sizable number of helpful comments from readers, and I wish to acknowledge the permission granted to me to use this work here from *First Monday, Harvard Education Review, Journal of Digital Information, Journal of Electronic Publishing*, and *Postgraduate Journal of Medicine*.

The Access Principle

1

Opening

The year 2003 signaled a breakthrough in scholarly publishing for what might be loosely termed the *open access movement*. After all, *Nature*, *Science*, *The Scientist*, and the *Wall Street Journal* all ranked "open access" among their top science stories for 2003. "Free for All" was the punning headline for *Nature*'s "2003 in Context" coverage on open access. The magazine dared to ask, with its own future potentially hanging in the balance, "Will the scientific literature in future be dominated by journals that do not charge their readers?" *Nature* placed "the 'open access' movement" right up there with the big stories on genetically modified foods, the elusive subatomic Higgs boson, the prospect of human cloning, and global access to clean water. What had catapulted open access into the top science stories for 2003 was the Public Library of Science's launch of *PLoS Biology*.

Reading the online version of *PloS Biology* is free to those who can find their way to an Internet connection, thanks to a $1,500 payment by the authors of each article published. Having authors (or their institutions) contribute to publishing costs in order to provide open access is not what distinguishes *PLoS Biology*; rather, what sets it apart is that this new journal is, as *Nature* notes, "competing for top biology papers with *Nature*, *Science* and *Cell*" ("2003 in Context"). However, the *PLoS Biology* editors, Patrick O. Brown, Michael B. Eisen, and Harold E. Varmus (2003), made it very clear in their opening editorial that their journal was about more than competing for the top papers in biology. As they saw it, the journal would, by virtue of being open access, "form a valuable resource for science education, lead to more informed healthcare decisions by doctors and patients, [and] level the playing scientists in smaller or less wealthy institutions" (1). For its part, *Nature* held a forum during the year on open access publishing, which was made freely available, on the magazine's otherwise subscription-only Web site. Suddenly, how scientists get their news—and how they get their news out—was itself front-page news and a hot political issue.

Within days of open access's ranking in the previous year's top five science stories, the U.S. House Appropriations Committee was expressing concern over public access to medical research that had been funded by taxpayers through the National Institutes of Health (NIH). The House instructed the NIH to arrive at a policy that would make NIH-funded research freely available through PubMed Central, a National Library of Medicine repository of open access biomedical research journals, within six months of the work's publication, with this delay in open access intended to protect subscription sales of journal publishers. To get a sense of the potential impact of a legislated measure for open access along the lines of the NIH policy, one should consider that the NIH currently supports $28 billion in biomedical research, resulting in, by some estimates, 60,000 articles, annually. The NIH measure has been supported by the newly formed Alliance for Taxpayer Access (which identifies itself, on its Web site, as "a diverse and growing alliance of organizations representing taxpayers, patients, physicians, researchers, and institutions that support open public access to taxpayer-funded research") and by a group of twenty-five Nobel Prize winners who have signed an open letter to the U.S. Congress in support of the measure ("There's no question, open access truly expands shared knowledge across scientific fields—it is the best path for accelerating multi-disciplinary breakthroughs in research") (Alliance for Taxpayer Access 2004).[1]

During the fall of 2004, the NIH invited public comment on this initiative, and among the 6,000 submissions that were received was an interesting "industry challenge" from Michael Keller (2004), Stanford University librarian, and the publisher of HighWire Press ("a not for

1. The Alliance for Taxpayer Access ⟨http://www.taxpayeraccess.org⟩ is sponsored by the Scholarly Publishing and Academic Resources Coalition (SPARC), which is funded, in turn, by the Association of Research Libraries; see also "An Open Letter to the U.S. Congress Signed by 25 Nobel Prize Winners" (Alliance for Taxpayer Access 2004).

profit enterprise of the Stanford University Libraries") and Stanford University Press. Keller's approach was to point out how much better HighWire Press and the publishers using its services were doing than the government's PubMed Central at providing "enormously improved public access" to research, with "over 770,000 articles in the life sciences and medicine" among HighWire back issues made freely available to readers (2004). Although there is no conflict between the NIH proposal and HighWire Press's back-issue access, Keller's stance that these things are better left up to the industry reflects how this move to extend the access principle is already part of the plan for at least some publishers among the not-for-profit sector.

On February 3, 2005, the NIH released its Policy on Enhancing Public Access to Archived Publications Resulting from NIH-Funded Research. The policy states that "NIH-funded investigators are requested to submit an electronic version of the author's final manuscript upon acceptance for publication" to PubMed Central, to be released to the public "as soon as possible (and within twelve months of the publisher's official date of final publication)." Understandably, a number of open access advocates were disappointed by the policy's final form. The twelve-month delay was bad enough, but then authors were only "requested" to comply with it, or as Suber (2005a) put it: "The policy is not only a retreat from the previous policy, but a retreat from clarity and coherence." However lobbied into dilution, the NIH policy still represents an important government acknowledgment that what has been changed by this new publishing medium is not only the public's right, but public expectations around that right.[2]

At the same time, in Great Britain, the House of Commons Science and Technology Committee was holding hearings on the state of scientific publishing and issued a report on July 20, 2004, entitled *Scientific*

---

2. A year earlier, on June 26, 2003, Representative Martin Olav Sabo (D-Minn.) had introduced in Congress a Public Access to Science Act that focused on the copyright of federally funded research. See Trosow 2003 for a defense of the government's withholding copyright protection from funded research, which is the basis of the act, on the grounds that "works resulting from extramural research that has been substantially subsidized by the Federal Government should enter the public domain in the same manner as works resulting from intramural government research undertaken by federal employees" (80).

Publications: Free for All? (presumably without intending the pun *Nature* had with its use of "free for all"). The report included a number of recommendations in favor of an open access approach to scholarly publishing. The committee proposed that universities be supported in establishing open access archives in which faculty could deposit copies of the articles that they otherwise published in journals; that funding agencies make depositing articles in such e-print archives, as they are known, a condition of the agencies' grants; and that the government look at ways of fostering open access journals, while having the Office of Fair Trading monitor the publishing industry. Although the government announced in November of that year that it would not be acting on the committee's recommendations, something is clearly afoot in the media and political circles over access to scientific and scholarly information.

The major corporate publishers of academic journals—the ostensible source of the access problem and target of these measures—had to blink in the midst of all the attention being paid to "free" journals and access to knowledge. In May 2004, Reed Elsevier, the largest of them with 1,800 journal titles, changed its policies on its authors' rights. Under the new policy, the authors of articles published in Elsevier journals are granted the right to post their own version (that is, not Elsevier's published version) of the final text in an open access e-print archive at their institution. This policy change meant that Elsevier authors were suddenly in a position to offer open access to all of the material they had published in Elsevier's journals. The unlikelihood of anything close to that happening is suggested by how few faculty members, outside of a few disciplines, such as high-energy physics, have uploaded their work to e-print archives, even after many publishers have granted them permission to do so. Some less generous-hearted critics have suggested that this figured in Elsevier's decision. Still, the publishing corporation that is most often portrayed as the villain in this story was no longer turning a deaf ear to open access.

A month later, Springer Verlag, another major scholarly publisher, with more than 1,000 journal titles, took matters a step further. Springer already permitted its authors to post their versions of published articles in e-print archives, but it went on to introduce Springer Open Choice

("Your research. Your choice."). Authors of articles accepted for publication in a Springer journal can opt, for a fee of $3,000, to have their articles made "freely available for anyone to read, download, or print," as Springer's Web site puts it. In a very short time, open access went from an untested upstart of an idea, posed by those who were accused of knowing nothing about the real business of publishing, to a way of doing business.

Of course, the open access story goes back much farther than all of the media, government, and corporate attention over the last year might suggest. The access principle that underlies this book—namely, that a *commitment to the value and quality of research carries with it a responsibility to extend the circulation of this work as far as possible, and ideally to all who are interested in it and all who might profit by it*—has a history that dates back to the great libraries of the past visited by scholars, whether one thinks of the fabled collection at Alexandria founded in the third century B.C. or the mosque libraries, such as the one at al-Azhar in Cairo, which flourished in and around the sixteenth century, or the small-town libraries that spread through nineteenth-century America.

Opening access is also what the printing press did for the emergence of experimental science in the seventeenth century, when Henry Oldenburg decided to print segments of the scientific correspondence that he was handling for the Royal Society of London. It is what *Nature* first set out to do when it started publishing in 1869, as it then made so bold as to promise its readers "to place before the general public the grand results of Scientific Work and Scientific Discovery, and to urge the claims of Science to a more general recognition in Education and Daily Life," a promise that *Nature* keeps current by citing on its *Science Update* Web site. However, hundreds of journals are delivering on this promise to place the grand results before the general public today in a new way, greatly expanding the circulation of knowledge by making their contents freely available to read online. There are now open access journals in every field and discipline, from every corner of the world, with some dating back a decade to the earliest days of the Internet. The open access journal is simply taking advantage of new Internet technologies to place its contents within reach of the growing number of readers who are able to go online. Increasing access to knowledge is an ongoing story, and what *Nature* identifies as the open access movement is but the most recent chapter.

So how is it that *PloS Biology* decided to charge authors $1,500 to have their article published and made free to readers, when its competitors sell subscriptions? How can the peer-reviewed journal *First Monday*, for which neither author nor reader pays, forsake a print edition and gain the respect it has, as a leading venue for scholarly inquiry into the whole Internet phenomenon? Why would the *New England Journal of Medicine* seemingly jeopardize its subscription list by offering open access to its entire contents six months after their initial publication? The first thing to note is that scholarly publishing runs on a different economic basis than the rest of the publishing world. Researchers and scholars are not paid a penny by journal publishers for original manuscripts presenting the results of perhaps thousands of dollars' worth of research. Rather, in publishing their work, the authors are banking on a longer-term investment in what might be cast as human rights and vanities. This inextricable mix of a *right to know* and a *right to be known* drives the academy's knowledge economy.

Money is hardly absent from this publishing picture. Although journals pay authors no royalties, faculty members do profit at least marginally as their research reputation grows. As a result of publishing well-received articles, faculty members can look forward to salary increases, job offers, speaker fees, consultancies, and other opportunities. Yet the immediate and direct value of publishing a work is realized in the circulation of knowledge. The extent of that circulation, as a work is made widely available to knowledgeable and interested readers, and as it weathers critique and garners praise in the process, stands as the work's claim to qualify as *knowledge*. The access principle is all the more at issue today for scholars and students throughout the world, as the pricing of journals over the last few decades has been leading to a decline in the availability of this academic work, as I go on to argue. The principle was, in a sense, identified at the very outset of the Western version of the scholarly project when Aristotle opened the *Metaphysics* with the statement "All humankind by nature desires to know."[3] As this desire is rightly identified, I believe, as part of our nature, it stands as a human right to know.

With its recent rise as a front-page news story, open access has also drawn its share of critics, who are alarmed at what this approach could mean for the future of scholarly publishing. The editor of *Chemical and Engineering News*, Rudy M. Baum, does not mince words in identifying the threat posed by open access: "The open-access movement's demand that an entirely new and unproven model for STM [science, technology, and medicine] publishing be adopted is not in the best interests of science" (2004). Baum is all for a free-market solution to the current serials pricing crisis—"the marketplace is responding to those high prices in a predictable way as libraries make hard choices and cancel subscriptions"—while seeking to portray open access as somehow an unnatural, extramarket economic force of mythic proportions: "It's human nature to want something for nothing. Unfortunately, excellence rarely comes without a price. Perhaps that's the most dangerous myth being fostered by the open-access movement: that access to high-quality STM literature can be had on the cheap."

It is easy enough to point out that it is no myth that an increasing number of journals, from the *New England Journal of Medicine* to *Essays in Philosophy*, are delivering high-quality literature in various forms of open access, as I go on to discuss. But then one might ask, What sort of market drives subscription prices and cancellations up to the point of forcing libraries to cancel journals? What sort of market ensures that the labor invested by faculty authors and reviewers results in journals that their own libraries can no longer afford? Well, it is a

---

3. I have taken one liberty with the standard W. D. Ross (1958) translation of Aristotle's *Metaphysics*: "All men by nature desire to know" (1.1). Aristotle goes on in that initial paragraph to give a proof for this proposition, based on delight, sight, and difference: "An indication of this is the delight we take in our senses; for even apart from their usefulness they are loved for themselves; and above all others the sense of sight. For not only with a view to action, but even when we are not going to do anything, we prefer seeing (one might say) to everything else. The reason is that this, most of all the senses, makes us know and brings to light many differences between things."

market that gives rise to an open access movement that takes advantage of new publishing technologies to restore the primacy of the right to know.

Baum's dismissal of open access needs to be compared to the publishing picture presented by Vitek Tracz, a member of BioMed Central Ltd., a for-profit open access publisher. Tracz was one of those who testified before the U.K. House of Commons Science and Technology Committee, which met through the winter of 2004 to consider the matter of scientific publishing. As an employee of a publishing company, albeit one pursuing an open access model, he pulled no punches on how skewed the publishing economy has become in terms of value and contribution: "I think that the role of publishers in the process of publishing scientific papers is wildly, incredibly exaggerated and overblown, completely out of proportion" (2004). What was being lost sight of, Tracz insisted, was that "it is the scientists who do the research, who publish, who referee, who decide. Most of the referees are chosen by another scientist. This is a process run by scientists and for us publishers to presume that we have some major scientific role or influence is wrong."

Still, the same parliamentary committee also heard from John Jarvis, managing director of Wiley Europe, who again returned to the threat posed by open access, this time to the public: "This rather enticing statement that everybody should be able to see everything could lead to chaos. Speak to people in the medical profession, and they will say the last thing they want are people who may have illnesses reading this information, marching into surgeries and asking things" (2004). Well, many doctors have already recognized and begun to deal in a most positive way with this age-of-information epiphenomenon. It is a point that has not been lost on Harold Varmus, one of the founders of the Public Library of Science, who also spoke to the British parliamentary committee about why he is committed to open access: "We want to put the best that biomedical research offers on the internet so that patients read information which is solid. We want physicians who are not associated with major medical funders, who are working in a farm town in Idaho, to be able to look up information which has been made available through publicly funded research and see the answers. We want, as emblazoned on the front of the British Museum and stated by the librarian of the British

Museum in 1836, every young poor student to be able to satisfy his learned curiosity just as a rich person does" (2004).

This concern with people "marching into surgeries and asking things," as well as with "every young poor student," is also the point at which I come into the conversation, having started out as a schoolteacher before becoming a faculty member given to studying how systems of knowledge, whether embodied in school curriculums or the *Oxford English Dictionary*, shape the way people think and act. Public education, in the broadest sense, has been my beat. While much of the discussion around this alternative publishing model known as open access has been directed toward increasing access to research for researchers, open access is also, for me, about turning this knowledge into a greater vehicle of *public education*, in its broadest sense. I am fortunately not alone in harboring this broader educational interest in the access principle. It is a theme taken up, for example, by the American Association for the Advancement of Science when it points out how "users" of scientific research include "historians and philosophers, editors, consultants, students and educators, journalists, consumer advocacy groups, government regulators and policy makers, and members of the legal community, as well as that diverse group we refer to as 'the general reader'" (Frankel 2002, 8).

What makes research and scholarship such a natural topic for thinking about setting up knowledge commons and publishing cooperatives devoted to providing open access is this work's standing as a *public good*. A public good, in economic terms, is something that is regarded as beneficial and can be provided to everyone who seeks it, without their use of it diminishing its value. The example commonly given of a public good is the lighthouse, which provides a guiding light to each ship equally, no matter how many ships pass its way. Fritz Machlup, a pioneering economist of the concept of *knowledge industries*, has described knowledge as a near-perfect public good: "If a public or social good is defined as one that can be used by additional persons without causing any additional cost, then knowledge is such a good of the purest type" (1984, 159). He allows that "to seek knowledge, to create, acquire, transmit, or retrieve knowledge" entails costs, but that "to use existing knowledge ... may be costless" (159). This lighthouse property of knowledge, as the quintessential public good, is worth pausing over. The growth in government support for academic research has led universities to develop an elaborate and extensive technical infrastructure. I argue that it is well within the capacity of the information technology provided by this infrastructure to provide greater public access to this public good known as research and scholarship, without diminishing its quality and quantity. The universities' capacity to make this work widely available is part of what drives this call for open access.

At this point, however, scholarly publishing is struggling to maintain a terribly inefficient triple-sided economy in the transition of journals from print to digital editions. First of all, publishers continue to employ the traditional industrial apparatus of print, even as manuscripts are prepared and managed electronically. Secondly, publishers are developing sophisticated Web-based systems for publishing, distributing, and indexing electronic editions within their own portals, as well as continuing to produce print editions. And finally, libraries have developed no less sophisticated technical infrastructures for providing their patrons with access to these and other digital resources. The redundancies will be reduced as academic publishing grows comfortably digital. In the face of the inevitable economic shakeout, viable publishing alternatives need to be put forward and tested for not only sustaining but also growing this public good, alternatives that, at the very least, go beyond restricting access to those who are associated with well-endowed institutions.

Now in playing the public-good argument as part of the case for open access, I stand both cautioned and encouraged by political scientist Jane Mansbridge's point that "the public good is essentially contested, that its evocation is open to demagogic exploitation, and that its meaning in any given case is likely to be heavily shaped by the interests of dominant groups" (1998, 5). The public good is, then, a "dangerous concept," but one that Mansbridge is more than willing to support because of how it highlights "the contrast between the growing weight of reason to act only in one's narrow self-interest," as she starkly puts it, "and the growing necessity, in an increasingly interdependent world, for sophisticated forms of cooperation that require a leaven of public spirit" (5). Presumably, some of the knowledge at issue in this body of research literature can sharpen the very perception of dominance, demagoguery, and contested meanings that gathers around the idea of a public good.

Creating additional sources of public knowledge would also contribute to what Mansbridge values most about the public good, which is that it serves "as a site for analytically fruitful contestation" where people can "formulate their views and test their arguments against others" (12). My concern with increasing access to research and scholarship here is very much about "sorting out which institutional arrangements in which contexts," as she puts it, allow self-interest to serve the particular view of the public good that welcomes "the contest over what is public and good" (17).[4]

I cannot help thinking that, however slightly the question of access to the journal literature may figure in the larger contest today over what constitutes the public realm and what stands as a public good, this innovative approach to publishing journals is the one institutional arrangement that Mansbridge and so many other scholars have immediately within their reach, not simply to explore, but to control, shape, and transform. If indeed, as Mansbridge maintains, the scholar's "job is to make good contextually based guesses [about institutional arrangements], which can then be tested in practice" (1998, 16), then let us in good faith begin with our own publishing arrangements when it comes to journals. It might also seem that finding ways of increasing the global reach of scholars and researchers would provide, if not the purest, then at least a fine opportunity "to let the engine of self-interest do its useful work without infecting the motivation to do good" (5). The self-interest of researchers, editors, and scholarly associations needs to be harnessed, in this case, so that their involvement in scholarly publishing is seen to have no conflict with the motivation to do this greater good. "One can do well by doing good" is how Mansbridge puts it, in describing such an alignment (14).

4. Mansbridge's point that there can be "rational and often even disinterested disagreement on the public good" has its parallel in the rational (if not always disinterested) disagreements that frequently take place within the research literature, while open access to the sheer variety of, and conflict among, research studies should reduce instances in which expert knowledge is used to end public deliberation, which she regards as a public good in and of itself (1998, 10).

2

Access

Scholarly and scientific journals have by this point enjoyed a successful print run of some 340 years. It has been that long since the shaky, understated launches, within a few months of each other in 1665, of the *Journal des sçavans* in Paris and the *Philosophical Transactions* in London. Since then, the journal has assumed a myriad of forms and sizes, covering every discipline, subdiscipline, and academic niche imaginable, all neatly summed up, for example, in the succinct simplicity of *Cell*, the narrowly and distinctly cast *Journal of Negative Results: Ecology and Biology*, and the entirely contemporary *Web Semantics: Science, Services and Agents on the World Wide Web*. Over the course of the journal's long publishing history, its pages have been the site of scientific discovery and scholarly breakthrough. Journals have launched stellar careers and ruthlessly exposed frauds; they have hosted hotly contested disputes and provided a refuge for fellow-travelers and like-minded thinkers.

Although the number of journals had steadily grown over the centuries, it was the growth in postsecondary education after World War II, along with the huge influx of government research funding, particularly in the United States, that led to a profusion of new journal titles, with many of the new entries coming from commercial publishers, which were, as a group, just beginning to move into this area of publishing. New titles continued to appear at a rate that exceeded the growth in the number of faculty, which began to slow in the 1980s. What drove the increase in journals was greater government research funding, particularly in the biomedical fields.[1] Between 1998 and 2003, for example, 783 new journal titles were launched by 149 publishers, with many additional ones appearing from scholarly associations and other groups (Cox and Cox 2003, 5). Although many a journal created out of the vision and hope of scholars and publishers has gone the way of all publishing ventures—namely, out of print—the estimate is that 50,000 scholarly and scientific titles are currently being published worldwide.[2]

Even as the journal's print run has continued into the twenty-first century, it has also struck out on an entirely new publishing course. Over the last dozen years, the typical journal has assumed a parallel digital life, with as many as half of the current titles available online (Tenopir 2004). What began in 1982, with the first electronic edition of the *Harvard Business Review*, which was given limited circulation by Bibliographic Information Services, has quickly grown into a global distribution system for journals in every discipline and field (Thapa, Sahoo, and Srivastava 2001). To have perhaps 20,000 journals or more move to online editions in less than the last dozen years suggests that this is where journal publishing is headed.

It is certainly true that the readability of a journal article on a computer screen does not compare to the ease of reading ink on paper. Still, electronic journals do offer scholarly readers certain advantages. Compared to the print edition of a journal, the online version can be far more readily and exhaustively searched, whether for a concept or term. Readers can quickly move online from citation to work cited, and when they find something that serves their needs, they can, with a click, copy

---

1. See Roger L. Geiger (2004, 177, 147) on how "the autonomous research mission" of the university grew out of United States federal government agencies that wanted access to the academic expertise that they had had during World War II, as well as on the growth of research support, between 1980 and 2000, by over 100 percent while faculty and student numbers grew by less than 20 percent during the period.

2. Carol Tenopir (2004), a leading scholar on academic publishing, puts the estimate this way: "I can say with confidence that as of the end of 2003, there are just under 50,000 scholarly journals and somewhere between one-third and just over one-half of them are in digital form. One thing I've learned is that these numbers are a moving target and somewhat suspect. Keep checking and keep definitive statements necessarily vague."

the article's bibliographic reference, and perhaps a quote or two, without leaving their keyboard and mouse. They can press Print or Save, if an article they come across is a keeper and worth reading with a pencil in hand.

Online journals have in this relatively short time won over the hearts of my colleagues and our students at the University of British Columbia (UBC) in Vancouver, where I work. Some 40 percent of those recently surveyed by the university's library (2003) ranked online journals ahead of books, print journals, and other resources; there was no such level of agreement on the value of any other scholarly resource. This favoring of the online journal is about to change the very nature of the library. A number of university libraries, including the one at UBC, are eliminating the overlap between print and electronic editions of the same journal in their collections by canceling the print edition. In 2004, UBC cut the print editions of 1,500 journals and plans to reduce its print holdings among a major portion of its 23,000-title serials collection in a similar way. Not long from now, scholars may well be overheard nostalgically recalling to a new generation of graduate students fond stories of the productive discoveries that once came of those serendipitous strolls through the racks of freshly printed journals placed on display in their university library, during the days when you had to be on your feet to browse.

If the journal has readily taken to the Internet, the scholarly book has not, up to this point. Certainly, the initial rumors of the book's imminent death at the hands of this new technology appear to have been greatly exaggerated. Still, many classic works of literature, from Austen to Shakespeare, are available online (although they are still read, I trust, most often in paperback editions).[3] This was not the case with scholarly

3. Project Gutenberg, a public-domain archive that dates back to 1971, has been mounting many of the great books (with expired copyrights). There is the Million Books Project at Carnegie Mellon University, with France's National Library sponsoring Gallica, another open access book archive. The Internet Archive project, led by Brewster Kahle, has a target of a million books pulled from libraries in five countries, with open access to all public-domain titles. The Alexandria Library, with its own historical hopes of reestablishing a universal library, has dedicated itself to providing online access to as much of the world's literature as possible, as well as to its own online archives of Islamic and Arabic literature.

books, at least not until very recently. The digital standing of the scholarly book was radically altered by Google's announcement on December 14, 2004, that it would digitize fifteen million books over the next decade, including the entire seven million volumes of the University of Michigan's library, along with portions of the collections held by Harvard, Stanford, Oxford, and the New York Public Library, with perhaps others to follow. As Suber observed in the wake of this development: "We don't know what it will do to teaching and research, let alone pleasure reading and autodidacticism. But we can be sure that removing access barriers to collections of this magnitude and utility will change basic practices" (2005b). Although only books in the public domain can be read online (but not printed or downloaded), Google Print will allow free searching of all the works, creating an encyclopedic guide to who deals with what.

As promising a development as this is, and as much weight and publicity as it has drawn to the idea of greater access, Google Print is not about faculty members doing what they can to ensure that their current work circulates openly and freely. Google Print does not directly address the crisis of access that has beset the journal literature. It does not provide a means for altering a publishing economy that continues to cut into the scholarly vitality of periodical literature.

Of course, the journal is hardly the whole of the academy's knowledge business. Yet the journal has arrived at a critical point in its own digital transformation, and how its future plays out, in terms of access, rests in the hands of researchers, editors, librarians, scholarly associations, and publishers. Although online scholarly resources are now available in a variety of forms—from online courses to scientific databases—the research article in particular is currently at the center of a struggle over the economics of access that may determine the global presence and impact of the research enterprise.[4] It is a struggle over whether online publishing will further contribute to, or whether it will begin to reverse, what can only be described as the current state of *declining access* to re-

---

4. For a review of the complete "multidimensional continuum" of scholarly electronic publishing activities that go well beyond the journal, and in relation to tenure and promotion, see Anderson 2004. On the economic benefits of open access to data and public-sector information, see Weiss 2004.

search and scholarship within an otherwise expanding global academic community.

How can access to research be declining, one might well ask, in a knowledge society? This age-of-information paradox follows on the successful transformation of knowledge into a capitalized commodity and economic driver. The university community, at least in some quarters, has caught hold of this wave (see, for example, Gibbons et al. 1994). And as a whole, the academy has been growing increasingly productive in patents, research articles, and doctorates. At the same time, the major journal publishers have been all about merger and acquisition as part of this know-biz phenomenon. The resulting corporate publishing concentration, with its relentless focus on knowledge capitalization and shareholder value, has seen journal prices increase well above inflation rates, and university libraries cannot keep up.

It has been hard enough for libraries to try to keep abreast of the increased quantity of research arising from the billions of dollars now invested in research, as well as the growth of postsecondary education and the professoriate more generally. But libraries are now facing a journal economy in which less is more. That is, the inevitable cancellation of journal subscriptions and reduced circulation resulting from higher prices is still leading to greater publisher profits. The publishing goal is not necessarily increased circulation for the journals. Profits are coming not only from increased prices and publishing efficiencies, but from taking greater advantage of the growing number of titles publishers hold, through such strategies as "bundling" titles in licensing arrangements with libraries that carry no-cancel policies for all of the titles in the bundle. The effect is to increase the publisher's share of subscribing libraries' budgets beyond the number of titles that libraries might have otherwise ordered (leading to cuts in other titles).[5]

5. Elsevier accounted for 50 percent of the University of California online serials budget in 2002, although its titles accounted for only 25 percent of journal use (Suber 2004b). A Credit Suisse First Boston financial report on the scholarly publishing industry points out that Elsevier has a higher profit margin on its lower-quality journals (with fewer submissions), which is one of the reasons for a bundling strategy that does not allow libraries to cancel these lower-quality journals without canceling the higher-quality ones in the same bundle (Suber 2004c).

What this corporate concentration in scholarly publishing looks like can be seen in the holdings of three of the major players: Reed Elsevier with 1,800 journals, Taylor and Francis with over 1,000 titles, and Springer with more than 500 titles. According to one industry report, these three companies now control 60 percent of the materials indexed in the world's leading citation index, the ISI Web of Science ("Merger Mania" 2003). The mergers with smaller publishers, and the resulting acquisition of journal titles, that have made those corporations giants of journal publishing are consistently associated with subscription price increases, amounting to, in the case of one publisher, an average increase of more than 20 percent for each journal moving from a smaller publisher to the larger one.[6]

The growth of the knowledge economy, which might otherwise have been thought to herald the university's ship coming in, has produced a "serials crisis" that threatens the basic access principle otherwise critical to production of research and scholarship. As the Association of American Universities and the Association of Research Libraries solemnly put it in an unprecedented joint statement from the two organizations: "The current system of scholarly publishing has become too costly for the academic community to sustain" (ARL 2000).[7]

Not surprisingly, there are different versions of how this unsustainable impasse in scholarly publishing was reached. I have attended the presentations of representatives from large corporate scholarly publishers, and their PowerPoint slides typically illustrate how a number of corporate academic publishing interests, such as Elsevier (with its august academic publishing pedigree dating back to the sixteenth century), began in the

6. Elsevier, for example, has acquired the academic publishing houses Harcourt, Academic, and Pergamon. See McCabe 1999 and McCabe 2002 on mergers and monopolies among corporate academic publishers: "According to these empirical estimates, each of these mergers was associated with substantial price increases; in the case of the Elsevier deal the price increases appear to be due to increased market power. For example, compared to pre-merger prices, the Elsevier deal resulted in an average price increase of 22% for former Pergamon titles, and an 8% increase for Elsevier titles" (McCabe 1999). Also see Tamber 2000.

7. Similarly, the Wellcome Trust study *Economic Analysis of Scientific Research Publishing* concluded that "[t]he current market structure does not operate in the long-term interests of the research community" (SQW Ltd. 2003, iv).

1950s to respond to Western-government increases in research funding by launching a wide range of new journals. In this way, the corporate publishers initially expanded publishing opportunities for researchers and advanced the circulation of knowledge. The academic community tends to forget, in today's fervor over pricing, the publishers' representatives are quick to point out, that the corporations stepped in to provide the new journals needed to ensure that advances in many fields had a proper venue, as the old-guard scholarly societies were extremely cautious when it came to adding new titles to their well-established lists.

The publishers' story is not without merit. At least one economics study lends this potted history credence, even as the study further fuels the outrage felt in the academic community over the current state of affairs by quantifying how much this corporate incursion into scholarly publishing costs on a journal-by-journal basis. Economist Theodore C. Bergstrom (2001) found that in 1960, economics was served by some thirty journals, almost all of which were nonprofit ventures sponsored by scholarly associations or other academic organizations. By 1980, the number of titles had increased to 120, of which half were published by commercial concerns, and by 2000, that corporate share was two-thirds of the 300 journals then available. The corporate sector was clearly creating or acquiring journals at a faster rate than the nonprofit sector.

Bergstrom also found that the average subscription fees for the commercial journals that were ranked among the top twenty for the field (according to the ISI Web of Science) was $1,660 per year (Bergstrom 2001, 183). Compare this to an average subscription cost of $180 annually for the economic journals published by the nonprofits in the top-twenty list, and you can see the basis for concern. Just as disconcerting is Bergstrom's finding that price has little to do with quality, at least as determined by a particular journal's impact factor.[8] Nonprofit economic journals held the top six positions in the ISI list of most influential economic titles according to their impact factors. The titles owned by

8. A journal's impact factor is an ISI Web of Science measure of its influence based on the average number of times articles in the journal have been cited in ISI-indexed journals over the previous two-year period.

commercial publishers held only five places within the top twenty titles.[9] Through the disproportionately high prices it charges for the journals it produces, not only is the corporate sector taking a much greater share of library budgets, but it exercises a much greater degree of control over the circulation of knowledge than the number of titles it holds would otherwise warrant.

Still, how can a market bear such price differences between commercial and association titles that are so unrelated to quality? How, in this world of consumer savvy, can you sell a product that is more than nine times as expensive as an equally good if not better alternative? And how can you sell it to the same set of relatively wealthy customers year after year, in a pricing spiral, with journal cancellations, resulting from increased prices, leading to further price increases as a smaller number of customers must bear the publishing expenses of the journal?[10] You can do it only if the consumer is blind to price differences and is interested only in acquiring a wide range of top-ranked products. That is, faculty members at leading institutions expect to be able to access all of the

9. Also see Bergstrom and Bergstrom 2004, which reports that "in economics, for example, the average inflation-adjusted price per page charged by commercial publishers has increased by 300 percent since 1985, whereas that of nonprofit economics journals has increased by 'only' 50 percent" (897); Mark McCabe (1999) reports that between 1988 and 1998, biomedical journals published by the leading corporate publishers increased their subscription prices by 224 percent compared to 129 percent for journals from nonprofit publishers.

10. In addition to noting how cancellations caused by price increases lead to further increases for the remaining subscribers, who are asked to generate the same revenue levels to produce the journal, Roger G. Noll (1996) observes an additional cost of these increases: "In addition, the high institutional price causes institutional libraries to be far smaller than would be socially optimal. Of course, for publications in science and engineering, this inefficiency ripples throughout the entire economy, for it means that education, applied research and development, and direct diffusion to the production of goods and services will proceed at a slower rate than otherwise would be the case" (12). McCabe (1999) estimates that a 1 percent increase in the price of a journal results in a 0.3 percent drop in the number of subscriptions to it. The American Physical Society, with fourteen journals, reports "an overall decline of an average of about 3 percent a year (less lately) across all our journals since the 1960s," and the Institute of Physics, with more than forty journals, indicates that "the general attrition slope has not changed" (Swan 2005).

high-impact journals in their field, and the pricing issues that their libraries face are neither here nor there for them. Faculty members run on a different journal economy than the library, one that is determined by the scramble among them for greater research impact: the vanity factor.

To speak of faculty *vanity* may seem terribly unfair to hard-working researchers, toiling away in lab coats and laboratories or in sensible shoes and dusty archives. This is clearly not about the vanity of rock or movie stars. It is something far closer to professional pride, to the pride one cannot help but take in seeing one's work, dare I say, "in print," or in seeing it cited in someone else's work. I would use the term *pride* to capture the economic driver of scholarly publishing for faculty members, except it doesn't do as good a job in capturing the special case of scholarship. Academic publishing is an end in itself. As such, the recognition of one's peers does not simply follow from what one achieves in one's field; this is the very field one plows with the work. That is, recognition of one's peers is the principal measure of one's contribution to a field of inquiry, although there may also be patents or other ways one's work has an impact outside the academy. The particular ego economy of being cited by name, and of being so closely identified with one's published work, even in collaborative endeavors, is not entirely without other kinds of rewards, which follow on this recognition factor. To be widely cited by other researchers and appear in high-impact journals can lead, as I have noted, to improved salaries and working conditions and can also present other incentives for faculty members.

This vanity factor, on first blush, may seem removed from the access question. Differences in costs and access policies among journals mean little, if you are entirely focused on impact factor or some other measure of the journal's reputation. The biggest corporate publishers have carefully cultivated highly reputable journals. To have an article accepted by one of these high-priced journals, or to be asked to sit on its board, or perhaps even to serve as an editor, can easily blind a faculty member to what can seem to be the librarians' issue over the journal's pricing. This vanity factor can be blamed, for example, for frustrating the efforts of the Public Library of Science in organizing, among researchers, an effective boycott of overly expensive journals in 2000. It may account for why only a small handful of editors have revolted over the escalated pricing of the corporate journals they edit (more on these editors in chapter 3).

Yet the evidence and argument that I go on to present make it clear that the vanity factor is not at all the enemy of open access. Open access is not only about human rights and the greater circulation of knowledge. It is about increasing *research impact*, to use the constant focus of Stevan Harnad's (2003a) compelling campaign for open access. Research impact speaks to the particular vanity or ego economics (or should that be *egonomics?*) of authors writing research articles as part of an otherwise royalty-free publishing system. A work's research impact is not only a measure of what it contributes to the work of others. It speaks, as well, to the recognition and reputation of the author. The vanity at issue amounts to more than a researcher's looking up, in a moment of weakness, the citation scores of colleagues down the hall. In this age of accountability, the need to have one's name in print and on the screen, in the right places and as often as possible, is institutionally reinforced at every turn in academic life.[11] So it is hardly surprising that during discussions of open access, the necessary vanity of academic life—publish well or perish badly—quickly surfaces, as faculty members ask about what this new publishing approach will mean for the current order of things.

Yet at the very point in the discussion when the air is charged with exposed vulnerabilities and vanities, the wise and experienced open access advocate looks up and asks, "Did someone mention journal impact factors and citation counts?" The advocate then quickly sets up a prepared PowerPoint presentation, with slide after slide showing, in study after study and discipline after discipline, that open access is associated with increased citations for authors and journals, when compared to similar work that is not open access. Readers of this book can experience

11. Kamran Abbasi (2004), in a recent *British Medical Journal* editorial, presents an informal international survey of how publications have, in the words of one researcher he cites, "become more important than teaching and the actual research itself," with examples provided of a number of publications and journal ratings determining recognition and reward among "deans, sponsors, government agencies, and employment panels." On the detrimental impact of performance indicators, including such bibliometrics as citation counts, on higher education, see Bruneau and Savage 2002.

the study-after-study effect themselves by accessing the regularly updated Web page "The Effect of Open Access and Downloads ('Hits') on Citation Impact: A Bibliography of Studies," maintained by Steve Hitchcock (2005). Going back to Steven Lawrence's (2001) study, which demonstrated that open access computer science papers garner 4.5 times as many citations as their print equivalents, Hitchcock's annotated bibliography offers access to dozens of studies: past, recent, and ongoing.[12]

When it comes to the vanity of journal publishing, it is as if the open access advocate is declaring, across the poker game of academic life, "I see your necessary professional vanity and raise it with open access by a factor of two, three, or even four times as many citations—depending on the discipline, journal, and other factors." Yes, the advocate insists, bring us your vanities. But do it now, for at some point, as open access spreads, its citation advantage will obviously evaporate. But still, the research impact, in the sense of an increased contribution, will continue.

The citation impact studies on open access reveal interesting nuances of the movement. Kurtz et al. (2004), for example, establish that the citation advantage for open access articles found in astronomy is not attributable to the articles' being freely available online. Those who publish in astronomy need to have access to astronomical data and resources, which, in turn, is associated with being at an institution with sufficient access to the literature. The citation advantage in astronomy at the moment is based on the earlier access afforded by open access e-print archives: first up, first cited. There is also a self-selection bias operating with the archive, which sees better authors archiving more. Kurtz et al.

---

12. In support of Lawrence's initial finding, for example, Brody et al. (2004) found that with a large sample of pre-2001 physics articles, the ratio of citations for open access articles compared to those that are not is between 2.5 to 1 and 5.8 to 1. Stevan Harnad, in collaboration with others, is also analyzing the relationship between an article's "hits" online and citations using arXiv.org E-Print Archive: "The correlations [between hits and citations] are quite big, and range from .3 to .6 or higher, and seem to vary somewhat with field and subfield" (2003d). In contrast, Kent Anderson et al. (2001) found that with the journal *Pediatrics* in 1997–1999, "an [open access] online article could expect 2.16–4.02 fewer citations in the literature than if it had been printed," although the faculty surveyed felt these open access publications counted as much as other publications for tenure.

do see the open part of open access as playing a greater part in the future. For as astronomy data sets are now being openly shared, a new generation of astronomers at institutions without sufficient library resources to otherwise tap into the astronomy literature will be using the open access arXiv.org E-Print Archive because there is no charge for doing so. So, to speak of rights and vanities in relation to open access is not to set up a tension between doing *good* and doing *well*. They are cojoined in this matter, as both can be enhanced by open access. Taking them together suggests the breadth of the case for open access.

In suggesting that faculty and librarians are driven by different economic factors when it comes to journals, I do not want to overlook how librarians have sought to bring faculty members in on the problems libraries face. During the 1980s and 1990s, if not earlier, librarians sent faculty members lists of current holdings in their fields, from which the faculty members were to identify titles they could not live without (the ones they appear in?) and titles that were not essential to their work (the ones their colleagues appear in?). The lists were consulted as the libraries were forced to make cuts from their serial collections. The numbers were substantial, and at the University of British Columbia, a librarian pointed out to me, 2,000 titles were canceled during that period. The librarians also solicited faculty support in calling during the period for increased budgets to keep up with the corporatization of this knowledge economy.

A comprehensive picture of what even the best research libraries were facing during this time is provided by the Association of Research Libraries (ARL) (2004), which represents the top 120-odd research libraries in North America. Between 1986 and 2003, ARL members managed to increase their budgets for journals by 260 percent. Even with this increase, however, the average library's collection had fewer titles throughout this period than it did in 1986, until finally in 2002 these leading libraries pulled slightly ahead of 1986 levels—by all of 14 percent (ARL 2004).[13] The increased cost of journals has also eroded the libraries'

13. Recent gains in the number of journals are likely a result of major publishers bundling larger numbers of electronic editions to which libraries purchase a license, which reduces library control over subscription lists, with a similar situation taking place among U.K. university libraries (SQW Ltd. 2003, 5–6).

ability to purchase books, with the numbers only returning to 1986 levels in 2003, despite the growing number of books published annually since 1986. What might seem like a game of catch up and keep up has been just as much a game of slow down the falling behind. The ARL initially responded to this situation with a series of information campaigns directed at raising awareness among faculty members, among others, of the need for alternative publishing models, which I return to later in the book.

Yet more recently, individual libraries have also taken direct action. A number of these research libraries have begun to say *no* in a very public way to high-priced journals. Harvard, Cornell, University of California, Duke, MIT, and others canceled Elsevier subscriptions in 2003, some dropping hundreds of titles, with the cancellations often accompanied by pointed letters directed to faculty, publishers and the public documenting and protesting journal pricing policies (Suber 2004b). Sidney Verba, director of the Harvard University Library, which subscribes to more than 100,000 serials, well ahead of any other library in North America (if not the world), explained that the decision to reduce the number of Elsevier titles to which Harvard subscribed was "driven not only by current financial realities, but also—and perhaps more importantly—by the need to reassert control over our collections and to encourage new models for research publication at Harvard" (2003).

Now, if the leading research libraries in North America have been unable to keep pace with the growth (and increased pricing) of scholarly publishing, it should give us pause to ponder what is happening to less fortunate universities, especially in developing countries. As I go on to discuss in more detail, access to books and journals has always been a major struggle for these institutions, but over the last two decades, whatever modest progress they have been able to make in the development of their print collections has come to a virtual standstill. University populations are growing, and the number of qualified and interested researchers is increasing, but the global contribution of this potential research capacity is threatened at its root by empty library shelves and out-of-date literature. It adds up to a picture of declining access to knowledge across a global academic community. The one ray of light and hope in this picture, however, has come by way of this variation in online access known as open access. The open access movement may have but a toehold when it comes to its current share of journal titles—with close to 1,500 listed, for example, on the *Directory of Open Access Journals* Web site run by Lund University (Lund University Libraries 2004)—but the idea behind it, of using the Internet to increase access to research and scholarship, has had an impact on every aspect of scholarly publishing.

On one level, the journal's large-scale move to digital publication has provided only a modicum of relief from the problems created by high journal prices. Subscription prices for online editions of journals do run a little less than those for the print editions of the same title, if only by 10–25 percent. This reduction is not enough, however, to reverse the declining state of access in the face of price increases that have continued into this century at a steady 8–10 percent a year (van Orsdel and Born 2003). This is why it is indeed fortunate that the Internet has also given rise to an alternative economic model for scholarly publishing.

When it first became possible to post a work on the World Wide Web during the 1990s, a number of journals, as well as newspapers and encyclopedias, briefly experimented with making their contents freely available to readers. That free phase for most of these sources passed quickly enough, as they instituted subscription and pay-per-view access models. However, a small number of researchers persisted in taking advantage of the relative ease of posting materials online to make their work freely available to readers, finding that it made their work far more widely available than traditional subscription-based journals, whether in print or online editions. Some faculty members uploaded their working papers and preprints (which they had had accepted for publication) to their own Web sites, and a few disciplines, such as high-energy physics, established preprint archives that have become hot spots for tracking developments in the field, as more and more faculty members in those areas contribute to them, even as they also send their work to the traditional journals for publication. At the same time, a few journal editors set up free electronic journals, through various combinations of e-mails, listservs, and Web sites.

These various methods of providing free access to the research article are now commonly referred to as *open access*, as in an *open access archive* or an *open access journal*. Exactly what constitutes true and complete "open access" in scholarly publishing has been carefully defined by a number of groups.[14] This book is less concerned with such definitions, although they are clearly helpful in establishing goals and making it clear what this movement is about. It is concerned with the value and viability of *opening* access to this knowledge, and by that I mean *increasing* access and *improving* access to the journal literature, largely through the use of the Internet. It is about ways of making a greater part of this literature accessible to more people. For journals that are not prepared to make their articles freely available to readers immediately on publication, there is now a range of options for increasing access: Journals can enable authors to deposit articles (in preprint and postprint stages) in an e-print archive run by the authors' institutions or to post them on the authors' own Web sites immediately on publication. Journals can make their contents free to read online some six to twelve months after initial publication. Journals can make their contents freely and immediately available to those working at universities in developing countries.

Up to this point, much of the media attention paid to this topic has been focused on those open access science journals that provide free and immediate access to their entire contents. The launch of the open access journal *PloS Biology*, from the Public Library of Science, in 2003 provides an excellent example. The arrival of *PLoS Biology* made a big splash in the press, if not one well understood, judging by such less-than-newsworthy headlines about the launch as "Science Journal to Put Research Online" (2003), from the Associated Press. *PLoS Biology*, which is funded by author fees and foundation support, and whose editors and authors are well-known leaders in the field, has clearly put open access on the map in a way that no other publishing event has up to this point. Yet the open access journal is only part of the story in increasing access to the research literature.

14. The Budapest Open Access Initiative (2002), for example, offers the following: "By 'open access' to this literature, we mean its free availability on the public internet, permitting any users to read, download, copy, distribute, print, search, or link to the full texts of these articles, crawl them for indexing, pass them as data to software, or use them for any other lawful purpose, without financial, legal, or technical barriers other than those inseparable from gaining access to the internet itself." Also, see the Bethesda Statement on Open Access Publishing (Brown, Eisen, and Varmus 2003). See also appendix A, table A.1, note a.

One reason to focus on the variety of open access models is to dispel the idea that greater access to the knowledge represented by scholarly publishing is an all-or-nothing proposition. The term *open access* may suggest that, like a door, a journal is open or it is not. The still-emerging realities of opening access to this literature are otherwise. Having recognized the importance of increasing access to knowledge, publishers have found ways of offering greater access to journals without severing the journal's entire revenue stream, or even reducing the number or cost of subscriptions, in some cases. To help clarify the complexities of the emerging scene, I have set out in appendix A what I would cast as ten current flavors of open access, along with their underlying economic model, each of which is currently being employed by authors and journals. I have already referred, for example, to open access archives or institutional repositories, in which authors deposit copies of the papers they have published in subscription-based journals, and journals that continue to sell subscriptions while opening access to the contents of each issue six months after publication. There are also the open access arrangements made by some publishers for developing countries and the open access sponsored by fees that authors, institutions, or countries pay. I go so far as to include in the appendix one of the largest publishing conglomerates, Reed Elsevier, among the contributors to open access, not only because it recently agreed to allow its authors post the final versions of their papers to open access e-print archives, but because its portal ScienceDirect provides free access to bibliographic information and abstracts for its 1,800 journals. This may seem little enough to offer readers until one recalls just how vital and potentially expensive access to good indexing is for scholarly work.

Each flavor of open access demonstrates how alternative knowledge economies have rapidly taken shape in journal publishing over the short life of the Internet. Each of these flavors—from e-print archives to open access indexes—offers a gain in the circulation and exchange of this knowledge over what might have been achieved in print in its late-twentieth-century hyperinflated economic state. Each of them is a further way of realizing what I am calling the access principle, which is concerned with making choices about publishing that improve the circulation of research and scholarship. By the time you are reading this book, there could well be more or fewer ways of opening access, as the idea grows, consolidates, and takes myriad forms. It is often shaped by the different publishing cultures that have formed around the various disciplines that journals represent. (Is there a preprint culture in a particular field for sharing work prior to publication? Do editors or board members expect to be paid? Is the journal used by a scholarly association to raise money for other purposes?) Although I do at times play favorites among these flavors, what matters is not the particular form that open access takes, but adherence to this principle of increasing and improving access, impact, participation, and circulation.

As for the number of open access archives and journals available at this point, the answer is no less a moving target than the total number of learned journals. There are places, however, to catch sight of the progress in this direction. The Core Metalist of Open Access Eprint Archives, maintained by the Open Citation Project at the University of Southampton, currently provides a guide to hundreds of open access archives with access to papers totaling in the range of hundreds of thousands.[15] As I have already noted, the *Directory of Open Access Journals* maintained by Lund University Libraries (2004) provides another guide. Still, open access journals may, at the point at which I am writing, represent no more than 3–5 percent of the journal market. On the other hand, there are substantial open access journal developments afoot. Brazil, for example, is moving toward open access for its scientific journal publishing activities, virtually as a national policy, through institutional and other grants to its just under 200 scholarly journals (Sabbatini 2003).

Whatever the proportion of the literature involved through journals and e-print archives, open access is demonstrating dramatic and striking gains in the circulation of knowledge. The journal *Education Policy Analysis Archives* provides an excellent example of what a difference open access can make. I mentioned it in the introduction, as the *New Yorker* had picked up one of its articles within days of publication. It was started a decade ago by Gene Glass, a professor of education at

15. The Core Metalist of Open Access Eprint Archives can be accessed at ⟨http:// opcit.eprints.org/explorearchives.shtml⟩.

Arizona State University perhaps best known for developing the statistical technique for marshaling the results of statistical studies on a common question, otherwise known as *meta-analysis*. As of 2003, Glass's *Education Policy Analysis Archives* had published 312 articles (including 24 in Spanish and Portuguese), and it was attracting some 2,500 visitors each weekday, which vastly exceeds the typical audience for an academic journal in a field in which a circulation of 600 copies, if largely to libraries, is common (Glass 2003). More than that, the journal's readers came from seventy-five to eighty nations and, according to a survey of readers Glass conducted, included teachers (16 percent), parents (3 percent), and a small number of journalists (1 percent). The journal's two most popular articles (one on home schooling and the other on teacher characteristics and achievement) had had well over 50,000 visitors each, with the readership of many articles still increasing years after publication, again bucking the typical academic trend of initial and then declining interest in work published in journals.

The open access idea is not simply a child of these new publishing technologies. Efforts to improve access to knowledge have a long and venerable history. Open access could be the next step in a tradition that includes the printing press and penny post, public libraries and public schools. It is a tradition bent on increasing the democratic circulation of knowledge, with a lineage that can also be traced back, for example, to the "invisible colleges" of the seventeenth century, which were comprised of informal study clubs that would gather in coffee houses, otherwise known as "penny universities" (Ellis 1956). When the public-library movement took hold during the nineteenth century, local communities and groups of workers came together to establish collections, often without outside government and philanthropic support, such was their determination to access this knowledge and literature (Rose 2003). And of course, many of today's public libraries now provide the surrounding communities with a point of public Internet access to those resources that are freely available online. Further historic parallels to this current access-to-knowledge movement can be found in the university extension movement and mechanics institutes of the nineteenth century, which gave rise to the "open universities" established during the twentieth century. At the heart of these developments was a belief in the right to knowledge, and at every point people have sought the means to ensure that a greater proportion of the population was able to exercise its right to know what is known.

In presenting the case for open access, this book works from historical precedent and global perspectives, as well as with the development of new technologies and economic models. In all of this, the goal is incremental advances in the circulation of knowledge within the academic community and beyond. I do not assume that the open access movement will somehow lead to universal access to academic knowledge, given the inevitable persistence of a digital divide based on persistent economic inequities. It is already, however, leading to considerable improvements in the access afforded to e-journal literature, well beyond what subscription-based print and electronic journals have been able to achieve within the current knowledge economy. And with the extended circulation of research facilitated by open access come greater opportunities for a larger proportion of the global academic community to participate in and contribute to this body of knowledge.

I realize that greater access to this research and scholarship will not always be welcomed. Some may object that the last thing the world needs at this point is access to more information, let alone more people participating in the production of it. But this stance smacks of the privilege that comes of already having considerable access to research resources. The information-overload argument makes a far less compelling case if one's research library has had its serial holdings decimated by increased prices, currency fluctuations, and budget cuts.

Others may ask what greater access will mean, for example, for the tight and constant hold of Islamic fundamentalism on Iranian universities at this point. Azar Nafisi describes in her book *Reading Lolita in Tehran* (2003), for example, how as an Iranian professor, she found that her every public gesture in the university, let alone her teaching and research, were constrained by what she sees as the politics of a cultural puritanism. The one form of intellectual salvation that she managed to create for herself and a small group of students was through their courageous work with a proscribed body of literature, which took place outside of the restricted sphere of her classroom and after she had resigned from the university.

Nafisi and her students' illicit encounter with Nabokov's novel is not the making of a political revolution. Instead, access to photocopies of *Lolita* fostered a wide-ranging encounter with ideas about literature and morality, for the group, in intersecting discussions of Humbert, Lolita, and their own lives. Nafisi had organized what was at once a secret reading group and a literary theory seminar. The experience raises the question, for me at least, of how the larger academic community, which so believes in the value of such encounters, could do more to support those who gather in such settings. The community could, for example, find ways of making more of its scholarship freely available for others to read, whether for, in this case, the sort of literary underground that Nafisi staged in her Tehran home or during the periodic liberalizations that Iranian universities go through, as they did during her time teaching there (2004, 9).

Now, one might well think: Better they should read photocopies of Nabokov than, say, Colin McGinn's article "The Meaning and Morality of *Lolita*" in the *Philosophical Forum* (1999), and one might be correct to think that. Yet that is not a reason for McGinn and other faculty members to keep from these students what others are making of Nabokov's work when it lies so readily within those faculty members' reach to offer it to them. Nafisi and the students could, of course, read both, and respond in turn. The other side of such access, as I have been stressing, is about the participation it enables in the circulation of knowledge.

Open access is not only about helping faculty and students take in this literature; it is not only about extending the Westernization of that literature, in approach or language. Open access can also lead to the introduction of other scholarly traditions into the research literature, extending that metaphorical conversation that defines one ideal for this body of work. To find new ways of increasing access is to extend an invitation and to acknowledge a right, for scholarship exists only as it is shared and circulated, only as it is open to new and diverging voices.

To stay close by Nafisi's book, the need for greater access has been made all the more pressing with the current rebuilding of Iraq, not only after war but after the universities were bled dry by Saddam Hussein's Baath Party, with faculty reduced, in many instances, to selling their personal libraries to survive financially (del Castillo 2003a). In the aftermath of the U.S. invasion, the universities were pillaged, with the library at Basra University, which once held two million volumes, reduced to "a mess of twisted metal shelves atop ashes from the books set ablaze by looters," according to a *New York Times* reporter (Santora 2003, A13). In the face of such destruction, it does not seem all that much to explore ways of making more of the journal literature freely available to these struggling faculty and students, who, in the case of Basra University at least, continued to show up each day among the ruins of their campus. Having online access to journals may well be a very small piece in a large puzzle, and it stands well behind the basic restoration of electricity to the campuses. Still, it is the one thing that academics elsewhere can help with, by self-archiving their published work in institutional repositories and by submitting work to open access journals. By the same token, as Iraqi universities gradually get back on their feet, help can be provided to set up online publishing systems that are able to provide the means of furthering Islamic engagement (in Arabic, as well as in English) with the larger body of research. Nothing is going to come easily in Iraq, and after the American invasion, there are ways for the academic community to reach out, without relenting in its analysis, critique, and search for understanding.[16]

Open access models of scholarly publishing hold out some promise for broadening the circulation and exchange of knowledge while more generally expanding research's presence in the world. Open access holds the promise of moving knowledge from the closed cloisters of privileged, well-endowed university campuses to institutions worldwide. Such an approach also opens a new world of learning to those outside the academic realm, to dedicated professionals and interested amateurs, to concerned journalists and policymakers. In this way, an open access approach to scholarly publishing is not simply a side issue, a matter of business plans and delivery systems, in the pursuit of truth. It is about more than the mechanics of moving an idea from point *A* to point *B*, and now perhaps to points *C* and *D* as well. Rather, the potential

16. The United States Agency for International Development has set aside $20–30 million to enable up to six American institutions to help Iraqi universities reach international standards in their curriculum (del Castillo 2003b).

expansion in the circulation of ideas is very much about the quality of the truth pursued in such settings.

I would argue that the global scale of knowledge's circulation is critical to its very claim as *knowledge*. I am drawing here on the work of philosopher of science Helen Longino, who demonstrates in *The Fate of Knowledge* that "the social [dimension of knowledge] is not a corrupting but a validating element in knowledge" (2002, 122). This is why, Longino argues, we need to pay more attention than we currently do to the social dimensions that arise in the day-to-day conduct of scientific work. For example, she draws our attention to how the economic disparities that affect one scientist's efforts or the gender discrimination that affects those of another amount to a form of "cognitive failure" on the part of science as a whole (132).[17] Cognitive failure suggests a slip of the mind, which does not capture, for me, the larger sense of a human research capacity that is being wasted or going unrealized because of what may now be an unnecessarily restricted access to the circulation of knowledge. In that way, I see the social dimensions of knowledge dissemination, within the current economics of reduced circulation, as a moral failure as much as a cognitive failure. Those involved in science could conceivably accomplish far more, and achieve a greater understanding of the world, if the conditions of access were improved. Or to put it another way, using Longino's term, this cognitive failure diminishes the quality of knowledge we possess.

Although Longino pays little enough attention in her book to questions of how research circulates, she adds to the open access argument by stressing that the scientific community "must also take active steps to ensure that the alternative points of view are developed enough to be a source of criticism and new perspectives" (2002, 132). This requires, to her mind, "publicly recognized forums for the criticism of evidence, of methods, and of assumptions and reasoning," which is what the journal literature already represents, although in ways that are currently limited

17. Longino: "The exclusion of women and members of certain racial minorities from scientific education and the scientific professions constitutes not only a social injustice but a cognitive failing. Similarly, the automatic devaluation in Europe and North America of science from elsewhere constitutes a cognitive failing" (2002, 132).

by the current states of access (129). Without unduly tying Longino to my argument for open access, the publishing approach I am proposing here can be said to be aligned with her concerns over access to science. It does address the "limitation of space" argument for publishing complete scientific information, which she raises, as well as "the privatization of information and ideas," which "contribute[s] to the marginalization of critical discourse" (129). Expanding open access to the research literature would also support what she feels needs to be done to "help citizens acquire a tolerance for the provisionality, partiality, and plurality of knowledge" (213). Nowhere is this aspect of knowledge more readily apparent, after all, than in the give and take of journal literature. What better way to build a little epistemological tolerance among the citizenry than to make these objects of partiality and plurality part of its information landscape, if only off toward the horizon and subject, at best, to occasional visits?

As noted earlier in the chapter, during the Cold War, the U.S. government greatly increased the amount of research funding in both basic and applied areas that it made available to the universities. The commercial publishing houses, more so than the scholarly societies, saw the need for new journal titles and increased numbers of issues to absorb new levels of scholarly output. But while the number of titles increased, the actual circulation of this knowledge was gradually curtailed during the final decades of the twentieth century, as increasing subscription prices forced journal cancellations.

Open access is a direct and immediate response to this state of affairs in scholarly publishing. This utopian upstart of an idea developed out of opportunity and experiment. It was initially the work of those who were intent on taking advantage of the new technology offered by the Internet and World Wide Web to improve the vital circulation of knowledge. Open access, even in the very loose and open way I am using the term, takes advantage of automated processes, open source software, and existing technical infrastructure in the university. And its spirit of openness is not strictly an academic notion. Open access journals, e-print archives, and institutional repositories are part of a larger movement to create an open and public space online that would carry forward the continuing life and legacy of print culture.

The spirit of openness extends beyond publishing in the sciences, and Dominique Foray, in *The Economics of Knowledge* (2004), speaks of the emergence of an "open science model" based on establishing an intellectual-property-right-free zone that "has proven to extremely socially efficient" (147). "Open source biology" provides perhaps the best instance to date of this new spirit.[18] Take the Alliance for Cellular Signalling, for example, with 500 scientists worldwide sending in molecular information that Alfred Gilman and his team are using to develop a virtual cell for testing cellular responses to different conditions (Thompson 2002). Then there are the U.S. National Institutes of Health, which began more than two decades ago to provide an open genetic sequence database, GenBank, which scientists can use to compare DNA sequences, as well as contribute their own findings, along with annotations and links to published articles.[19] There is also a movement afoot toward creating "open government information policies" for public-sector information, including scientific, environmental, and statistical sources (Weiss 2004).

Bodies of knowledge that would advance human understanding and benefit humankind seem so clearly a public good that it might well be hard for someone who is not thoroughly a part of the current system of scholarly publishing to understand why the research and scholarship literature is not being made as open as possible. One might argue that the print economy of journal publishing was once as open and far-reaching

18. A third of research geneticists in a recent survey agreed that there had been a decrease in data sharing over the previous five years (as opposed to 14 percent who saw such sharing as having increased). Reduced access was seen to be hurting their ability to evaluate the research, whereas the principal reason given for not openly sharing data was that it was too much work to do so (Campbell et al. 2002).

19. GenBank is a project of the National Center for Biotechnology Information ⟨http://www.ncbi.nlm.nih.gov/Genbank/⟩. Patrick O. Brown, Michael B. Eisen, and Harold E. Varmus referred to the example of GenBank (as well as the European Molecular Biology Laboratory and the DNA Databank of Japan) in launching their open access *PloS Biology*: "Imagine how impoverished biology and medicine would be today if published DNA sequences were treated like virtually every other kind of research publication—with no comprehensive database searches and no ability to freely download, reorganize, and reanalyze sequences" (2003, 1).

as is economically possible. Had journal prices not skyrocketed over the last few decades, it is possible that the idea of creating open access would not have taken the form it has, or at least the idea would not have the force and urgency that it has now assumed. Given that open access has demonstrated how a much wider and more equitable access to the journal literature can be achieved, the issue is no longer about a return to reasonable pricing for journal subscriptions. Rather, at issue is a greater understanding of the potential implications of this approach to the access question, as opening access stands to further the scientific and public quality of research and scholarship.

3

Copyright

Small ironies abound at the intersection of copyright law and digital technology when it comes to scholarly publishing. Consider how the digital network that makes it all too easy for millions of people to illegally swap copyrighted music files is, at some level, the same technology that is used by journal publishers to further exploit and enforce their ownership of scholarly literature and by researchers to make their work available through open e-print archives with the permission of journals that otherwise hold and protect the copyright for this work. The same technology is used by the U.S. government to build PubMed, an open access index to the life sciences, which then serves as a pay-per-view marketing device for corporate journal publishers, increasing the value of their copyright over publicly financed research.[1] This public-private overlap in technology, financing, and ownership is raising new possibilities for the digital future of journal literature. Or as the American Association for the Advancement of Science pointedly notes, given how the information age "challenges the traditional balance between public and private rights," scientists would do well to seek publishing arrangements that "actively foster the public interest in promoting access to and broad use of scientific information" (Frankel 2002).

1. With PubMed, Harold Varmus, as director of the National Institutes of Health, during the late 1990s, had originally proposed "a system that would make results from the world's life sciences research community freely available on the Internet" (1999). The corporate journal publishers balked at giving away their principal assets, portraying his suggestion as a government threat to free enterprise that would cripple the journal-publishing industry.

The defining legal feature of this digital future is copyright law. In the United States, recent amendments and extensions of the Copyright Act have become a point of concern for a number of legal scholars who see in these changes a worrisome erosion of public rights. These scholars have taken to portraying the current state of copyright as "the enclosure of the intangible commons of the mind," in James Boyle's (2003, 37) elegant analogy with the historic enclosure and loss of shared grazing lands or commons.

In response to this contemporary enclosure, Lawrence Lessig and James Boyle have helped to form the Creative Commons. Founded in 2001, the Creative Commons (2005) seeks to establish a new kind of "reasonable copyright" by providing creators with a new set of copyright licenses that fine-tune an author's right to grant free use for noncommercial purposes or to developing nations, while protecting an author's right to be identified with the work and to keep the work intact. In 2005, Creative Commons plans to launch a Science Commons that will offer licenses that permit authors to retain preprint, postprint, republication, and related rights (including those affecting technology transfer and data sharing). The Creative Commons licenses provide authors with a way of formalizing their legal right to offer, in effect, open access to their work, and in this chapter I review how copyright law is, ultimately, an ally of this greater openness, particularly in the case of research and scholarship.

The changes to copyright law that are intended to bring intellectual-property rights into the digital era have tended to further delimit the public domain, reducing creative possibilities and ultimately restricting freedom of speech, according to the legal shepherds of the commons, Boyle, Lawrence Lessig, and Yochai Benkler.[2] These three have challenged the recent copyright extensions before the Supreme Court and

2. James Boyle: "The expansion of intellectual property rights has been remarkable—from business method patents, to the Digital Millennium Copyright Act, to trademark antidilution rulings, to the European Database Protection Directive. The old limits to intellectual property rights—the antierosion walls around the public domain—are also under attack" (2003, 38). On the creative loss, see Lessig 2002, and on the threat to the freedom of speech, see Benkler 1999.

are part of organizations that would reassert the rights of the public domain and provide alternative formulations of intellectual-property rights.[3] Justice Louis Brandeis expressed what is at stake for them in a dissenting opinion he delivered in a 1918 Supreme Court case involving the press: "The general rule of law is, that the noblest of human productions—knowledge, truths ascertained, conceptions, and ideas—become, after voluntary communication to others, free as the air to common use."[4]

No one in this revolt against enclosing the commons of the mind is opposed to the basic principle of copyright, which protects and balances the rights of author and public. The issue is whether changes to the Copyright Act pay sufficient regard to the public interests that the act is intended also to protect. For my part, this interest in balancing the interests of both author and public is what makes copyright a strong and natural ally of open access for research and scholarship. Given the rise of an open access alternative in scholarly publishing, I think that researchers and scholars need to pause, when faced with a form for transferring the copyright for their work to a journal publisher, rather than simply reach for a pen and sign away "all rights to the above-named work of whatsoever kind and nature" (as I have done countless times). Authors now have a new range of options for protecting their rights, not just out of concern for public interests, but out of unmitigated self-interest and vanity, as well.

This tug between public and private interests in university research is not, of course, unique to this digital era. In a 1942 essay on science and democratic social structure, sociologist Robert Merton bravely pointed out how "'communism,' in the non-technical and extended sense of common ownership of goods," was integral to the scientific ethos, along with universalism, disinterestedness, and organized skepticism (1968, 610). With the great increase in federal funding for research after the

3. Examples of such organizations are the Creative Commons ⟨http://www.creativecommons.org⟩, the Center for the Public Domain ⟨http://publicdomain.org⟩, and Public Knowledge ⟨http://www.publicknowledge.org⟩.

4. The case is cited by Benkler (1999, 354): *International News Serv. v. Associated Press*, 248 U.S. 215, 250 (1918) (Brandeis, J., dissenting).

Second World War, for example, universities were soon being called to account for their tendency to "turn the results of publicly funded research over to some private corporation on an exclusive, monopoly basis," as Horace Gray, at the University of Illinois, put it in response to a Senate committee on the question in 1945, while suggesting that corporate patents on university research amounted "to public taxation for private privilege" (quoted in McSherry 2001, 148). By the end of the 1950s, economist Richard R. Nelson was arguing for the effectiveness of having knowledge "administered as a common pool, with free access to all who can use the knowledge" (1959, 306). Merton was to later remind us that "only by publishing their work can scientists make their *contribution* (as the telling word has it) and only when it thus becomes part of the public domain of science can they truly lay claim to it as theirs" (1979, emphasis in original).[5] Publishing research in a print journal or book was, until not so very long ago, the only way to enter scholarship into the public domain. Today, a two-tiered "public domain of science" has emerged—the one based on fee-restricted access and the other offering open access—with a very small minority of articles existing in both realms, thanks to authors posting their published work in e-print archives. This divide radically affects "the status of scientific knowledge as common property," to use another of Merton's expressions from this earlier period (1968, 611).

More recently, legal scholar Melville B. Nimmer (1970) has argued that public interests should be allowed, in special circumstances, to override copyright claims or should at least be used to restrict such claims to the immediate and actual economic damage done by the free flow of the information in question. Benkler (1999) takes a similar line when he argues that in a democracy, freedom of speech should trump copyright restrictions that prevent the public use of certain materials.

The courts have recognized limits in the application of copyright to research. In 1981, the U.S. Fifth Circuit Court ruled, in *Miller v. University Studios*, against the right to copyright research results: "The valuable distinction in copyright law between fact and expression cannot be

---

5. Merton also held that "an idea is not really yours until you give it away" (quoted in Mahoney 1973, 7).

maintained if research is held to be copyrightable.... [T]o hold that research is copyrightable is no more or no less than to hold that the facts discovered as a result of research are entitled to copyright protection" (McSherry 2001, 204).[6] What journals own, then, if not the research, in the sense of the facts discovered or truths uncovered, is the exact expression of the results in an article. This is why copyright does not necessarily bear on charges of plagiarism, which can be about using, without attribution, the facts and truths that someone has discovered (and cannot copyright), as well as someone else's words. Plagiarism represents more than issues of proprietorship, as it is concerned with a cultural ethos of respect for how the use of others' work should be credited.[7]

To better understand the role that copyright plays in the journal-publishing programs of the major corporate journal publishers, I contacted five professors who had served as the editor for a journal published by one of the leading corporate journal publishers, Elsevier, Springer, Kluwer, and Wiley. Each of the editors had at some point in the not-too-distant past resigned his or her editorial post with the corporate-published journal in order to work in the nonprofit sector of academic publishing. While my five editors hardly represent an unbiased source of insight into the relationship between editor and publisher, they did set out in clear terms not only what publishers do and do not do as part of the publishing process, but how copyright is being used to distort the relationship among author, editor, and publisher.

In describing why they took on editorial roles for these commercial publishers, the editors spoke of *honor* ("it is hard to refuse a board

---

6. The content of databases is another area of dispute over intellectual-property rights that is extremely relevant to the research enterprise that the U.S. courts have held is not covered by copyright unless the database meets the originality claim (*Feist v. Rural Telephone*, 499 U.S. 340, 1991).

7. Publishers use copyright in cases of plagiarism when elements of the wording are the same, but non-copyright-infringement tempests over plagiarism also arise when a study fails to sufficiently credit an earlier work that may cover the same ground, use similar methods, or produce similar, if not identical, results; see, for example, Monastersky 2003. Martin Blume (2003), editor-in-chief of the American Physical Society, reports using the concept of copyright violation to prod editors into publishing retractions for plagiarized work they have published.

position with a prestigious journal," as one put it) and *ignorance* (another credited the Association of Research Libraries with eventually educating him, long after he had taken on the editorial role, on the consequences of increasing corporate control of journal publishing). Editors did receive perks from the publishers, although there was certainly no standard editor reward package. One editor received no more than a free subscription to the journal, while another editor spoke of receiving "a nontrivial amount of $9,500" in 1991, which was, to his initial surprise, then paid to him annually. The editorial services provided by the publishers also varied. Where one publisher provided proofreading services for the journal and offered to support copyediting costs, the editor actually opted to do both the proofreading and copyediting himself, as he felt his scientific background enabled him to do a better job. Another publisher provided neither copyediting nor proofreading. In one case, the publisher of the journal would, in its former editor's opinion, "typically introduce typos rather than remove them," with the result that some authors insisted on submitting their copy camera-ready in LaTeX rather than risk having it typeset. Still, when it came to leaving these well-respected publishers to start an alternative journal in their field, one editor noted "the huge cost of breaking away." The cost includes having to rebuild subscription lists and having the new journal slowly earn its way into the ISI Web of Science citation index as a ranked journal.

Then there had been the matter of copyright for these editors. The terms of the copyright held by a journal's publisher are set out in a contract, typically with the editor. These contracts make it apparent how important it is for the publisher to secure copyright control over the journal and its contents. For example, in providing one editor with $16,000 per year for office expenses—as any payment directly to the editor or the reviewers, the publisher explained to the editor, would taint the process—the publisher made it clear that this was "in consideration for" his services, as well as for the transfer of copyright for all materials in the journal. The transfer of copyright from author and editor to the publisher is not to be misconstrued, these contracts make it clear, as a gift or otherwise considered potentially non-binding or contestable. One publisher's contract went beyond that to transform the journal's contents, and the editor's efforts, into "work-made-for-hire," or as the publisher's legal department worded the contract:

The Journal and all material contained therein and the work product of the Editor and the Editor's staff produced hereunder shall constitute a "work-made-for-hire" under the U.S. Copyright Act and all rights comprised therein shall automatically, upon creation, vest in and thereafter be solely owned by the Publisher. To the extent, if any, that the Journal and/or any Contribution or other material contained therein do not qualify as a "work-made-for-hire" or copyright or other proprietary rights thereto might otherwise vest in the Editor, the Editor hereby grants, assigns and transfers all such rights exclusively and in perpetuity to the Publisher, in all languages and formats, in all media of expression now known or later developed, throughout the world.

Even apart from the "in perpetuity" phrase, which mistakenly suggests that copyright has no temporal limits and that the work in question will not eventually enter the public domain, this "work-made-for-hire" clause is a particularly troubling turn of legalese overkill. The first thing this contract does is reverse what would otherwise seem to be the case, namely, that the academic community hires the publishers, in effect, to provide a service necessary for the circulation of knowledge. Instead, this contract positions the editor, and by implication the author, as working for the publisher. The contract situates the publisher as an employer, having received work-made-for-*hire* by virtue of seeing the manuscript through to publication, and thus gives the publisher the right to sell, or rather rent (as the publisher retains ownership), the work back to the researcher's actual employer, through the serials budget of the university library.

Now, the very fact that a researcher, whether as author or editor, is able to enter into such a contract as a free agent speaks to the public trust invested in academic work, often celebrated by faculty members under the banner of *academic freedom*. The contract voids this element by positioning the author as working for the publisher. A business's employees are typically considered to be engaged in just such "work-for-hire" (think of Microsoft programmers), which ensures that an employer owns the copyright for "a work prepared by an employee within the scope of his or her employment," according to U.S. copyright law. Under that same law, academics have long been entrusted with the copyright for their research articles. This is known in copyright law as the "teacher's exception" or "academic exception," and it has continued to withstand challenges in the courts.[8] This exception recognizes that a scholar's research is self-directed, owing more to free inquiry in the pursuit of a public good than to the direct financial well-being of the institution employing the researcher. On the other hand, universities now have a recognized claim on patents resulting from faculty work and on distance education course content (in which they invest substantial amounts developing).[9]

Although the courts have upheld an author's right to control his or her scholarship in the name of academic freedom, faculty members have remained rather indifferent to this right. Or rather, they are all too happy, as a rule, to turn that ownership over to publishers, "in all media of expression now known or later developed, throughout the world," as the publisher's contract quoted earlier puts it. The use of new technologies is only adding to the significance of the ownership transfer, with digital rights management, content repurposing, pay-per-view transactions, and licensing agreements increasing research literature's commercial value. Still, regardless of how a publisher may word its contracts, copyright protection cannot be conveyed to the publisher "in perpetuity," as even the Copyright Term Extension Act of 1998 limits corporate

8. 17 U.S.C. Section 101. Also, see Frankel 2002 (14) on the "teacher exception," upheld most recently in *Hays v. Sony Corp. of America*, 847 F.2d 412 (7th Cir. 1988); *Dolmage v. Erskine* [2003] OJ No. 161 (Ontario Superior Court of Justice—Small Claims Court) for a recent Canadian ruling; and more generally, McSherry 2001 (101–143). On a freedom-of-speech interpretation of university assertion of research copyright ownership as placing an undue chill on faculty freedom to explore, discuss, and share ideas, see Meyer 1998 (13–14).

9. American universities were given the right to own patents resulting from federally sponsored research (as long as federal government access is not restricted) by the Bayh-Dole Act of 1980. Patents cover human creations that are novel, useful, and nonobvious, compared to copyright, which protects the exact expression of an idea (McSherry 2001, 170). In 2001, U.S. universities earned $857 million in patent royalties and filed for 9,454 U.S. patents (Blumenstyk 2003). This "second academic revolution," as it has been called, is worth comparing to the capitalization of knowledge in scholarly publishing (Etzkowitz, Webster, and Healy 1998).

owners in the United States to a ninety-five-year hold on copyrighted material before it enters the public domain.[10]

Whereas authors routinely transfer copyright ownership to journal publishers, whether corporate or nonprofit, this is not the case, interestingly enough, for books, judging by those sitting on my desk. The authors hold the copyright for some of the books sitting here, whereas the publishers hold it for others. What this suggests is that journal publishers do not necessarily need to hold the copyright of materials they publish, much as they might protest otherwise. The publisher needs only *first-publication rights* from an author to protect the journal's position in the marketplace of ideas by being the first outlet in which the article appears.[11] Copyright and publication rights are not different terms for the same principle. The author's retention of copyright asserts an ownership that includes, in many jurisdictions if not yet the United States, a moral claim over the work, intended to protect its integrity, which in the case of research includes its status both as the author's personal work and as a public good.

The current journal economy seems to be about something more than protecting the author's right to benefit from this creative and intellectual act of publishing original work. As things now stand, copyright is too often used to protect the publisher's right to charge what it will for its journals, placing what can be a prohibitive price on entry into what is otherwise thought of as the public realm or as common property, to use Merton's term. Copyright is being used by some publishers to ensure that the transfer from print to digital publishing does nothing to diminish the profitability of scholarly publishing and, if possible, increases it.

10. When this copyright extension was unsuccessfully challenged recently in the Supreme Court in *Eldred v. Ashcroft* (537 U.S. 01-168, 2003), an editorial in the *New York Times* bemoaned that the "public domain has been a grand experiment, one that should not be allowed to die. The ability to draw freely on the entire creative output of humanity is one of the reasons we live in a time of such fruitful creative ferment" ("Coming of Copyright Perpetuity" 2003).

11. I owe this point to Henry Hardy's (2002) letter to the *Times Literary Supplement*. With the open access e-journal *First Monday*, for example, the author retains copyright, while granting the journal a publication right or license which "allows *First Monday* to publish a manuscript in a given issue," as its Web site puts it.

Thus, the greater access to the research literature afforded by the Internet, when compared to what it took to send around print journals, is being exploited by some to generate new revenue streams through such systems as pay per view that allow readers to purchase access to an article on the spot, instead of having to subscribe to the journal or order an offprint in order to read it.

Publishers have granted two substantial exceptions to their increased marketing and control of materials for which they hold the copyright. One important copyright concession many publishers have made is to offer universities in developing countries open access to their journals (Smart 2003). The other concession, owing much to Harnad's efforts, is found in publisher policies enabling authors to self-archive the work they submit to the publisher's journals in open access e-print archives (available in more than a few university libraries), which makes the work freely available to the world. Among 100 publishers polled in one ongoing survey, authors were permitted to self-archive in 92 percent of the close to 9,000 journals those publishers represent, with 79 percent of the journals allowing postprints or final versions to be posted and 13 percent restricting self-archiving to preprints (EPrints.org 2005; see also Gadd, Oppenheim, and Probets 2003). In one sense, the self-archiving concession follows on the tradition of publishers sending neat bundles of offprints to authors, who then sent them off with a warm note to colleagues, students, and family or in response to preprinted postcards that arrived from abroad. The difference is that in archiving a work, the author opens and extends access to it on a more democratic and global basis (although by no means making it universally available, in light of the digital divide).

Still, a final contradiction in this transfer of ownership from author to publisher remains to be considered, one that makes it clear how copyright law, at least in spirit, stands as an ally of the open access journal and archive. The relevant clause in the U.S. Constitution (Article II, Section 8, Clause 8) grants Congress the power "to promote the Progress of Science and useful Arts, by securing for limited Times to Authors and Inventors the exclusive Right to their respective Writings and Discoveries." This exclusive right to their work is intended, of course, to enable authors and inventors to profit sufficiently that they have an incentive to continue this creative contribution to society. Yet copyright is also intended to protect the public's interest by allowing the work to enter the public domain, as copyright is only secured "for limited Times."[12]

The key to copyright is the right of authors to *profit* from their work. Yet journal publishers have not made their editors or authors financial partners in the publishing economy they have created (whereas the same publishers pay royalties to the authors of the books they publish). Authors turn their work over to publishers in exchange for having the work reviewed and published. Though they may not have come to recognize it yet, those authors who choose to publish their work in journals that do not offer some form of open access, and do so without also submitting the article to an e-print archive, may be working against their own best interests. I mean *best interests* in three senses: a professional sense (as they wish to contribute to a greater public good), a vanity sense (in the search for recognition), and a financial sense (given the recognition-based academic incentive system in which they work). In failing to take advantage of the journal or archive routes to open access, not only are these authors reducing public access to knowledge, they are undermining the level of career-enhancing recognition that they might otherwise receive for their work.

There's no question that to appear consistently in the leading journals does a career a world of good, whether they be open access journals or not. But when it comes to adding up the number of times one is cited, at the end of the day, self-archiving one's work in a repository or choosing an open access journal in the first place may make a critical difference, or so an increasing number of studies are suggesting, as I noted in chapter 2 by drawing attention to Hitchcock's (2005) regularly updated Web site bibliography devoted to such work.

Even choosing to publish in a journal with what I am calling *delayed open access* can make a difference for an author. *Teachers College*

12. The first U.S. copyright statute in 1790 limited copyright protection to a period of fourteen years, and the period has been repeatedly extended, to the point where the average copyright is now in effect for ninety-five years for corporate holders of copyright such as publishers, a length of time that some argue serves only to diminish creative and inventive cultural possibilities (Lessig 2004).

Record, a journal from Teachers College, Columbia University, has been publishing for more than a century, and it now offers delayed open access to its online content, which it provides through its own Web site, while continuing to publish with Blackwell. Whereas Blackwell handles its print and electronic subscription editions, the *Teachers College Record* Web site provides open access to articles six months after their initial publication. Gary Natriello, executive editor of *Teachers College Record*, reports that in 2001, one popular article which the journal tracked was downloaded 100 times from Blackwell's subscription service in its first six months and then, after it was placed on the journal's open access Web site, it was downloaded 4,000 times from that site over the next few months. But that shouldn't be surprising, given that *Teachers College Record*'s free notification service for its open access site goes by e-mail to 65,000 people. As for how often the journal's articles are being cited, *Teachers College Record*'s impact factor doubled between 1998 and 2002, according to the ISI Web of Science. Also speaking to the increased presence of the journal, Natriello reports that submissions to *Teachers College Record* have gone up, since launching the open access site, from 75 submissions a year in 1995 to 600 submissions in 2002, leading to a greater frequency of publication for the journal.[13]

These very preliminary indications—including my earlier reference to the open access *Education Policy Analysis Archives* being visited 2,500 times a day and having over 50,000 hits on its best articles—point to open access papers' being cited and consulted more often than toll-access work. And to have one's work read and cited more often than before, or more often than a colleague's non-open-access papers, is certainly in the best interests of one's career and financial standing. Open access journals and e-print archives also hold the promise of increasing the exposure and circulation of knowledge. In this way, open access is consistent with the

13. *Teachers College Record* gradually increased its frequency of publication from quarterly to monthly between 2000 and 2004, and it has increased subscription costs accordingly, without hurting the number of libraries that subscribe to the print edition (around 1,500); an additional 2,300 libraries receive the digital edition alone through bundling deals with the publisher, Blackwell. On the other hand, personal subscriptions are down to 300 (personal communication, Gary J. Natriello, July 31–August 1, 2003).

copyright principle of protecting the interests of the author, while honoring the rights of the public. Of course, were everyone to publish in open access journals or place his or her work in open access archives, any career and remunerative advantages to doing so would disappear. (Would that the case for open access might be diminished in this manner.)

If open access takes care of the author's interests, what, then, of the other party to copyright law, the public? Open access could be said to increase freedom of speech, in contrast to many uses of copyright law today, which undermine it, according to legal scholar Yochai Benkler (1999).[14] Although the Supreme Court has repeatedly upheld the principle that "the widest possible dissemination of information from diverse and antagonistic sources is essential to the welfare of the public," as Justice Hugo Black put it in a 1945 decision, this diversity is being curtailed by corporate concentration in media ownership, or in Benkler's words, "A world dominated by Disney, News Corp., and Time Warner appears to be the expected and rational response to excessive enclosure of the public domain" (377, 359).[15]

The danger is not simply with an economy that favors corporate concentration—in academic publishing no less than with other media—it is in how this concentration reduces the opportunities for (and increases the costs of) initiating new alternative sources of information. In the name of preserving freedom of speech, Benkler proposes that we restore an information commons that supports more open communication: "To secure this freedom, however, we must build a core common infrastructure that will allow commercial and noncommercial, professional and amateur, commodified and noncommodified, mainstream and fringe to interact in an environment that allows all to flourish and is biased in

14. Although appeals to freedom of speech have traditionally been used as a check on government powers, Benkler points out, the issue is now one of corporate concentration in the media creating an "information flow ... [that] will tend to prevent effective political challenge to the prevailing order," as fewer and fewer companies control "the resources necessary to effective communication" (1999, 380–381).

15. Some years later, U.S. courts took a similar stand in striking down the Communications Decency Act of 1996 on the First Amendment grounds that the Web represents a "vast democratic flora ... [where] any person with a phone line can become a town crier" (Romano 2002).

favor of none" (2001, 3).[16] Benkler's vision of an information commons is not all that removed from the "core common infrastructure" that underwrites open access e-print archives and journals, with their shared indexing systems and open source code, designed to improve the scholarly and scientific contribution to this larger commons. That is to say, public access to research provides its own support for freedom of speech. Not only does it enable greater participation in scholarly communication, but it facilitates the informed deliberation on which democracies depend (which I treat in more detail in chapter 8).

The copyright interests of researchers are to have their work reproduced, read, and accurately cited among as wide a readership as possible. The economic interests of faculty are not hurt, for example, as are those of publishers, by the distribution of free copies of their published work. Just the opposite. A 1999 study by Alma P. Swan and Sheridan N. Brown of "what authors want" within the academic community speaks of authors' overriding interest in finding the widest possible audience through the journals in which they publish, while also keeping an eye on their prestige and inclusion in the major indexes, which are also related to the size of readership.[17]

In a further survey conducted just a few years later, Swan and Brown (2004) were able to poll a sample of 314 authors evenly divided between those who had published in open access journals and those who had not. They found that those who had chosen open access on occasion

16. Benkler proposes both a publicly financed fiber network, drawing on the model of the National Highway Act, and a national software foundation devoted to open source software. It is well worth noting in that regard that open source systems are currently being supported by the National Libraries, National Science Foundation, Association of Research Libraries, Mellon Foundation, Free Software Foundation, and others.

17. One premise of PASA is that "the Internet makes it possible for this [scientific] information to be promptly available not only to every scientist and physician who could use it to further the public good, but to every person with access to the Internet at home, in school, or in a library" (Weitzman 2003). In a 1998 report, the American Academy of Arts and Sciences proposed that authors retain the copyright for federally funded research: "Federal agencies that fund research should recommend (or even require) as a condition of funding that the copyrights of articles or other works describing research that has been supported by those agencies remain with the author" (Bachrach et al. 1998).

expressed "a belief in the principle of free access to research information," while also thinking open access journals offered a higher readership and a greater number of citations; on the other hand, those who did not publish in open access journals felt that such journals offered reduced readerships and citation.[18] The goals for both sets of authors are the same; the understanding of the best means of achieving them just differs. A similar form of ignorance lag is at work with self-archiving, as the majority of faculty slowly learn about the publishing issues surrounding self-archiving and catch on to what open access really has to offer.

Up to this point, few authors have been taking advantage of publishers' self-archiving policies, and many e-print archives have little in them. Despite the high number of journals explicitly permitting authors to make their work open access in this way, rough estimates are that no more than 15–20 percent of the journal literature is archived annually (Hitchcock 2005). Swan reports that among those in her faculty survey who had yet to self-archive a paper, close to 80 percent were "not aware of the possibility of providing open access to their work by self-archiving" (2005). The whole thing has led Harnad (2004a) to call on universities to mandate self-archiving by their faculty.[19] The publishers are no longer the roadblock to open access, in Harnad's book, given the number that permit self-archiving. The problem is the authors. They remain blind to the greater research impact they could achieve by uploading a paper to an archive, which takes all of about six minutes (according to e-print archive Web logs, Harnad reports, at the University of Southampton). As Harnad impatiently puts it, "10 years of evidence have since suggested that although it might not take till the heat death of the universe, that voluntary road of rational self-interest is proving

18. A counterpoint comes from Robert P. Parks, who contends that "although authors desire greater readership, that is not the major goal and in fact may be counterproductive because more readers demand more time from authors to explain their writing" (2001). This was certainly the case with Isaac Newton, as I discuss in chapter 13.

19. Up to this point, a half-dozen or so departments and universities have mandated self-archiving policies for their faculty, according to the Registry of Departments and Institutions Who Have Adopted an OA Self-Archiving Policy maintained by the EPrints.org Web site at ⟨http://www.eprints.org/signup/fulllist.php⟩.

far too slow. So it was wise of the UK and US [committees considering the issue] to recommend mandating [self-archiving] instead, just as publishing itself is already mandated ('publish or perish')" (2004a).

When there was but one economic model for publishing research in a form that could be sent far and wide, there was little argument against readers' and libraries' bearing reasonable publishing costs that were obviously associated with delivering to them a print edition of the journal. Nor was there any reason, in the era of print, for researchers to be concerned about turning over the ownership of their work to publishers. Yet over the last couple of decades, the journal economy has reached certain limits in the dissemination of research, even as the world of scholarly activity has continued to expand on a global scale. Corporate journal publishers have chosen to concentrate their marketing efforts (and profits) on well-endowed research libraries that have no choice but to continue to subscribe to the journals that the publishers hold and continue to acquire. Although some publishers are making admirable concessions for self-archiving and others are providing open access to older material, there is still a long way to go in establishing a balance of rights and interests between author and public. As long as the greater part of the publishing industry falls short in promoting the best interests of the authors and the public, it fails to honor the spirit of copyright law.

4

Associations

Whether in representing the professional interests of an academic discipline (such as the American Psychological Association) or in giving voice to new areas of research (as does, for example, the Cognitive Science Society), associations publish journals to provide a focused venue for the work of their members and to define their leadership and professional identity in the field. As these associations grow in size, it often takes more than one journal to represent the scope of interests that they represent. With more than 150,000 members, the American Psychological Association (APA), for example, lists no less than fifty journals on its Web site, ranging from the *American Journal of Orthopsychiatry* to the *Review of General Psychology*. The Institute of Electrical and Electronics Engineers, Inc. (IEEE), with over 360,000 members and over 100 journals, manages to publish 30 percent of the literature in electrical engineering and computers. Both of these associations have a membership made up of faculty researchers and practicing professionals, with the journals serving to increase the flow of information between these two groups. Many associations generate a considerable budget surplus from journal sales, which they use to support other society activities. Associations work hard to ensure that their journals are among the top titles in their field, and they use free or discounted subscriptions to their journals as a membership incentive.

Historically, it actually took some time for associations to discover the value of publishing journals. As I describe in chapter 13, the Royal Society of London held back for almost a century before becoming more than nominally involved in the publishing of the *Philosophical*

Transactions, which essentially published the correspondence of the society, which began as a private publishing venture in 1665, albeit operated by the secretary of the Royal Society, Henry Oldenburg. By the eighteenth century, the society's members had realized that the journal could well further the goals and reach of the organization and its members. Today, a scholarly association wouldn't be caught charging membership fees without offering those members at least one journal. Now, however, these associations face a new set of challenges associated with journal publishing. They have to manage the transition from print to electronic publishing while contending with basic changes in the way that people are reading research, which is now far more often by selecting articles from an index rather than by subscribing to a journal and reading a smattering of articles in it.

According to researchers Carol Tenopir and Donald King (2001), "the average number of personal subscriptions per scientist ... roughly halved" over the last two decades of the twentieth century.[1] Scientists are now doing a third of their reading in electronic form, drawing on a broader range of journals than they did even a decade ago, when they might typically read through a single journal. There are just too many journals today that touch on a scholar's work, which discourages individual investments in a single journal.

Although some have accused the associations of riding the upward subscription price spiral of corporate publishers to their advantage, what is perhaps more troubling is the number of scholarly associations that have turned their journals over to these publishers, effectively moving the journals out of the nonprofit sector. For example, Reed Elsevier announced in 2001 that it was offering thirteen new journals, ten of which it had acquired from scholarly societies, and Sage Publications pointed to the fact that ten of its thirty-five new titles for 2002 repre-

1. Nearly forty years ago, it is worth noting, Fritz Machlup (1977, 224) found that between 1966 and 1977, the number of individual subscriptions to five out of the six journals in science and technology he was examining had declined, with the number of institutional subscriptions going down for all six journals. Machlup observed that despite the decrease in the number of noninstitutional subscriptions, the revenue from these subscriptions did not decline but actually rose between 76 and 167 percent, as a result of price increases.

sented "society contracts," according to the Web sites of these two corporate publishers. Some of the major journal publishing houses, such as Sage, are offering the associations the equivalent of "signing bonuses," in the tens of the thousands of dollars, for turning their well-established titles over. Other services, such as Ingenta, charge associations for setting up and maintaining online access for their journals, with a promise of royalties from licensing and pay-per-view fees.

Placing an association's journals with a commercial publisher or service may raise the journals' profiles among librarians, as the corporate publishers have excellent marketing arms. In addition, an association's journals, once placed with a commercial publisher, may well be bundled with other journals, increasing their likelihood of further sales. Yet the increased subscription fees that typically follow on the corporate acquisition of journals could as easily result in a drop in subscriptions and readership for a society. On the other hand, some associations are experimenting with different forms of open access. They are permitting authors to use open access e-print archives for their published work (as are many of the corporate publishers at this point).

Adding urgency to the need for scholarly associations to plan for the future is an inevitable undermining of the subscription-based membership model. The problem is that most members and potential members of the associations are beginning to have ubiquitous access to association journals—at the office, at home, and on the road—through their research library's subscription to electronic editions. That is, membership confers no additional advantage for those who belong to subscribing institutions, or at least it won't after the associations drop their print editions, as increasing numbers of readers move online. This obviously undermines the subscription benefits of association membership.

Let me offer an example, from the high end (financially) of the scholarly association field, of how access redundancy can affect an association. The American Astronomical Society (AAS), with around 6,500 members, publishes three journals, which, taken together, contributed $5,834,020 in revenue to this nonprofit society's total budget of $8,683,893 in 2000 (see appendix B). The AAS operates a very successful publishing operation. The society's two principal journals, the *Astronomical Journal* and the *Astrophysical Journal*, are published for the

AAS by the University of Chicago Press, whereas the AAS itself publishes the *Bulletin of the American Astronomical Society*. A membership in the AAS costs $110 annually, and although that does provide members with a number of newsletters, it also entitles members to purchase online access to the society's two journals and bulletin at a discounted rate of $50, which is a considerable bargain compared to the normal fee.[2]

The advantages of AAS membership (at least those regarding journal access) quickly evaporate, however, when one considers that the journals are no longer the first or exclusive source of the material they publish. The field of astrophysics may not be typical among scholarly fields of inquiry, given how much of its literature is freely available online, but where it finds itself today may well be where other sciences are headed, especially with the prospect of mandated self-archiving policies among institutions and funding agencies.

David Rusin's (2002) paper "The Expected Properties of Dark Lenses" provides a typical instance of how the new state of redundant access works with the AAS. Rusin's paper, by the way, is not about astronomers carrying on like the Blues Brothers, which Dan Aykroyd and John Belushi made famous in the movie by that name, with their ever-present dark lenses, but about the effects of "multiple-image gravitational lens systems formed by dark matter halos" (2002, 705). It was published in the *Astrophysical Journal* in June 2002. By that point, however, it had already been read by every scholar and student of astronomy with a particular interest in the issues Rusin raises. When the editors of the *Astrophysical Journal* notified Rusin, in February 2002, that they had decided to accept the article for publication, he did what many researchers in physics do: He posted a copy to the open access database known as the

2. The annual subscription fee for *Astronomical Journal* for 2005 was $525 for twelve issues a year covering print (including shipping) and electronic versions, with the electronic version alone costing $425, and the thrice-monthly *Astrophysical Journal* had an annual subscription fee of $1,800 for paper (including shipping) and electronic versions, with an additional $200 for its *Supplement Series*. For research libraries that require airfreight delivery of the print edition, the charge can add another $440 to the cost of the two journals. The society does have a "journal donation" program, in which members offer complete sets of the journals, covering various years, but again the acquiring libraries must pay shipping.

arXiv.org E-Print Archive, supported by the National Science Foundation and the Energy Department of the U.S. government (Kling, Spector, and McKim 2002). As I noted in chapter 3, physicists all over the world make a point of visiting arXiv.org every working day to check what is new in their field, and many papers go up there long before they are even seen by a journal. After Rusin's paper went through the editorial process with the *Astrophysical Journal*, Rusin then updated the arXiv.org version, on May 2, with the comment: "Final version, minor corrections, 18 pages, ApJ June 20 2002."

By June 2002, identical versions of Rusin's article were available from multiple sources. The article first appeared publicly in the arXiv.org E-Print Archive, which made it available free to anyone with Internet access. This was followed by the publication of both print and electronic versions in the *Astrophysical Journal*, published by the University of Chicago, and circulated among individual and institutional subscribers. Thus a member of the AAS who took advantage of the discounted electronic subscription would have four possible routes of access to Rusin's article.[3] Members, as well as libraries, are paying for something that is otherwise available for free.[4] All three electronic versions are virtually indistinguishable on a computer screen in the office, at home, or on the road. Association membership is losing its associated privileges, at least in regard to access to its journals. (The Rusin example does not even exhaust the current redundancies within the current scholarly publishing economies, as the overlap extends to the indexing of the article, which I treat in more detail in chapter 12.)

It may not be all that surprising that journals making the substantial transition from print to digital publishing media would take some time

3. As for the copyright legality of this redundancy, the University of Chicago Press was still in 2004 among a minority of publishers (14 percent) that did not permit self-archiving in e-print services such as arXiv.org (see the Web site of the SHERPA Project at ⟨http://www.sherpa.ac.uk/⟩), although the press does not appear to have sought legal redress for the placement of its property in such open access archives.

4. To reduce this redundancy, a "peer review overlay" for arXiv.org E-Print Archive has been tested in various forms but has yet to become a feature of the archive.

to sort out redundant and overlapping services. However, what is clear is that the personal-copy-of-the-journal advantage of membership does not transfer to the online medium. The library's electronic edition is available everywhere, for the vast majority of potential members who, if they can afford to join AAS, are likely to work at an institution that subscribes to its journals. But the eventual e-print archive buildup of articles from the journal, whether placed there voluntarily or by institutional mandate, puts the association's retention of the library's subscription in jeopardy.

So what is a scholarly association to do, where is it to turn? Well, as always, it should turn to the best interests of its membership. What other purpose does it have? From a researcher-as-author perspective, increased readership (and citation) will always trump journal revenues. Associations need to recognize, if they have not already, the declining value of a membership copy of an association's journals. On the other hand, opening access to the journals increases their readership (and that of the association's author-members). The question for the associations is, Why keep the membership's research from those in their field who do not belong to the association or have access to a good research library if a form of open access to this literature can be provided without destroying the viability of the association's journal publishing? The time has come to explore different routes for increasing access to the work that the association is devoted to supporting.

Associations may be tempted by schemes that try to ensure that a library's electronic copy does not replace a member's copy (for example, by limiting the number of users of an electronic edition at any one time, as some publishers do), or they may seek to provide members with "value-added services," such as reference linking to which members alone have access. These approaches seem a little shortsighted and again not in the best interests of the membership, as they hamper rather than advance access to the membership's work by a larger realm of potential readers.

To help associations realistically address this question, I have assembled budgetary information for twenty scholarly associations in the United States (see appendix B). Just how much do the scholarly associations make on the sale of their journals to libraries and other institutions? The associations in my sample (which leaves out the large organizations taking in tens of millions of dollars annually) saw, on average, $691,873 in publication revenue in 2000 (a figure that does not include membership fees). The range in revenue is considerable among associations. The Cognitive Science Society and the International Association for Feminist Economics (which publish their journals through Elsevier and Taylor and Francis, respectively) declared no revenue from the sales of their journals. The American Astronomical Society (which as I noted above publishes its journals through the University of Chicago Press) claimed $6.4 million in publishing revenue. The associations' publishing revenue is supplemented by the royalty sales of material previously published, which averages $22,918 for the twenty associations, suggesting that the after-initial-sales market of back issues and reprints is not all that strong.

The revenue and royalties obtained through journal publishing need to be set against, of course, the publishing costs. The average annual publishing expenses for the sample of scholarly associations considered here is $921,250. Although these costs may include other of the association's publications, it is safe to conclude that journals make up the bulk of it. What this means is that selling subscriptions to institutions covers close to 80 percent of the publishing costs, on average, for the twenty associations. Some associations do much better than that and are able to devote their entire membership dues to other aspects of the association, while at the same time making a profit on their subscription sales. But more often, the library and other institutional subscribers cover a good portion of the associations' publishing costs, with the rest of their publishing expenses, averaging 22 percent of the costs, covered by membership fees. Open access would seem to place the revenue from subscriptions at risk, leaving associations scrambling to make up close to 80 percent of their publishing costs.

This may seem to pose an insurmountable problem, but pioneers in open access have demonstrated that it need not be. Some sense of the details behind a viable transition to open access is provided, for example, by John Hawley, executive director of the American Society for Clinical Investigation. Hawley sought to fill in my account of association practices, when I initially published this analysis (2003a), by describing the economics of the open access *Journal of Clinical Investigation.* The journal is published bimonthly and runs to 350 articles and 3,000 pages a year and thus requires, not surprisingly, a full-time science editor and executive editor. The journal costs $2.5 million per year to produce, including $200,000 in honoraria paid to its editorial board and unstated compensation for the chief editor. The journal charges its authors a manuscript-processing fee of $50 and has publication charges, on a per-word basis, that can run up to $1,500 an article. It also continues to sell subscriptions to its print edition. Against all of that, the society has been able to offer immediate and complete open access to the electronic edition of the journal since it went online in 1996. As Hawley (2003) explains in a *Journal of Clinical Investigation* editorial, since the journal's move to open access, institutional subscriptions to the print edition have fallen by 40 percent, whereas its Web site is now receiving some 20,000 unique visitors each week. The journal is managed online, with reduced costs and improved efficiency in its publishing operations, but it has also been increasing its author fees, compensating for the reduced number of subscriptions and allowing it to maintain its revenue levels a little ahead of a decade ago. Its impact factor increased 66 percent between 1998 and 2002, although Hawley attributes this increase to the reduced number of papers it accepts and publishes, rather than open access.[5]

The *Journal of Clinical Investigation* provides but one instance of how an association can increase access to its publications without suffering any loss of revenue. Associations have a number of options in this regard. At the most basic level, they can support their members' self-archiving of articles that are published in their journals, as well as in

5. Also, see Hawley 2004. In addition, John Vig, a vice president with IEEE, wrote to me in response to an earlier version of this chapter (2003a) with an open access proposal that he was developing for the more than 100 journals published by his institute. His approach is driven, he explained, not by "revenue replacement but profit (surplus) maintenance" (personal communication, January 30–February 3, 2004). He also attempted to correct my assumption that an association's primary mandate is to serve its members. Such a stance did not stand up to IEEE's lawyer's advice on nonprofits; the position nonprofit organizations were instead advised to take is neatly summed up in the IEEE mission statement, which Vig cited: "The IEEE promotes the engineering process of creating, developing, integrating, sharing, and applying knowledge about electro and information technologies and sciences *for the benefit of humanity and the profession*" (IEEE 2005, emphasis added).

other journals, making it explicitly part of their association's and their journals' publishing policies, as some associations already do. They can further support self-archiving by establishing an open access e-print archive for their discipline. I would take that to be the most basic and responsible of responses to what is otherwise the prospect of declining access to research and scholarship on a global scale, in the face of an opportunity for greatly increased circulation. Authors who self-archive the work they publish do not appear to pose a threat to associations' subscription lists. So one might conclude from Alma Swan's (2005) study of arXiv.org E-Print Archive's impact on subscriptions, with authors self-archiving 42,000 papers annually in high-energy physics, condensed matter, and astrophysics. Swan surveyed the relevant associations, namely, the American Physical Society (APS) and the Institute of Physics (IOP), both of which report that arXiv.org has not affected subscriptions to the journals that carry articles that appear in the archive. However, speaking to points made earlier in this book about the current state of access, both organizations noted a long-standing and continuing decline in their overall subscription numbers, which affects journals in areas outside the realm of arXiv.org, as well as those that deal with topics covered by the e-print archive.[6]

To move beyond support of self-archiving, scholarly associations can continue to sell subscriptions to their journals, but offer delayed open access to their journals' contents, as do the National Council of Teachers of English and the Massachusetts Medical Society (publisher of the *New England Journal of Medicine*). The impact of delayed access? The American Society for Cell Biology, with 10,000 members, started (in 2001) to provide open access to its flagship journal, *Molecular Biology of the Cell*, with a two-month delay from initial publication. Ray Everngam (2004), director of publications for the society, reports that three years later, subscriptions to this journal, which began publishing in 1989, were continuing to increase, although Everngam suspected that its open access policy is not widely known. Other associations are offering print subscriptions and online open access simultaneously, as the Staff Society of Seth G. S. Medical College and K. E. M. Hospital in Mumbai, India, does with its

6. See note 10 in chapter 2.

Postgraduate Journal of Medicine. Associations are also giving authors the option of purchasing open access for their own work by paying a fee, as the Florida Entomological Society does with the *Florida Entomologist*.

These approaches can be thought of as transitional strategies in the move to digital publishing, during which both print and online editions need to be maintained. They do not make for sound long-term publishing policies, given that publishing in two formats is hardly efficient, especially as readers and libraries are moving from the far more expensive print edition to the electronic version for its greater ease of searching, access to its growing archives, and the linking of references from an article to the work that is cited in the article.

That being the case, what about strategies that would see the associations into a postprint future? What if a scholarly association went to one of the library organizations that represents the vast majority of its subscribers, such as the Association of Research Libraries or the Association of College and Research Libraries, and proposed a different kind of agreement between publisher and library that indeed furthered the access principle? That proposal would take the form of a publishing cooperative between scholarly and library associations that would be guided by two principles: providing sustainable support for managing and publishing the association's journals and providing immediate open access to the journals. The key to the cooperative's sustainability, especially for scholarly associations with memberships that do not typically have research grants sufficient to cover author fees, would be reducing publishing costs. The cooperative would move toward dropping the print editions of the journals it publishes, while at the same time implementing, with the libraries' support, open source journal management and publishing systems.[7] Recent data from a sample of social science and humanities journals suggest that the savings from such initiatives could be as high as 50 percent (see appendix D, table D.1).

The libraries could contribute to further savings by utilizing some of their technical infrastructure to host the journal and its management sys-

7. The targets for cost reduction in publishing include printing, layout, mailing, filing, duplicating, postage, and other clerical support, which can be eliminated by online management and publishing systems (with details on how this works in the next chapter, on economics).

tem, as well as providing archiving, preservation, and indexing support. The libraries would be looking at reduced storage and personnel costs, with the electronic editions of the journals, in addition to the reduced outlay to obtain access to the journal. Then comes the kicker to this cooperative idea: With the cooperative in place, the journals would have a sustainable model for offering the rest of the world open access, to the benefit of authors, associations, and libraries. (Let me stop here with this idea, as I devote chapter 6 to the publishing cooperative model. I introduce it here only as it grows directly out of the situation of the associations.)

Still, having set up the open access imperative for scholarly associations, I fully recognize the risk it poses to them. An association's members may decide, when renewal time rolls around, to leave it up to their colleagues to join and do the work, while they ride into the glory of this greater readership by publishing in the association's open access journals. We are faced, in other words, with the tragedy of the commons, in which when some leave it up to others to act responsibly with property held in common, and when that doesn't happen—with the farmer who brings one cow too many to graze on the commons, in the classic case—the value of the commons rapidly declines, and this prospect constantly haunts the open access movement.

Yet a scholarly society is, in addition to a vehicle for publications in the field, a means for faculty members to contribute to the development of their profession. It gives them a chance to be part of a larger academic community and to increase, through the association, their level of public service. This is not a minor consideration, according to a Stanford e-journal user survey of 10,000 participants, which found, among other things, that the "most popular reason for joining societies was to support the society's mission" (e-Journal User Study 2002). Still, "the second and the third most frequent motivations given were economic benefits— receiving journals free or discounted with memberships and attending conferences at a reduced rate." I am not suggesting that it will be easy to change ideas about associations' journals. Yet associations will need to seriously reconsider the journal as a revenue stream for supporting the rest of the organization, when maintaining this revenue stream is costing the journal's authors the readership they deserve and desire.

The privilege of exclusive access to the journal, which individual subscriptions afforded members, can no longer be the basis for membership recruitment. Here then is a need and opportunity to demonstrate disciplinary leadership around issues of access and ownership, not only in publishing, but in the sharing of data sets and related research databases to strengthen the quality of research and encourage the scientifically productive notion of an information commons against increasing efforts to privatize data (Reichman and Uhlir 2001).

Fritz Machlup noted, at one point in his economic inquiries into scholarly publishing, that "in a wide sense of the phrase, any activity is 'economically viable,' if its product is promoted to the ranks of public good and its cost is borne largely out of public funds, such as an actual or potential tax revenue" (1977, 217). Scholarly inquiry is economically viable, in the first instance, as a public good—with research costs prior to publication largely borne by public funds—and the scholarly publication of that research should be no less viable for the same reason, as colleagues edit, review, and join in nonprofit societies, to further the very work of that inquiry, with public support. With so much scholarly activity supported by public money, it is only natural to ask whether there is now a way to distribute the resulting research in ways that make it open and available, as a global public good.

Scholarly associations have to ask themselves whether they are about to use this new publishing medium, already integral to the scholarly process, to extend and advance the circulation and exchange of knowledge. The associations need to add to their agendas items on the principles of access and the viability of open access publishing in an immediate, transitional, and long-term sense. They need to do so, given that this public good that we work so hard to produce can be made unequivocally part of a larger and revitalized public sphere. They need to consider working in greater cooperation with research libraries and otherwise attune themselves to what is in the best interest of their members and authors, as well as the cause of research and scholarship which they serve.

Having said all of that, what of my colleagues who have told me that their scholarly associations cannot consider dropping the print editions of their journals? It is not only the revenue stream that is at issue, although it is that too. It is because, well, the members count on receiving the journals in the mail. They are fond of the journal's fine paper, and of the ease with which they can take it out to the back deck to read an article or see who is up to what. And while I, too, appreciate the scholarly pleasures of working with a desk full of well-bound journals, this may no longer be a sustainable means of circulating knowledge or of building an association's membership among a new generation of print-less and wireless colleagues. The pleasures of the printed page—at least when it comes to the journal—may no longer justify denying the rights of tens of thousands of interested faculty and students access to this knowledge, in the face of open access alternatives that would expand the circulation of knowledge. Print does not need to be dropped immediately to increase the circulation of the knowledge in question. The options for opening access are many. What does need to be considered is whether, in the long term, going digital will mean more of the same or will extend not only the right of access to scholarly literature, but the opportunity to participate more fully in this public good.

5

Economics

When I first began to speak publicly about the prospects of open access during the late 1990s, I found myself running into difficulties over the most obvious of questions. I was asking faculty members to consider two things, doing an electronic edition of the journals with which they worked as editors, board members, and reviewers, then exploring whether they could make those online journals free to read in some way. Even as I asked people to give the advantages of these two ideas some serious thought, I had no real idea of what moving a journal online would cost, as more than one of them politely pointed out to me. The solution to this embarrassing moment in my presentations seemed easy enough. I simply had to pin down what it cost to put a journal online, and to do so I hired Larry Wolfson, as a research assistant with an economics background, to scour the emerging literature on online publishing for costs, as well as conduct a small survey among editors of online journals on this matter. It was not hard to find an answer to the question, although that gave rise to a new problem. There were far too many answers to the question, with huge differences among the answers.

Our inquiry certainly got off to a good start. Larry sent off e-mails to editors of electronic journals asking about their costs, while he started to scour the literature in search of published figures on online journal costs. However, before he had sent more than a handful of e-mail queries, he had an answer back from Gene Glass, who had founded *Education Policy Analysis Archives* (EPAA) in 1993 as a "born digital" peer-reviewed journal. Glass was blunt and multilingual about his business model: "Zero, *nada*, no budget, no grad assistant, no secretary" (personal communication, October 21, 2001). I described earlier the success of Glass's online journal, which receives some 2,500 unique visitors a day (Glass 2003).

As you might imagine, we were greatly encouraged by how easy Glass made it all seem, both to gather figures and then to convince others what a sensible, viable idea open access is. We were still in the early stages of our search, and of course, we did not see anything even close to that figure for publishing costs again. Even the most successful of the automated repository models, the arXiv.org E-Print Archive, in which authors file their own papers, and there is no reviewing or editing, has costs that, according to its founder Paul Ginsparg, run to nine dollars per paper (Glanz 2001).[1]

We went on to identify a small group of electronic journals that were spending in the area of $20,000 a year. For example, the *Electronic Journal of Comparative Law* had had its books reviewed by the accounting firm PricewaterhouseCoopers, which calculated that the Dutch open access quarterly was costing $20,084 annually (Bot, Burgemeester, and Roes 1998; also see Fisher 1999; "Integration" 2002). Adding up the author fees of $525 per published article (for most of its 100 or so open access journals, although a few charge more) yields a similar figure for the journals published by BioMed Central, a corporate venture in an entirely online and open access approach to journal publishing. Some journals contract out their e-journal edition, and HighWire Press, at Stanford University Library, was charging $35,000 to $125,000 in the late 1990s to set up an electronic journal, with ongoing operating fees of several thousand dollars a month (Young 1997). Additional figures are to be found in the report on e-journals from Donald W. King and Carolyn Tenopir (1998), who put the cost of an electronic edition of a journal at $368 per page or about $175,000 per year for a typical journal. Then, there was the Electronic Publishing Steering Committee at Cornell University (1998), which estimated that it would take $2,700,000 to establish an electronic publishing program at the university, serving a number of journals, although a member of the team at Cornell later told me that

1. The National Science Foundation, the Department of Energy, and Los Alamos National Laboratory provided $300,000 annually in support of arXiv.org E-Print Archive prior to its move to Cornell University in 2001 (Kling, Spector, and McKim 2002).

what had been spent was more like $600,000. Finally, Reed Elsevier estimates that it has spent $360 million developing ScienceDirect, which hosts electronic editions of its 1,800 journals (Davis 2004).

All told, the breathtaking range in the cost of mounting journals online bespoke nothing but risk, risk, risk. How could we advise editors to consider open access as a viable option when we could not provide a reliable picture of what it cost to run an online journal? Well, we could tell those skeptical editors that it might cost them nothing, or more likely $20,000 a year, although it might run to more than $100,000, especially if there were a number of journals involved. It seemed to leave the entire open access journal-publishing movement with a less than credible case to make with editors, scholarly associations, and funding agencies. The open question of what it costs to move a journal online would seem to discourage all but die-hard risk takers and do-it-yourself adventurers from considering the move from print to online publishing, unless one had a very sound business plan to cover the unpredictable costs.[2]

It is true that there are a number of economic models for open access publishing, as I review in appendix A, but in all of the models I discuss, there is this initial hurdle of setting up shop online. It appeared that if we wanted to speak with some authority on what it cost to put a journal online, the Public Knowledge Project, with which I work at the University of British Columbia, would have to build, test, and cost out a system of our own for putting a journal online. This would seem to require having a journal to put online, which we did not. Alternatively, we could build a device for others to use to put their journals online. After all, our survey of journal costs had revealed a myriad of approaches to publishing online, many of which entailed creating an ad hoc publishing system for each journal, which is bound to keep expenses high. Tenopir and King (2001), for example, use this software development point to argue that

2. A similar picture emerges for the cost of "institutional repositories" such as e-print archives: "Practically speaking, both development and operating costs can range from virtually no incremental costs (for institutions that reallocate resources) to hundreds of thousands of dollars (for institutions recognizing incremental systems and staff resources)" (Crow 2000, 28). For open source solutions to repositories and archives, see the Massachusetts Institute of Technology's DSpace Federation Web site ⟨http://www.dspace.org⟩ and that for EPrints.org ⟨http://www.eprints.org⟩.

electronic publishing does not lead to great savings: "Electronic access avoids these costs [of printing and distribution], but has a substantial additional fixed cost—putting up full text on the web, staffing, software and other technology issues including design, functionality, searchability and speed" (673).

What if, we wondered, we could control one part of publishing's financial model by reducing the journal's software design and development costs to zero? We could do this by creating open source software that was specifically developed to manage and publish journals online. The software could be designed so that it required no more technical skills of journal editors than word processing, e-mailing, and Web browsing. It could also keep costs down by utilizing the technical infrastructure already in place in most university libraries to place the journal online.

This was, after all, the model that had proven itself with the self-archiving EPrints.org software developed at the University of Southampton, which enables libraries and other organizations to set up sites for authors to self-archive their preprints and postprints. It was to follow the well-established path of such open source systems as Linux, otherwise known as "the impossible public good" (Smith and Kollock 1999, 230).[3] Just as Linus Torvald began working on Linux as a graduate class project in Finland, the academic community continues to play a vital role in open source software development, most recently with the Sakai coop-

---

3. Josh Lerner and Jean Tirole (2000) identify "career concern" and "ego gratification" as the central incentives for those contributing to the development of Linux; then these two economists pause to wonder if such an open source phenomenon could happen in any other industry. Why has it not occurred to them, I wonder in turn, that their own academic "industry" of scholarly publishing should be the next logical site for such a phenomenon? Many of Linux's 90,000 registered users have contributed, if only in a small way, to its development, largely by following their own interests and "itches," as Steven Weber (2000, 15) puts it. Eric Raymond also plays on Linux's impossibility: "Many people (especially those who politically distrust free markets) would expect a culture of self-directed egoists to be fragmented, territorial, wasteful, secretive, and hostile. But this expectation is clearly falsified by (to give just one example) the stunning variety, quality and depth of Linux documentation" (2003). On the inappropriateness of drawing analogies between open access and open source, see Harnad 2003e.

erative, which has formed among forty-four institutions and is devoted to developing, with the support of the Mellon Foundation and Hewlett Foundation, open source course management software (Young 2004).[4]

Now, I realize that it would be easy to confuse *open access* and *open source*. Just to review, *open access* principally refers to research literature which has been made free to read online. *Open source* is a term used exclusively in referring to software the code for which can be used, modified, and distributed by anyone.[5] So what the Public Knowledge Project has done, in response to this economic question, is build a piece of *open source* software that would make *open access* journal publishing not only economically viable, but well-indexed, through its compliance with the protocols set by (to add one more *open* term to the mix) the *Open Archives Initiative*. The Open Archives Initiative has established an open, nonproprietary protocol for "harvesting" and then searching a prescribed set of metadata or indexing items from research databases and documents, such as journals, which I discuss in chapter 12.

Drawing inspiration, then, from the open source movement, as well as from efforts afoot with open access e-print archives and journals, the Public Knowledge Project team set to work in 2001 on what has become Open Journal Systems (OJS). It has cost roughly $100,000 in hard-won research grants to develop thus far, even as upgrades of the software continue to be released. Launched in November of 2002, two years later it was being used by some 250 journals, based on those that have contacted us, including 210 African journals that are using a version of OJS adapted by the African Journals Online program to give these journals an online presence (Smart 2003). A community of users and developers has grown up around the software (typical of open source projects)

4. See the Web site for the Sakai Project at ⟨http://sakaiproject.org/⟩. See also Gleason 2003 on the use of open source systems in universities: "Open-source initiatives stand the best chance of success in higher education because of the traditions of sharing and cooperation among institutions and software developers. Open systems and open standards all lead in the same direction: promotion of interoperability among applications, a lessening reliance and dependency on the proprietary technology of a single application-software vendor, and reduction in costs to higher-education institutions of all sizes."

5. On the contentious issue of "open source" versus "free software," see Stallman 2001.

pushing it in new directions—with delayed open access for example—as well as translating it for international use. It has worked with the LOCKSS (Lots of Copies Keep Stuff Safe) team at Stanford University Library to ensure that it can take advantage of the team's open source archiving and preservation strategy.[6]

As part of the open source economic model, OJS is designed to be downloaded and installed on a local Web server, enabling local control within a distributed system for journal content indexing and system development. A number of university libraries are hosting OJS on their servers, which makes a great deal of sense given the libraries' expertise, technical infrastructure, and interest in improving access to such resources. Once OJS is installed, the editor can readily configure it by filling in templates (for example, "Title of the journal:") that reflect the journal's editorial structure, policies, sections, review process, and publishing schedule. Through this process, OJS creates a customized Web site for managing and publishing the journal. Authors can submit their work directly to the Web site; editors can work on the journal from computers in hotels or airports; reviewers can similarly pick up assigned papers and post their reviews; accepted papers are edited, laid out, published, and indexed all on the site. OJS is designed to reduce the clerical, management, and publishing costs of journals (see appendix C). Such cost reduction was necessary, of course, if there was to be any hope of journals' being able to make their contents free for readers in some form of open access.

In one sense, Open Journal Systems is no more than a proof of concept. It is testing the degree to which an open source (freely distributed) and easily configurable piece of software can reduce the cost of running a journal by moving the process online, not only in the publishing and distribution of the journal, but in its actual day-to-day management. It may indeed seem something of a heartless approach to place experienced and

6. The LOCKSS initiative is producing open source software that will enable journals to synchronize the archiving of their content across a handful of institutions to ensure its long-term preservation. The expense for libraries hosting this service (which can be used for the preservation of more than journals) has been projected by the LOCKSS team to be down to $0.07 for a year of a journal by 2007 (Reich and Rosenthal 2003).

knowledgeable editorial assistants' jobs on the line through the use of automated systems to, in effect, file, record, date, notify, look up, assemble, calculate, and on and on. Yet where cost reductions are used to support open access, at least, a trade-off is being made that brings to the fore the very purpose of the journal, which is to extend the circulation of knowledge. I have laid out the advantages and savings that a journal management system such as OJS can provide, as it would support journals moving to open access forms of publishing. However, this obviously raises a question about the rest of the publishing industry's use of these tools. Sarah Milstein (2002), in a column for the *New York Times*, identified journal management systems as belonging to that coveted class of "killer app," and she estimated that some 30 percent of journal publishers were using these management tools in 2002. She predicted that the rest of the industry would soon follow. While the publishing industry may not be using open source versions of these management systems, one still has to wonder where the savings these systems produce might figure in the ongoing transfer to this digital publishing medium.[7]

An online management system does more than simply reduce costs. It allows energy and money to be reallocated from clerical tasks to editorial quality, including copyediting and proofreading, which can be an issue for small and struggling journals. The ease with which the editor can take care of business means more time and attention for working on manuscripts and otherwise helping authors improve their research (see appendix C). The system's meticulous record keeping and reminders improve the journal's accountability to authors and readers, which should reduce some of the career-imperiling delays and confusion that are too often experienced with journal publishing. The ideal justification for the use of this technology was summed up by Steinway Pianos Vice President Werner Husmann, commenting on the use of new technologies in the building of his company's pianos: "What is your relation to machines?

---

7. Milstein (2002) quotes a typical setup charge of $5,000 to $20,000 for commercial journal management systems, and a processing cost of $12 to $50 a manuscript, with editors repeatedly citing advantages of speed and efficiency, which is thought to attract better papers, and savings that run to $60,000 in mailing costs, at least for *Journal of the American College of Cardiology*.

It's simple. A machine has to provide an increase in quality" (quoted in Barron 2003).

Exactly how much going online with a system such as OJS can reduce a journal's publishing costs depends on how the journal is currently being run, whether it will continue with a print edition, and how important it is for it to reduce costs. I present figures from a survey of sixty-one journals in appendix D (in association with chapter 6, on publishing cooperatives) that demonstrate how, with the elimination of print editions and the use of an open source management system such as OJS, the savings can be in the area of 50 percent over current figures. Among current users of OJS, a number are managing and publishing their open access journals entirely online, using university hosting services and volunteer editors, reviewers, copyeditors, and proofreaders, resulting in a zero-revenue and zero-expense budget. The goal here, however, has not been to simply package a version of the Gene Glass nada-expense journal publishing model. (Would that we all had Gene's resourcefulness and dedication.) It is about using open source and open access principles and technologies to extend the quality and circulation of this knowledge. One way of doing that is by reducing publishing costs to enable journal editors and publishers to consider alternatives to the dominant publishing models. One can think of it as increasing competition within the oddly shaped marketplace of scholarly publishing.

While the publishing industry may have been the principal means of achieving journal quality and circulation during the age of print, its business model has been taken to the point at which, according to the leading research libraries, the scholarly community has no choice but to begin "declaring independence" (from corporate journal publishers) by seeking ways of "returning science to scientists."[8] The considerable difference in journal prices is bound to raise questions about the value of the services that publishers provide, an issue that arose in chapter 1 as well.

As Janet Boulin of Oxford University Press, which publishes 184 journals, recently pointed out, a publisher's staff is highly knowledgeable about the review process, skilled at staffing editorial boards, and adept

8. The quotations are from materials for recent campaigns of the Scholarly Publishing and Academic Resources Coalition (2001) in association with the Association of Research Libraries.

at using software to mange the flow of manuscripts in an efficient manner (ALPSP 2003). Boulin also held up the extensive marketing campaigns that publishers mount on behalf of the scholarly materials they handle, and she emphasized how responsive publishers can be to market changes. Publishers are there, she concluded, to support the authority, quality, accessibility, longevity, and recognition of scholarship. And publishers have done this indisputedly well for a good long time, and a great many scholars have benefited by it. But what is perhaps most striking about the skills that Boulin identifies is that they are (with the exception, perhaps, of the marketing campaigns) possessed by scholars and their associations as well. However, marketing campaigns cannot help seeming something of an extravagance when librarians are deciding on which journals to cancel, rather than on which to purchase. Otherwise, it would seem fair to surmise that the qualities held up by publishers as representing their contribution regarding the state of the journal are rooted in the countless editors, authors, and reviewers involved in the production of these periodicals.

Whatever publisher or journal they are working with, these scholars are at the heart of the *authority*, *quality*, and *recognition* that Boulin identifies as distinguishing this body of literature. By the same token, improving *accessibility* (the very point of open access) and *longevity* (with the LOCKSS software) is very much a part of the economic alternatives that are now available under a broadly construed open access. The services of a good copyeditor, on the other hand, cannot be matched by faculty or system. As we saw in chapter 3, the major publishers do not always provide copyeditors for their journals, but fortunately, copyeditors are available on a freelance basis and offer a quality investment for journals that are saving money by automating other aspects of the editorial process.

Still, the current economics of scholarly publishing no longer allows one to pit the big publisher against the open access rebel with a cause, at least not in any simple sense. Boulin's Oxford University Press, after all, is moving its flagship journal, *Nucleic Acids Research*, to open access in 2005 by shifting from subscriptions to author fees. Such moves, with other journals presumably to follow suit at Oxford with time, point to how open access is becoming part of the peculiar economics of scholarly publishing. Open access's corporate champion, BioMed Central, is certainly part of that picture, as are publishers rethinking what the low costs of access mean for their responsibilities to research access in developing countries, as reflected in the Health InterNetwork Access to Research Initiative (HINARI) and International Network for the Availability of Scientific Publications (INASP) projects.[9] And Elsevier chairman Derk Haank is right. Elsevier Science is "making scientific information more accessible to the community at large than ever before" ("Integration" 2002; see also Haank 2001). Not only does Elsevier's ScienceDirect provide an open index to that portion of the literature that it controls, but its endorsement of Elsevier authors' self-archiving their work makes the company party to the most expedient, as Stevan Harnad (2003a) rightly notes, and most easily achieved form of complete open access.[10]

Where does that leave the economics of access, if not with blurred lines between the heroes and villains of access? The blurring speaks, however, to the remarkable range of opportunities that journals have for increasing access to research and scholarship. This greater realization of the access principle through this digital medium offers tenable options to large corporate publishers and small society journals. And the development of these options is bound to continue, given that the American Association for the Advancement of Science, among others, is encouraging the U.S. National Science Foundation to "fund experiments intended to bolster alternative models of licensing and publication" with a goal of promoting "wide access to and the preservation of scientific information in a cost-effective way" (Frankel 2002, 25).

Yet while open access is making gains in almost every sector of scholarly publishing, journal prices go on increasing well ahead of infla-

9. The Association of Learned and Professional Society Publishers (2004) reports that 60 percent of publishers participate in some form of assistance program for getting their wares to developing countries.

10. Parent company Reed Elsevier, fifth-largest media company in the world, had revenues of $8 billion in 2002, of which $1.5 billion came from online delivery of information to both scholars and professionals (physicians, lawyers, etc.) through services such as ScienceDirect, with an operating margin that Forbes .com called "fabulous" at 22 percent (Morais 2002).

tion rates. Restrictive licensing agreements and near monopolies persist among journal publishers bent on mergers and acquisitions (McCabe 2002; Susman and Carter 2003). That is, there is little reason to let up in pursuit of the access principle. The need for new forms and alternative journal-publishing models continues, even as the case for opening access must be carefully worked out to ensure that this idea continues to play its part in what is most exciting and promising about scholarly publishing today.

6

Cooperative

A recent, if somewhat obscure, crime story throws further light on the economics of digital access. The victim of this intellectual-property crime was JSTOR, a nonprofit organization that offers online access to the back issues of scholarly journals. JSTOR was founded in 1995, as an initiative of the Andrew W. Mellon Foundation, which is playing a leading role in the introduction of new technologies into scholarly communication. JSTOR offers institutional subscribers, largely university libraries, online access to *complete* sets of journal back issues. It provides readers with digitized images of the original journal pages, and an ability to search the journal, for what is currently 600 journal titles, from the *Academy of Management Journal* (launched in 1963) to the *Yale Law Journal* (founded in 1891). As it continues to add back-issue sets to its collection, it brings considerable historical depth and reach to the online journal literature, dating back to the first issue of the *Philosophical Transactions* from March 6, 1665.

However, in the autumn of 2002, this nonprofit archive "experienced a sophisticated attack," according to Kevin M. Guthrie, then president of JSTOR. The breach enabled someone to "to systematically and illegally download tens of thousands of articles from the JSTOR archive" ("Unauthorized" 2002, 16). The hacker had apparently entered JSTOR by tunneling in through an unprotected proxy server on a campus (left unnamed) where the university library had a JSTOR license. As a result of the hack, 51,000 articles, drawn from eleven of the journals in the archive, were downloaded to an unlicensed computer without being detected in the process.

The Mellon Foundation set up JSTOR "to improve dramatically access to journal literature for faculty, students, and other scholars," according to William G. Bowen, president of the foundation, as well as "to mitigate some of the vexing economic problems of libraries by easing storage problems" (1995). The foundation, which might be thought of as the great venture capitalist of scholarly publishing start-ups, has always been keen to see a sound business plan for any new endeavor. "From the outset," Guthrie explains, "JSTOR was given the charge to develop a financial plan that would allow it to become self-sustaining—the Mellon Foundation was not going to subsidize the concept indefinitely" (1997).[1] JSTOR went on to establish agreements with commercial and nonprofit journal publishers, enabling it to digitize the publishers' back issues and offer them at a fee to its institutional members.[2] As part of its arrangement with publishers, JSTOR agrees to maintain a "moving wall" by which back issues are added to the collection once they are three to five years old (depending on the publisher's agreement). This is intended, of course, to protect for publishers the value of subscribing to the journal.[3] The model has since given rise, with variations, to the Mellon-supported ARTstor, which provides access to art images.[4]

1. William G. Bowen: "Perpetual subsidy is both unrealistic and unwise: projects of this kind [i.e., JSTOR] must make economic sense once they are up and running. If users and beneficiaries, broadly defined, are unwilling to cover the costs, one should wonder about the utility of the enterprise. In this important respect, we are strong believers in 'market-place solutions'" (1995). Bowen broke down the JSTOR cost savings for research libraries in 1995 as follows: Journal storage runs $24 to $41 per volume of a journal; binding issues into volumes is $24 to $41 a volume; and retrieval for users can run $45 to $180 per journal. A more recent study demonstrates the storage costs per journal volume in print to be between $48 and $353 a year (Schonfeld et al. 2004).

2. At current rates, institutional access to the complete JSTOR archive of 600 titles can cost as little as $750 annually (after an initial $500 capital fee), for a high school with low college enrollment rates, and up to $35,000 a year (after an initial capital fee of $90,000) for a large research university.

3. JSTOR also attempts to protect the publisher's copyright by forbidding patrons to download "a significant number of sequential articles, or multiple copies of articles," according to its Web site ⟨http://www.jstor.org/about/terms.html⟩.

4. From ARTstor's Web site: "ARTstor's purpose is to create a large—and indefinitely growing—database of digital images and accompanying scholarly information for use in art history and other humanistic fields of learning, including the related social sciences" ⟨http://www.ARTstor.org⟩.

For faculty and student alike at subscribing institutions, JSTOR is much like a round-the-clock research assistant, with the winged feet of Mercury, ready to search the stacks for a classic or overlooked journal article. For the Dalton School or the Horace Mann School—to name two of the small number of high school subscribers—it adds a layer of intellectual depth and distinction to their college-prep libraries. For the few public library subscribers, from Cleveland to San Francisco, JSTOR offers the public a way of digging back into a research literature that is otherwise rarely available outside of a substantial university library. For the North South University in Bangladesh and the Institute for International Relations in Vietnam, it provides the basis for an English-language research library.[5]

What then of this crime committed against JSTOR? Of course, the journal articles are not missing as a result of the piracy, nor does the theft represent lost potential sales or unrecoverable expenses for JSTOR. A library of the sort that subscribes to JSTOR is unlikely to be the culprit, and it is just as unlikely to buy "hot" copies of articles from a shady salesperson. What the size and scope of this essentially worthless act of piracy committed against JSTOR demonstrates, for me at least, is the *surplus capacity* within JSTOR for providing access to the back issues of scholarly journals. Hacking into JSTOR did no one any good, but perhaps under different circumstances, this excess access could feed the hungry minds of hundreds if not thousands of interested readers, without damaging JSTOR or its business model.

I do not mean to condone the crime by speaking of a surplus capacity. It is a crime with a victim. Good citizen-scholars will ultimately have to pay for the hacker's pilfering. In response to this theft, Guthrie asked librarians to beef up their "access control," through authentication, authorization, and certification systems. Scholars will be the losers, as more of the library's budget is devoted to shoring up security systems designed to keep such hackers at bay. Subscription fees for journals and

5. On JSTOR's international fee structure, the organization's Web site explains that "fee levels are ... set taking into account the relative value of the JSTOR journal titles to the higher education community in the country as well as the local availability of fiscal and technological resources" ⟨http://www.jstor.org/about/intl_fees.html⟩.

JSTOR will be increased to cover similar measures within these organizations.[6] The librarians who responded to Guthrie's report of the crime on the LibLicense e-mail list (which connects librarians dealing with publishers' licenses and related services) were quick to recognize their need to protect intellectual property, although they cautioned that, as in any business, a loss from such forms of "shoplifting" is the price of doing business. They also wanted to ensure, given this talk of greater access control, that members of the public who visited their libraries could also use JSTOR without being members of the university, which is permitted within the current contract.

I want to suggest, however, that increased security systems may not be the only way to ensure that JSTOR's archive of research literature continues to be made available. Remember, providing free access to *additional* readers—beyond, say, the current set of subscribers—does not necessarily pose a threat to the system. If JSTOR represents one of the sustainable models for electronic publishing, is there a way to introduce an element of open access into its operations based on this surplus access? Piracy would no longer be an issue, certainly, but more importantly, the contents of these back issues would greatly increase in value as they became available to a much wider body of readers around the world.

Certainly, I am in no position to advise JSTOR on restructuring its current business model and am too filled with admiration for what it offers to risk losing it. However, I would like to borrow the JSTOR idea, for a moment, in ways that will not, I hope, be regarded as yet another intellectual-property hijacking. JSTOR has, in a handful of years, built up a clientele of over 2,000 institutional subscribers. This list continues to grow, although presumably at some point, that growth will level off. This JSTOR community of libraries, scholarly associations and publishers has every reason to continue to cooperate in providing access to back issues of the journal literature. In fact, it suggests the possibilities for a *cooperative* economic model for open access publishing. In terms

---

6. See Gallouj 2002 on how restricting access to knowledge only becomes more expensive and complicated as its transfer is increasingly simplified through inexpensive digital formats.

of American history, the precedent for such an approach goes back to Benjamin Franklin, who founded America's first and oldest continuing cooperative, the Philadelphia Contributionship for the Insurance of Houses from Loss by Fire, two decades after he established the country's first lending library in 1731.

The current membership of JSTOR, if you set aside the small number of public libraries and high schools that subscribe, could work in conjunction with the scholarly associations and other publishing bodies (such as university presses, publishers, research institutes, and groups of scholars), to form a cooperative involving both publishing and archiving. JSTOR has already demonstrated the level of cooperation that can be achieved among libraries, publishers, and scholarly associations. Donald J. Waters, Program Officer of Scholarly Communication at the Mellon Foundation, rightly refers to JSTOR as a "community-based organization" (2004). However, there may be a way to go a step further with this idea of giving back to the larger community, both academic and otherwise.

Membership in a publishing and archiving cooperative would enable libraries to participate more directly in journal publishing and archiving to ensure affordable access to research and scholarship. It would offer its members a means of containing and controlling costs, with cost containment far more of an issue for research libraries than reaping a wide-scale windfall from journals going open access. By drawing on the self-help initiatives of the cooperative movement, research libraries would simply be taking one step farther the consortia that they have formed to coordinate discount subscription and licensing fees from large publishers. Certainly, libraries are aware of a need to rethink their roles in this age of online resources from that of information procurers and providers. This sense of needed change is reflected, for example, in the Association of Research Libraries report on institutional repositories, of which e-print archives are a good example. The report notes that "library programs and budgets will have to shift to support faculty open access publishing activities in order for the library to remain relevant to this significant constituency" and that this is "a natural extension of academic institutions' responsibility as generators of primary research seeking to preserve and leverage their constituents' intellectual assets" (Crow 2000, 20).

Research libraries' greater involvement in publishing has its precedents, most notably with Stanford University Library's operation of HighWire Press, which I noted in chapter 1 is making a substantial contribution to the academic community by providing one of the largest open access archives in the world. And as I discussed in chapter 5, the library has also developed LOCKSS, an open source system for use in libraries for archiving electronic editions of journals, which has currently been installed by more than eighty research libraries worldwide. The system's software enables these libraries to automatically archive copies of electronic journal issues, preserving their content against loss and corruption. In other words, libraries are taking on new roles in reshaping scholarly publishing.

A publishing and archiving cooperative would capitalize on the technical infrastructure that research libraries have built up to support journals and other digital resources. It would utilize the collective information science expertise embodied in the library's staff to assist with the indexing and organizing of the publishing and archiving activities. The cooperative would, of course, draw on open source software for journal management, publishing, and archiving. The scholarly associations and other groups that joined the cooperative would bring their communities of authors, editors, publishers, and readers to manage and contribute to the journals and archives. Publishers might join or be contracted for editorial, design, portal management, and other services as needed. The member libraries would pay fees to the cooperative, perhaps based on some proportion of the subscription fees that they once paid for the journals that were now being published by the cooperative, as well as on institution size, as they do with JSTOR. Then there are the donor organizations that currently support developing-nation access to resources such as JSTOR and other publications; they might contribute directly to this open access cooperative, which would provide, in effect, greater access to more institutions in need. In appendix D, I present recent financial data from a sample of Canadian humanities and social sciences journals and JSTOR.

Of course, the idea behind the cooperative model is to turn the surplus access generated by online publishing to open access. With the surplus access afforded by digital distribution, not only would a publishing and archiving cooperative ensure that its membership was well provided for, but it would offer the rest of the world open access to the research and scholarship for which it was responsible. Such a cooperative would avoid the dual economy of the open access e-print archive, in which the institution both supports the management of the archive, where its faculty members archive their published work, and subscribes to the journals that review and publish the work. The cooperative is a way of organizing a large-scale implementation of immediate and sustainable open access, one that is particularly appropriate for the humanities and social sciences. Those are also the areas, as it turns out, that JSTOR represents particularly well and the areas that need an alternative to the popular author fee model of open access in the biomedical sciences.

Yet the cooperative concept is not that far removed from the author fee model, which can take the form of institutional memberships. In such an "institutional membership" model, an institution pays an overall fee to a publisher such as BioMed Central on behalf of its faculty members, ensuring their right to publish in its open access journals.[7] Institutional membership fees, as well as author fees generally, create a situation in which the more prolific institutions carry the extra weight of their productivity, while affording everyone else open access. The difference is that rather than simply transferring funds from institution to publisher, as with the author fee model, the cooperative draws on the members' existing expertise and infrastructure to create a more efficient and integrated model, to the benefit of the world at large.

There is already something of a cooperative's spirit operating with the current setup of JSTOR. The organization began with 199 charter members, largely research libraries, and more than a hundred institutions donated back issues of journals for digitization. Those who subscribe to JSTOR have first to pay an initial capital fee, as might well happen with membership in a cooperative or club.

The members of an open access publishing and archiving cooperative would benefit most from the increased global access to the research

7. Currently, 451 institutions, principally universities (from forty countries), have become members of the open access (for-profit) publisher BioMed Central, which affords their faculty members the right (without having to pay the otherwise requisite author fees) to publish in its over 100 journals.

archives maintained by the cooperative, as their faculty members' work will make up the greatest part of these scholarly resources. If open access were found to contribute, however slightly, to a global research capacity, the less-privileged institutions would not be the only ones to benefit, as the leading institutional members of the cooperative have a long tradition of drawing on a global pool of academic talent and are themselves deeply invested in a research culture of critique and take-up. And there are signs that the larger public would benefit as well. The cooperative's open access contribution could certainly draw inspiration from JSTOR's admirable Secondary Schools Pilot Project, which, when it ran (from 2000 to 2002), made an impressive case for opening access to this segment of the public, or as one participating teacher reported, "Access to JSTOR has been extremely helpful to my rare but treasured moments of being able to read about and research some of the material I'm teaching for fresh perspectives" (quoted in Bhattacharya 2003).

As for membership in this publishing and archiving cooperative, the university libraries that make up the overwhelming majority of JSTOR subscribers, from Alabama State to Yale, would hardly question the need to continue supporting services that increased access to digital scholarly resources while containing costs, whether out of a sense of pride or of responsibility for the circulation of knowledge that is so clearly of benefit to themselves and others. Still, issues of fairness might arise, namely, over those institutions, including corporations with research libraries, that by not joining appear to be freeloaders. While it would stand against the spirit of open access, the cooperative could always limit access to communities of users who clearly fall outside the scope of the cooperative's membership community. An open access cooperative could grant free access to students and scholars in developing countries, patrons of public libraries, and students and teachers in high schools, as well as private scholars and dedicated amateurs. This would add, of course, to the management costs, but limited forms of open access are already being employed by a number of organizations and publishers. Or a cooperative might agree to offer a number of free downloads annually, perhaps starting with the figure of 51,000 articles, in recognition of the great JSTOR hijack that made the principle of surplus access so apparent.

Yet I am not sure that we have to limit open access in this way. The "tragedy of the commons," as this freeloading problem (which I introduced earlier) is known, may not apply in this case. Typically, the prospect of this tragedy undermines efforts to establish a commons out of a fear that someone will "snatch some selfish benefit" from the public good, as economist Paul A. Samuelson put it, in describing "the heart of the whole problem of *social* economy" (1954, 389).[8] Take the current wave of cooperation among higher-education institutions on open source software development, with the benefits made freely available and open to all. Twenty such open source projects were recently featured in the *Chronicle of Higher Education*, the best-known of which is the DSpace Federation, which MIT has formed among university libraries and other institutions that are using DSpace, its freely available software for setting up institutional repositories ("Open Source" 2004). The DSpace Federation's commitment to "sharing in the development and maintenance of the DSpace source code" speaks well to how libraries' role is changing in ways that gives credence to their playing a greater role in JSTOR-like projects.[9] The federation approach to DSpace, which was developed with support from the Hewlett Foundation and, once again, the Mellon Foundation, is the perfect complement to a publishing and archiving cooperative, as are the well over 100 institutions that have set up e-print archives employing the open source EPrints.org software for faculty members to use to provide open access to their published and unpublished work.[10]

In terms of which research libraries would participate in such a cooperative venture, I was encouraged by the recent declaration by a number of library associations—including the Association of Academic Health

8. At least one economics study has found people willing to support a greater public good, even as it decreases their chances to maximize their benefit (Kemp 2002, 18–20).

9. The quotation is taken from the DSpace Federation Web site ⟨http://dspace .org/federation⟩.

10. The Mellon Foundation and the Hewlett Foundation have also supported the development of the Sakai Project, which, as noted in chapter 5, is devoted to creating an open source course management system through a cooperative of forty-four institutions, with members paying $10,000 a year to get advance releases and be part of the community of college developers (Young 2004).

Sciences Libraries, American Association of Law Libraries, American Library Association, Association of College and Research Libraries, Association of Research Libraries, and Medical Libraries Association—that they are "ready to work toward solutions in cooperation" with the fifty scholarly associations (representing 300 journals) that signed the Washington D.C. Principles of Free Access to Science (SPARC 2004). The Washington Principles include a commitment to ensuring that the "full text of our journals is freely available to everyone worldwide either immediately or within months of publication, depending on each publisher's business and publishing requirements" ("Washington" 2004). It is easy to imagine the publishing cooperative idea taking on an international dimension as well, or perhaps subchapters would form around different fields, such as law, medicine, or the humanities.

I realize that establishing a formal cooperative represents a considerable step from these loosely organized efforts to setting up e-print and journal archives. Yet it builds on the same spirit of collaboration, cooperation, and common purpose to further access to research and scholarship, just as it would take advantage of existing technical resources, expertise, and connections. For those in charge of research libraries, the cooperative can further the library's interests in containing journal costs, something that e-print archives are not intended to do. Indeed, Stevan Harnad (2004b) has admonished librarians that it would be "a great strategic mistake to cancel" journals that permit authors to self-archive.

By the same token, the executives of scholarly associations might say that we might do far better to join forces with research libraries to ensure a steady line of support for what we do best, rather than worry over whether increased open access threatens our ability to sell subscriptions to our journals. We need a place, they might argue, amid all the new technologies, for sustaining existing journals and supporting new ones, including those independent of associations like ours, as this, too, ensures the continuing development of the field.[11]

11. The American Association for the Advancement of Science has recently insisted, in its report on scholarly publishing, on the importance of enabling the launching of new independent journals, by keeping entry barriers low for new publications of scholarly quality (Frankel 2002, 7).

As for the granting agencies and donors, is there not, they might well ask, some way to consolidate these hosting, archiving, reviewing, and publishing processes to create a well-organized and sustainable system that would increase the circulation of knowledge on a global scale? After all, as Donald Waters, a program officer of the Mellon Foundation, has pointed out, the "sustainability of digital scholarly resources" depends on three factors, namely, "a clear definition of the audience and the needs of users," sensible "economies of scale," and a well-organized means to "manage the resource over time" (2004). A publishing and archiving cooperative should represent nothing less than such an approach. And to assist its potential members in thinking about a reasonable economic model for this new organization, we have two models to draw on, thanks to the work of the Mellon Foundation. The first comes from a proposal recently put forward by Ira Fuchs (2004), Mellon's vice president for research in information technology, for an open source software collaboration in higher education. Fuchs's proposed collaboration would be, in effect, a cooperative that according to Fuchs's vision "might involve more than 1,000 colleges and universities from around the world," with each contributing "between $5,000 and $25,000 per year, based on size," which would "produce more than $10-million per year, enough to coordinate the development, packaging, delivery and maintenance of many of the key academic and administrative software applications that higher education needs." The second Mellon model is found in the subscription fee structure used with JSTOR, presented in appendix D, which would seem, given the funding levels it has attained, to offer an encouraging picture for the viability of such a cooperative.

This idea of a publishing and archiving cooperative among libraries, societies, and other publishing groups draws on a range of precedents, from open source development communities in higher education to library consortia. It is intended to stand as an alternative to prevailing assumptions that free-market principles prevail, and need to continue to prevail, in scholarly communication. It is meant to suggest an approach to sustainability that goes beyond setting up corporate entities to sell services, recovering costs plus, to the higher-education community. A publishing cooperative realizes a common cause among research libraries, scholarly associations, and other publishing groups, as well as funding agencies. It makes sense for a core set of those research libraries to be directly involved in the hosting, indexing, and archiving of the literature, while the scholarly associations and related bodies oversee the management of peer review, editing, and layout, wherein lies their expertise and experience. Even apart from the potential efficiencies of such a cooperative, it is distinguished by its determination to turn the surplus access created by the Web into a far greater public good, at least when it comes to making scholarly resources available to a wider public and a global academic community.

7
Development

For those countries throwing off the yoke of Western colonialism during the latter half of the twentieth century, the founding of new universities represented a particularly promising assertion of modern nationhood. Certainly, many of these communities and cultures had long-standing scholarly traditions that dated back well before the spread of European imperialism. Across the Islamic world, for example, scholarly libraries and colleges, such as the magnificent Alhambra in Granada, had long been kept open to scholars from abroad (Singleton 2004). During the final decades of the twentieth century, however, the modern university took hold around the world, creating something of a global academic community. Certainly, the prevalence of Western-trained faculty in many of the new institutions contributed to the sense of a larger community. The scholarly journal also played a vital part, offering faculty and students a means not only of staying current in their fields, but of participating through their own research in what is increasingly becoming the global circulation of knowledge.

Among universities in developing countries, it was not as if academic journals ever came easily. The arrival of a new issue could at times represent a singular accomplishment, given the expense of overseas subscriptions in relation to local economies and currencies, as well as the uncertainties of mail service. Locally published journals faced their own set of problems. Many were typical scholarly journals published on a regular basis, but more than a few were marked by irregular publication schedules and titles that ceased to exist after a few issues. Still, research libraries in the developing world began to build journal collections in the hundreds, and even thousands, of titles during the 1960s and 1970s, only to have those collections decimated by subscription price increases, currency fluctuations, and local economic troubles. Addis Ababa University in Ethiopia, for example, lost 70 percent of its 1,200 subscriptions in the late 1980s (Rosenberg 1997). Thiagarajan Viswanathan, director of the Indian National Scientific Documentation Center, reports that "India, which used to receive about 20,000 journals in 1983, now gets less than 11,000, and fewer copies of each," and Autar S. Paintal, former director general of the Indian Council of Medical Research, paints an even grimmer picture by pointing out that "an Indian [researcher] is often unaware of the latest trends in science publishing [because] hardly 10 percent of our libraries get the top journals" (both quoted in Gibbs 1995, B13). The World Health Organization found that at the close of the twentieth century, more than half the research and higher-education institutions in the lowest-income countries simply had no current subscriptions to international journals (Aronson 2004).

With the transition to new publishing technologies over the last decade, the question that has arisen for those working in the Southern Hemisphere is whether the North "will continue to refuse to cooperate in the establishment of an equitable world information order," as Colin Darch, an academic librarian in Cape Town, South Africa, bluntly puts it, "based on entrenched principles of full disclosure and free flow" (1998). Darch's ideal of an equitable world information order, one that has moved beyond the colonial legacies of center and periphery in the geopolitics of knowledge, has everything to do with the goals of open access archives and journals, especially as greater access to the literature and to journal publishing can contribute to the research capacities of developing nations.

A United Nations report presented in Addis Ababa in 1969, for example, proposed that if the "vicious circle of underdevelopment" was to be overcome, an "indigenous scientific capability" needed to be fostered, which meant overcoming, among other things, "highly imperfect access to the body of world scientific knowledge" (quoted in Cooper et al. 1971, 107–109). More recently, the World Bank (2000) attributed the growth experienced by Asian economies in the 1990s to policies that "placed heavy emphasis on education and technology in order to close the knowledge gap with more advanced countries" (16). Avinish Persaud (2001), a State Street Bank analyst, has calculated the gap between the developed and developing world in number of scientists per capita to be ten times as great as the considerable differences in incomes. When the United Nations Development Program (1999, 66) examined scientific and technology output, using the number of scientific papers published per unit of population as its measure, it found that the knowledge output of the Arab world, for example, was 2 percent of that of the industrialized countries, and that China and the Republic of Korea had both realized a tenfold increase in the number of papers since the 1980s.

In a recent copy of their joint annual report on educational indicators, UNESCO (the United Nations Educational, Scientific and Cultural Organization), IFS (the Institute for Statistics), OECD (the Organization for Economic Cooperation and Development), and WEIP (the World Economic Indicators Program) (2002) speak of "a historic convergence of globalization, knowledge-driven economies, human rights–based development and demographic trends" that fuels a renewed interest in education as a vehicle for human capital and economic growth (5). Although it may be hard at times to sort the human-rights concerns from the human-capital perspectives fostered by UNESCO and OECD respectively, the report makes it clear that improvements in educational attainment are closely associated in developing countries with economic well-being, with each additional year of schooling among the adult population corresponding to a 3.7 percent increase in economic growth rate (9). This attainment, however, is not simply a matter of improving basic literacy levels, but "depends critically on participation in and the successful completion of higher levels of education" (10). The report goes on to identify how educational inequities, particularly at the postsecondary level, appear to "reinforce" broader social inequalities (12). The encouraging news is, however, that the number of students attending postsecondary institutions in Africa grew by 20 percent annually over the last two decades of the twentieth century, even if those institutions are often poorly equipped to do the job they must do (Banya and Elu 2001, 1).[1]

1. With postsecondary education, the costs per student can be as much as sixteen times those for primary schooling, and up until the 1990s, the World Bank tended to treat postsecondary education in the developing world as an inefficient enterprise compared to sending students abroad (UNESCO, IFS, OECD, and WEIP 2003, 14). But that has changed with the World Bank's recognition that higher education can foster knowledge and sensibility (as well as contribute to a global knowledge-based economy) that can lead to more democratic and resilient nations (Banya and Elu 2001, 1).

The need for developing countries to become a greater part of a new world information order has inspired a number of global initiatives by the private sector and aid agencies to build developing countries' technical infrastructure.[2] As a result, computers and connectivity are appearing, if only in very small numbers, in the research libraries and laboratories of universities in the developing world. In one United Nations Development Program (2002) project, the 5,600 students and staff of the Bangladesh Agricultural University were able, as part of a national wireless initiative focused on educational institutions, to shift from a single modem and an unreliable phone line to high-speed wireless connectivity linking them to the capital city of Dhaka, 100 kilometers away, and to the rest of the world. In India, Indira Gandhi National Open University is providing computer education courses to remote areas of India, while the Information and Library Network—which connects 150 university libraries, 50 postgraduate centers, and 200 research and development centers—is implementing library automation and database systems, with gateways to international research databases (Rao 2001). A corresponding development in the technological savvy of librarians also appears to be taking place in developing countries, judging by Lampang Manmart's (2001) study of Thailand, which elucidates how university degrees for librarians in that country are being recast as information

---

2. At this point, for example, the World Bank is devoting $800 million to increasing the Internet connectivity of developing countries; one example is the World Bank Group's Global Development Learning Network Project, a $3 million venture in Indonesia devoted to new communication and learning technologies for higher education. Vietnam has a $100 million World Bank Higher Education Project aimed at "capacity building, institutional development, and computerization." These projects are described on the World Bank Group Web site ⟨http://web.worldbank.org⟩. Other programs for improving Internet access in developing countries include the Digital Opportunity Taskforce, the United Nations Development Program, the African Information Society Initiative, and the Global Information Infrastructure Commission. In addition, the U.S. government has been supporting a five-year, $15 million Leland initiative to support Internet infrastructure in twenty-one African countries (Adeya and Oyelaran-Oyeyinka 2002, 31). Marine fiber cables now circle the African continent, with Internet connectivity having grown from two connected countries in 1994 to all African nations in 1999, although the distribution of that connectivity is still extremely sparse, especially in the interior.

science and information management programs, which are introducing a new generation of librarians to Internet technologies.

Despite limited access in most areas of Africa to a level of technical infrastructure that the West now takes for granted, it is clear that African access to e-mail has already made a significant difference in the circulation of research. In Zimbabwe, health workers are using e-mail to conduct searches on PubMed, the U.S. National Library of Medicine's online index to the life sciences, and then request articles to be scanned or downloaded. E-mail is also used to carry out research, as well as to circulate articles, for the Ethiopian Flora Project. E-mail has also become a means of getting the word out on the content of new issues of African journals, as well as assisting in the submission and review process (Teferra 1998).

University faculty in developing countries have not waited for their campuses to be wired to go online. In a study of computer use among faculty in Nigeria and Kenya, Catherine Nyaki Adeya and Banji Oyelaran-Oyeyinka (2002) found a few years ago that more than 90 percent of the 227 university faculty who responded to their survey were using e-mail and word-processing programs. The Kenyan faculty members reported that they had been doing so "for 5–10 years for an average of 2–4 hours a day" (43). In both countries, most of the faculty were covering their own Internet costs, in part because they found university systems too slow and congested for reliable use (49). Faculty in both countries (80 percent in Kenya and 58 percent in Nigeria) reported using the Internet for academic research: "While researchers devote a relatively small proportion of time to their own research, respondents still use the Internet to keep abreast of new research and developments in their areas of specialization" (50–51). Though noting that the "responding academics both in Kenya and Nigeria expressed the desire for greater interaction with their peers worldwide because they feel isolated due to poor access to the ICTs [information and communication technologies]," Adeya and Oyelaran-Oyeyinka conclude that enhanced infrastructure will not be as important, in the long term, as more active participation in research and the production of knowledge (51).

As connectivity in African universities (as well as those elsewhere in the world) slowly improves, it then falls to the academic research community to ensure that the knowledge gap is further reduced through a ready ability to access online resources. It is time for researchers in the developed world to consider just how easily they can contribute to the research capacity of the developing world by moving to a more open approach to scholarly publishing. More than that, researchers every-where only stand to benefit by the promise such increased access holds for the increased circulation of and participation in the critical work of their field.

Just what the access principle can mean in this context has been dramatically portrayed by Amartya Sen as nothing less than a matter of human freedom. This Nobel Prize–winning economist holds that prog-ress on the road to development is based on reducing "various types of unreason that leave people with little choice and little opportunity of exercising their reasoned agency" (1999, xii). Sen speaks of the need for "a broader informational basis," whether to increase a nation's pursuit of justice or an individual's exercise of reasoned agency (67).[3] The pub-lic's "participatory capabilities," he notes, which require "knowledge and educational skills," need to be encouraged in everyone, including girls and women, who have not traditionally had the same opportunities as boys and men (18, 32). India's continuing malnutrition problems, as well as its high illiteracy rates, require more effective use, in Sen's estima-tion, of "communication and political participation—in short, fuller practice of democracy" (154).[4]

3. Sen has famously claimed that India has not suffered a substantial famine since democracy was established, as a result of this greater information openness and a free press. Sen acknowledges, however, that democratic India does not pre-vent millions of Indians from dying of malnutrition annually and has not yet been able to increase the national literacy rate above 60 percent. He remains con-cerned with an "elitist concentration on higher education" in India that operates at the expense of the primary and secondary schools (1999, 42).

4. A practical example of broader participatory capabilities, which Sen wishes to see developed, is found in the M. S. Swaminathan Research Foundation program for setting up value-added centers, often staffed by women, which gather and dis-tribute information through a hybrid wired and wireless network, linking ten to twenty villages, helping the villagers check on prices, government entitlements for villages, health care information, and ocean weather conditions (Arunachalam 2002).

Given Sen's belief in the importance of building public capabilities, developing public reason, and inspiring a sense of freedom and choice, Indian universities do seem to have a critical role to play, in gathering data, testing new models, and positing new theories, within local and global contexts. Yet they cannot do this effectively if they are isolated from the work of the larger research community. Thus I am concerned that, for example, at Delhi University, one of India's finest research libraries, with over a million volumes, had been forced by the late 1990s to give up two-thirds of its subscriptions, with cuts felt particularly in the arts, in which 582 titles were cut down to 168 (Patel and Kumar 2001, 61). Although university budget allocations in India during that period certainly fluctuated, with years of increase as well as decline, the reductions in general funding to Indian universities were nowhere near as drastic as the unrelenting price increases that, combined with currency fluctuations, forced the cutting of journal titles.

At the Agricultural Sciences University in Bangalore, which I visited in 2003, nearly half the journal subscriptions had been canceled during the preceding decade, leaving it with somewhat fewer than 600 titles. That figure would have been much worse if the library had not had free online access to 150 journals, and if it had not been able to barter its way to another 150 titles in exchange for copies of its own journal, *Mysore Journal of Agricultural Sciences*. This mix of open access and bartered print copies exemplifies the sort of resourceful struggle that these universities are carrying on in an otherwise state of declining access to research.

In Africa, there is no less of a struggle underway to support the development of research capacities amid scarce access to the scholarly literature. The Development Policy Centre in Ibadan, Nigeria, for example, has become a magnet for scholars in the policy area, because funding from the World Bank, United Nations Development Program, and African Development Bank has enabled it to minimize its loss of journals, at least compared to other institutions in West Africa (Mabawonku 2001, 102). Still, the Centre's librarian, Iyabo Mabawonku, notes that visitors are more likely to browse the Internet in search of the resources they need, rather than consult the library's books and print journals, even though they have to pay for this browsing. As it is, the Centre's print journal collection is anything but sufficient, given that, as Mabawonku notes, the overseas vendors of the print journals to which the Centre subscribes "have never supplied more than 60 percent of the issues published each year," while her ongoing letters of complaint are "never acknowledged" (105). One source of hope for Mabawonku is that libraries could begin to offer more publishing and editorial functions and become directly involved in the circulation of locally produced research.

Kenya provides a similar example of difficult realities and continuing hope. The devaluation of the Kenyan currency during the latter half of the 1990s cost the libraries there about 30 percent of their purchasing power for foreign journals (Mutula 2001, 156). At Kenyatta University, the library's serials collection was down by 2003 to one "core" print journal per department (Muthayan and Muinde 2003). On visiting Nairobi University Library in 2003, I walked among seven well-crafted wooden racks for displaying current periodicals, all of which stood empty, with not a journal on display or a back issue stored beneath the hinged racks. When I asked about the empty racks, the librarian said that the current issues of the few subscriptions that they still had were eagerly being read by the students. However, on top of the empty display racks were signs notifying patrons that the Internet had recently "resumed" in the library and should be used for accessing journals. In a small lab with a handful of computers in a glass-enclosed corner of the library, students had suddenly acquired access to 10,000 electronic journals and a much greater number of abstracts through the agreements that had recently been negotiated by the International Network for the Availability of Scientific Publications.[5] INASP's initial three-year agreement with EBSCO (a major journal subscription service), Springer, Oxford University Press, Blackwell, and others provides for a 90–98 per-

---

5. The Web site for the International Network for the Availability of Scientific Publications is at ⟨http://www.inasp.info⟩. INASP's Programme for the Enhancement of Research Information has four components, with the delivery of information, through e-journal contracts with publishers being the first of these, followed by disseminating results of national and regional research, enhancing computer skills, and strengthening local publishing (Smart 2003). The Electronic Publishing Trust for Development (EPT) is also committed to supporting publishing efforts in developing countries, and eIFL.net, a project of the Soros Foundation, has been active in negotiating licenses for electronic access on behalf of libraries in transition and developing countries.

cent discount on electronic access to journals and covers over a hundred developing nations.[6] INASP, which currently covers these minimal access fees through its donors, plans to have this discount agreement negotiated by the individual developing countries in the future.

Another promising development in Kenya was the launch in 1991 of the African Virtual University (AVU) in Nairobi. Utilizing satellite technologies, AVU was able to serve students through thirty-four sites (with over 1,000 computers) in nineteen African countries during its "proof of concept" stage, with courses in technology, engineering, business, and the sciences ("sourced from leading universities in North America and Europe," according to the AVU Web site).[7] Having moved out of its pilot stage as a World Bank project, this independent intergovernment organization offers access to 1,000 online journals through its digital library and has helped institutions across Africa to set up AVU learning centers with high-speed connectivity to the Internet. The African Virtual University's library, according to Nancy Kamau, senior librarian at the Kenya Medical Research Institute, is devoted to "breaking through the information access barriers," as this "global platform" also seeks to make African content available to the world, while improving African access to resources (Kamau 2001). It understandably troubles African scholars to see companies, as Kamau puts it, "that market information products from the developed world … fail to recognize the potential that local content has as a part of a global knowledge."

The first major boon in open access for developing countries took place in 2002, when the World Health Organization (WHO) convinced the leading scientific publishing houses to provide these nations with free access to their biomedical research journals. The resulting Health Inter-Network Access to Research Initiative represents a partnership between WHO and (currently) forty-seven publishers of biomedical and health care journals (Aronson 2004). Institutions in the sixty-eight countries

6. The 90–98 percent discount figure is based on publishers' costs for managing access to their journals by the participating nations, a percentage that I take as further evidence of electronic publishing's surplus distribution capacity (Smart 2003).

7. The African Virtual University Web site can be accessed at ⟨http://www .avu.org⟩.

with a per capita GNP of less than $1,000 (according to World Bank fig-
ures from 1999) now have access to over 2,300 journals.[8] After the first
year of HINARI's operation (2002), 438 institutions had signed up from
fifty-six countries ("Health Interchange" 2003). Whether the INASP and
WHO initiatives are read cynically or optimistically—whether as a
public-relations flip for publishers or the moral arm twisting of international agencies—they represent a ray of light in what can otherwise be
portrayed as the gloom of the irresistible and heartless forces of economic
globalization. The HINARI model has since been extended to agriculture, with the Access to Global Online Research in Agriculture (AG-
ORA) project providing open access for institutions in fifty-one of the
poorest nations "to more than 500 key journals in food, nutrition, agriculture" and "related biological, environmental and social sciences" to a
similar set of impoverished nations, according to the project's Web site,[9]
with similar open access initiatives under discussion in fisheries, food
technologies, and environmental protection.

    "You cannot do science without information" was how Barbara
Aronson described the basis of the HINARI agreement, which in her capacity as a WHO librarian she helped put together. Researchers in some
of the world's poorest countries, she pointed out, now have, as a result
of HINARI, information equivalent to "a top-flight U.S. library" (quoted
in Peterson 2001). Think of the difference that access to 2,000 life science
journals will make to the University of Zimbabwe, for example, which
has seen its journal collection in this area dwindle from a high of 600
titles to 170 because of escalating subscription costs over the last two
decades (Nagourney 2001). Faculty there had reported in a study conducted in the 1990s that they were spending half their limited travel
opportunities each year visiting libraries and bookstores, while others
were successfully using personal contacts to obtain recent work as well
as writing to authors for reprints (Rosenberg 1997, 1:53). The recently

8. HINARI also includes an additional forty-two countries with per capita GNPs
of between $1,000 and $3,000, which pay $1,000 annually for national access,
with the money going toward the training of librarians in the use of the HINARI
catalogue and journals.

9. The AGORA Web site's URL is ⟨http://www.aginternetwork.org/en/⟩.

acquired access, through HINARI, to biomedical and agricultural journals amounts to a small triumph for the public sector of the global knowledge economy.

The other side of this access coin, however, concerns the publishing activities of researchers working in developing nations. Not so long ago, Diana Rosenberg, an expert in African libraries and scholarly publishing, concluded that it will take "a quantum leap in African publishing and distribution" to "reverse attitudes to local and African published material" (1997, 1:20). Among the many examples she offers is that of the University of the Cape Coast Press, which at the time of her study had several books in preparation, with pages camera-ready for printing, that could not go to press for want of funding (1997, 1:20). The *African Periodicals Exhibit Catalogue*'s list of scholarly journals went from 135 titles in twenty-two countries for 1997 to 70 titles from sixteen countries two years later, whereas earlier reports had identified up to 400 journals from forty-eight countries (Adebowale 2001, 30). During the 1990s, nine of the nineteen journals that had started publication in the 1960s in Nigeria met their demise (Zeleza 1998, 23). The cost of the raw materials for publishing, including paper and printing-machinery parts, had "more than doubled in the past five years," Jacob Jaygbay noted in 1998, with the overall result that it was just plain difficult for an African library to acquire African journals (66). Still, when it comes to the introduction of new technologies into publishing, Jaygbay, for one, remains wary, given many economic and cultural aspects associated with such technologies that need to be considered in light of the African context.

A further challenge for journal publishing in Africa has been the failure of major international indexing or journal supply services to include journals published there. Fortunately, the National Inquiry Services Centre in South Africa, headed by Margaret Crampton, has begun to address the indexing issue with its Global Information for Africa program, which issues a variety of bibliographic databases "for Africa, about Africa and by Africans" (NISC 2005). Additionally, Bioline International provides a portal, with indexing, pay-per-view, and open access services, for over thirty biology journals from developing nations, including a number from Africa. As Leslie Chan, associate director of Bioline

International, explains it: "The goal is to improve the visibility, accessibility and subsequent impact of research that would otherwise be 'lost' because few research libraries subscribe to developing countries' journals despite their importance.... Our experience suggests that open access not only enables free flow of ideas, it ensures more equitable scientific developments and their applications to social needs, including those of the developing countries" (2003).

On a larger scale, African Journals Online (AJOL), a site maintained by INASP, now offers the tables of contents and abstracts for over 200 African journals, accompanied by a print and e-mail document delivery service. The AJOL program also conducts workshops and provides other forms of support aimed at introducing African journals to ways of managing and publishing their content online (using systems originally developed by the Public Knowledge Project, as discussed in chapter 5), as a means of creating a greater global presence for this work and establishing a local and sustainable journal culture (Smart 2003).

Paul Tiyambe Zeleza, Director of African Studies at the University of Illinois at Urbana-Champaign, sees the need for indigenous publishing and local research agendas, out of a concern over how readily African university faculty "import appropriate packages of 'universal' theory and, at best, export empirical data," even as African universities are "increasingly forced to become service parks for private capital" (1998, 17). The lack of access leads, in Zeleza's view, to a lack of intellectual accountability in the study of Africa: "Today, Northern scholars writing on African countries do not need to worry about what their African colleagues think or say, especially if the latter are based on the Continent, because they are unlikely to review their work" (21). He calls for "mutually beneficial networks" that reinforce "the productive capacities" of all involved (21). Zeleza, above all, wants African researchers and scholars to be able to freely assert their intellectual autonomy, something they can achieve, he believes, only "by publishing, without apology in journals they control; by reading and citing each other, by demonstrating a greater faith in their own understanding of their complex and fast-changing societies—for no one else will do that for them" (1996, 300). This is precisely the promise of open access publishing systems, which can be installed and controlled locally, while offering a global presence through sophisticated indexing schemes (presented in more detail in chapter 12).

The challenges facing African scholars are little different from those experienced in Latin America, as noted by Ana María Cetto and Octavio Alonso-Gamboa, two information scientists working in Mexico: "We still look to the North to find out what we should be doing and how well we are performing; and we adopt and apply measuring standards defined abroad, regardless of whether they correctly measure performance according to our objectives, needs and conditions" (1998, 116). They point out that it is much easier, if far more costly, for Latin American scholars to get hold of North American or European journals than to obtain journals from another Latin American country, forcing Latin American universities seeking journals from the region to go through a "North American or European distributor so as to ensure as much as possible a safe and regular delivery" (120). They also tell of a librarian in a European university acknowledging that her library was unlikely even to allocate the space needed to house a print edition of a Latin American journal, even if it arrived at the library at no cost (120).[10]

When it comes to what these issues of access to the literature and a right to participate in it mean for someone working in a university in a developing nation, one can do no better than turn to A. Suresh Canagarajah's (2002) account of teaching literature at the University of Jaffna in Sri Lanka. Although the focus in most discussions of access to scholarly literature is on the scientific literature, Canagarajah reminds us that the humanities are no less vital a scholarly aspect of the academic community and that issues involving access to research in humanities fields are no less in need of redressing. He cites examples of stunningly insensitive peer reviews of articles that he and his colleagues submitted to Western journals, which included near-impossible demands made of them to be on top of the current literature. He records just how little time faculty

10. The open access response to this situation is found in the Scientific Electronic Library Online ⟨http://www.scielo.org⟩, a trilingual host for Iberian and Latin American journals with approximately eighty titles.

had for scholarly writing (given the very large teaching loads imposed by the university), as well as the paucity of incentives for conducting research and writing and resources for doing so (shortage of typewriters, paper, and typewriter ribbons, let alone computers).[11] Meanwhile, local magazines and newspapers welcomed contributions from university faculty, which made for much greater public engagement in their communities but drew them away from research activities that scholarly publishing opportunities might have fostered.

While Canagarajah makes little reference to publishing technologies and is duly cautious about the Internet, he turns repeatedly to issues and principles of *access*. For example, he calls for changes to "the relationship in the publication networks so that we can reconstruct knowledge—and presumably conduct international relations—in more egalitarian and enriching terms" (2002, 305). He reminds readers that the initial challenge faced by faculty members who wish to engage in scholarly research is getting a feel for the context of current scholarship. He describes how faculty members might come across perhaps a single, outdated issue of a journal, brought back by a colleague returning from abroad, or happen upon a notice of an exciting new journal in their field without being able to see it. In the most mundane details of access, Canagarajah makes poignant how the basic rights of participation—no less than "a rhetorical knowledge of scholarly publications"—are taken for granted by scholars who exist at the centers of publishing activity, even as they assume that these publications represent an open and free discussion of ideas, while in reality the limits to the circulation of the journals defines an intellectual periphery in which participation in this circulation is almost impossible (207).

Canagarajah uses this postcolonial metaphor of *center* and *periphery*, which he sees persisting in current knowledge production, to bring home the point that real change will take place only if "periphery scholars in-

---

11. Similarly, in the case of Kenya, according to Adeya and Oyelaran-Oyeyinka (2002), "lecturers at the public universities have complained that their research potential is stifled due to excessive teaching hours, outdated technology or lack of modern technology and insufficient access to scholarly materials and publications. Yet, most are keen to develop research in their disciplines in order to further scholarship worldwide" (27).

filtrate these publishing channels [of the center]" (2002, 29).[12] Yet he is no less concerned about creating space within these channels for local publishing efforts; he uses the Shri A. M. M. Murugappa Chettiar Research Center in Chennai, India, as an example: "Lacking the means to disseminate their own knowledge widely through print, peripheral communities have to be satisfied with having their research and scholarship receive limited hearing" (242). This, in turn, leads those working in the center "to assume that no knowledge exists on certain peripheral realities," so that they "go on publishing work based on limited data" (242). The result? "The journals thereby disseminate partisan knowledge globally" (43).

For Canagarajah, the alternative is to create a place for the distinct sensibilities of different academic cultures—"a plurality of rhetorics"—while avoiding a headlong rush into a one-voice, one-style, one-world sequence of cultural globalization (2002, 94). Using the impact that the Swedish journal *Lanka* has had on his colleagues in Sri Lanka, Canagarajah speaks of the sheer motivational power of being able to turn to a body of work that speaks directly—if nonetheless published at a distance—to the experience of peripheral scholars. Canagarajah also spells out the benefits for the intellectual center of the increased global dimension of scholarly activity, noting that "an engagement with local knowledge from periphery contexts can help enrich, expand, and reconstruct mainstream discourses and knowledge" (303).

12. For example, one study shows that of research articles concerning the forty-eight least developed countries in 1999–2000, only 30 percent had coauthors from local research institutes in those countries (Dahdouh-Guebas et al. 2003, 329). The authors of articles on those least-developed countries expressed confidence, when interviewed, in the "reliability" of local researchers and in the contribution of their own work to "development cooperation"; yet Dahdouh-Guebas et al. feel compelled to conclude that a form of "safari research" is still commonly being practiced among researchers conducting their studies in the developing world (336). Benjamin Acosta-Cazares and his colleagues (2000) first used "safari research" in a paper that calculated that, although 25 percent of the world's scientists live in developing countries, a scientist from the developed world is five times as likely to submit an article to, and 2.1 times as likely to have it accepted in the *British Medical Journal* than a scientist from a developing country. Additionally, scientists in developing nations are poorly represented on the editorial boards of such journals as *Lancet* and *Nature* (although they hold six of thirty-four positions with the *British Medical Journal*).

From my perspective, open source online journal management and publishing systems offer the potential of locally controlled scholarly publishing efforts on the Web utilizing the scant but emerging technical infrastructure that is gradually taking root in universities in Sri Lanka and elsewhere. This would allow a far more distributed journal culture to spread through the academic community, against an otherwise centralized model. Online journal systems can, for example, support far more extensive collaboration among international editorial teams—and such collaboration is what Canagarajah recommends—in further overcoming the lingering center-periphery divide (2002, 273–274).[13] The editorial gatekeepers of scholarship no longer need reside at the center, which undermines the very idea of the center. The digital divide will undoubtedly persist, but there are grounds for hoping that new information technologies can be used creatively to overcome aspects of what might be cast as the *print divide* that has hindered the full participation of the global academic community in research and scholarship.[14]

As Michael Hardt and Antonio Negri warn in *Empire*, it is nearly impossible now to step outside of what they awkwardly term "the informational colonization of being" perpetuated by a handful of communication industries that "not only organize production on a new scale and impose a new structure adequate to global space, but also makes its jus-

13. For example, according to its Web site ⟨http://pkp.ubc.ca/pocol⟩, *Postcolonial Text*, one of the first to use the Public Knowledge Project's Open Journal Systems, has its initial team of editors, assembled in 2003, distributed among the West Indies, South Africa, India, Sri Lanka, Australia, and Canada, with each able to oversee the editorial process from a Web browser.

14. In the sciences, at least, one promising sign of reduced influence of the center-periphery model is the very growth in coauthorship between scholars from developed and developing nations (Arunachalam and Doss 2000). This international collaborative strategy is particularly common with authors working in countries with a very weak presence in the ISI Web of Science, as with Indonesia's 266 papers, of which 88 percent had international collaboration (622). Although Arunachalam and Doss attribute the overall growth in international coauthorship to increased airline flights and international phone calls, it might also seem that enabling researchers in developing countries to have greater access to the research literature would only add to their capacity for this type of collaborative research.

tification immanent" (2000, 33–34). This new media empire, with its parallel in scholarly publishing's own forms of corporate concentration, only increases the importance of opening up alternative communication channels for scholarly inquiry in the name of open access. How else can the two-way knowledge gap suffered by both periphery and center be bridged? How else can the global scale of scholarly activity contribute all that it might to the democratic and public possibilities of a public sphere that is otherwise in danger of being overwhelmed by the proprietary interests of the communication industries?[15]

What this means is that scholars everywhere need to question their assumptions about what constitutes an adequate circulation of their and others' work. As scholars work against the partiality of knowledge, in the double sense of its being both biased and incomplete, they need to recognize that the best check on that partiality is to extend the global basis on which knowledge circulates, not only among university researchers, but among those working in related areas of health, education, welfare, and justice to draw on a few social science examples. Practically speaking, scholars and researchers need only ensure that the journals with which they are associated have a policy of offering open access at least to developing countries and that they upload published and unpublished work to open access e-print archives, when that work is not otherwise freely available online. It seems little enough to ask.

Yet there are undoubtedly risks to opening local cultures further to globalizing influences through their universities. Questions remain about whether the technology can reduce the information inequities and whether a balance can be found between global and local interests. Can technology indeed help rewire not only older patterns in the circulation of knowledge, but the spread of education and the growth of research capacities? Innovations in open access publishing are taking place

15. For Hardt and Negri (2000), what is at issue is the "right to reappropriation," and in particular a *"reappropriation of knowledge"* that, as a "political demand of the multitude," is all about "having free access to and control over knowledge, information, communication, and affects," as it is "articulated with the powers of science and social knowledge through cooperation" (404; 404, emphasis in original; 406; 407; 410).

against the chilling historical backdrop of earlier efforts at instilling universal education and global knowledge systems, when the West placed educating the native at the heart of imperialism's moral economy (Willinsky 1998). The way forward with new scholarly publishing models is not without dangers, but the academic community has reason enough to pursue this principle of increased access to the knowledge it produces and to do so consciously against the backdrop of this ever-present past.

8
Public

When a scholarly journal is free for online reading, or when a researcher places a published article in an open access e-print archive, it is first of all a boon for researchers and students the world over. However, open access is also public access. Open access is slowly making a greater portion of the research literature publicly available. This will mean little enough, admittedly, to most of the people most of the time. Still, it is not difficult to imagine occasions when a dedicated history teacher, an especially keen high school student, an amateur astronomer, or an ecologically concerned citizen might welcome the opportunity to browse the current and relevant literature pertaining to their interests. Increased access could also contribute context and depth to the work of investigative reporters and policy analysts. It could assist small-town physicians and lawyers stymied by difficult cases. Or this public right of access could turn up in a William Haefeli *New Yorker* cartoon, depicting a young son sitting on his father's knee and responding to the proverbial patriarchal wisdom with "Please don't be offended if I consult additional sources of information" (2004).

While the public use of research published in a scholarly journal will add little or nothing to the publishing costs of the journal—barring an overwhelming surge of interest in a particular title—it will increase the presence and impact of the work published. And this may lead, in turn, to greater public support for research and scholarship. That is, the public impact of open access forms part of the case for an open access approach to scholarly publishing.

To speak of public access once again raises the issue of a *digital divide* that limits many people's hope of ever visiting the Internet. The digital divide is obviously rooted in larger economic disparities that are unlikely to be overcome within the current world system, and yet when it comes to the public sphere, governments and philanthropic organizations have initiated a number of programs that have substantially increased the presence of the Internet in libraries, schools, and community centers.[1] At any rate, waiting for the divide to be closed somehow is a poor excuse for the academic community's not doing what it can now do about the inequitable distribution of access to research and scholarship. Critiques of the digital divide in hardware and software lose some of their sting if the authors are doing nothing to ensure that their own content contributions are made freely available online and not part of an information divide. On the other hand, increasing public access to relevant research could provide, say, antipoverty organizations in Vancouver, Aborigine organizations in Sydney, union organizers in Washington, and health organizations in Indonesia with the latest findings, historical patterns, international comparisons, and proven methods, all of which would further their efforts and improve the quality of their work (Williams 2002; Edejer 2000; Zielinski 2000).

Opening the research literature's virtual door to the public in this way bears a certain kinship to the nineteenth-century public library movement that took hold during the other age of information, during the nineteenth century. As Alan Rauch points out in his history of that earlier era, this "obsession with knowledge" was led by the Society for the Diffusion of Useful Knowledge, as well as by public libraries and mechanics institutes that operated as self-improvement societies, with libraries and regular lectures, for their craftsmen members. There was a corresponding growth in the publication of periodicals, encyclopedias, and societies, all concerned with fostering public knowledge

1. Bill Gates has provided support for Internet access to 95 percent of the public libraries in America, at a cost of $250 million (Egan 2002); in Cameroon, the universities are establishing satellite Internet hookups that will eliminate the faculty's current dependence on Internet cafés for access (Shafack and Wirsiy 2002). Also see the Web sites of the Digital Divide Network ⟨http://www.digitaldividenetwork.org/⟩ and PowerUP: Bridging the Digital Divide ⟨http://www.powerup.org⟩.

(2001, 1).[2] The public library, in particular, has long been a beacon of self-directed and deeply motivated learning on the part of common readers. It is not only a vital cornerstone of democracy, but a public site of quiet solace, intellectual inquiry, and literary pleasures. To increase public access to online research and scholarship would add a great deal to what has emerged over the last decade on the Internet as a wired and virtual public library, providing people with an opportunity to explore a new world of ideas that they may have only suspected existed.

Already, with only a limited body of literature freely available online, that portion of the public with Internet access has shown a surprising capacity for delving into studies of relevance and interest to them. As I discuss in this chapter, public interest in the life sciences has reshaped the U.S. National Library of Medicine Web site, as well as altering professional practice in health care. In astronomy, public access is enabling amateur astronomers to contribute to the professional literature. Whereas in chapter 11, I describe how presenting readers of research with related links can help more of them get more out of what they read, here I discuss why public interests already form part of the case for open access.

Nowhere has the democratic quality of the open access question played itself out more dramatically in recent years than in the doctor's office. The Pew Internet and American Life Project calls the new level of public access to medical information and research made available on the Internet an "online health revolution" that is helping "American take better care of themselves" (Fox and Rainie 2000).[3] This "new method of care,"

2. Rauch writes of the nineteenth century as "driven by remarkable changes in technology and science, [when] knowledge was both inspirational and irresistible in terms of its potential for social and cultural transformation" (2001, 1). It was an age given to "mental improvement" and scientific innovation, taken up in both public forums and private homes, giving rise to an influential knowledge industry, or as David Mason held, in 1862, "an encyclopedia chained at Charring Cross for public reference would be a boon for London worth fifty drinking fountains" (quoted in Rauch 2001, 39).

3. A related Pew Internet and American Life Project report found that 60 percent of Americans now have Internet access, of which 81 percent expect to find "reliable information about health and medical conditions online," while 45 percent of those who do not have Internet access also see the Internet as a reliable source of this information (Larsen and Rainie 2002).

based on patients' informing themselves on health issues, is being called by physicians—now that they have overcome any initial sense of intimidation by patients—"shared decision making" (Brownlee 2003, 54). I hardly need add that *shared decision making* sounds a lot like democracy on a personal level, and if what it takes is access to relevant and rigorously reviewed information, it could apply equally well to schools, neighborhoods, and workplaces. If nothing else, this public access to research might provide a slight democratic check on the tyranny of expertise, as the experts' sources can be verified and countered. The quality of the information available to the public, however, is dependent on the proportion of peer-reviewed research to which there is open access, compared to the vast amounts of other sorts of online information. As I mentioned in the opening chapter, the NIH is now considering a request that who have received federal funding from the NIH provide open access to any work resulting from the funded research within twelve months of publication, a measure that has attracted support not from Nobel Prize winners, but from the Alliance for Taxpayer Access.

Six million Americans go online each day in search of information about health issues (NIH 2003). A significant proportion of those people report that they have been influenced in their thinking and practice by the information they have accessed, although they also express some concern over the quality and reliability of that information (Fox and Rainie 2000). They are taking what they find to the doctor's office, as suggested by the fact that 85 percent of the physicians in one study noted that their patients had brought Internet materials on health issues when they visited, with some doctors holding that this led to "less time-efficient" visits (Murray et al. 2003; see also Freudenheim 2000). Of course, very little of the health information that patients access is drawn from peer-reviewed journal articles, as the vast majority of that literature is only available to them, if at all, if they come to their computer with a credit card in hand (Okamura, Bernstein, and Fidler 2002).

Still, one study, done with physicians in Glasgow, found that the accuracy and reliability of the information which the patients, working with what is available, brought into their doctors' offices was not a major cause of concern for physicians, although they observed that patients often needed help in interpreting it correctly (Wilson 1999). What was also encouraging in this study was that the majority of the physicians reported that the information brought in by patients was new to them. That patients are contributing, even in a small way, to the education of physicians and that physicians might in turn help patients interpret health information strikes me as a significant contribution to the general level of public education. Certainly, most doctors do not rely on their patients for online research. A great number of them already use the Internet on regular basis, or as one explained, the "newest and best in medical research [is] right at our own desks," leading them to discover, for example, that "leeches, for example, are now used on some patients to treat the pain of arthritis" (Sanders 2003, 29).

In an effort to feed patients' hunger for information, as well as address the right to know, doctors in Georgia are experimenting with a "health information prescription" (Brownlee 2003, 54) that will guide patients to reliable sources, including the U.S. National Library of Medicine's MedlinePlus, which combines a layperson's guide to health with the capacity to search for the latest medical research through the PubMed index.[4] As patients find themselves in a better position to make informed decisions, they may decide at times to exercise their right not to be influenced by the latest study. When the risks of menopause hormone therapy were reported, for example, one patient described her decision to stay with the therapy after learning about its dangers because, in her words, "for me, it's a trade-off," given the increased mental agility she experiences as a result of the therapy (Kolata 2003).

The government's development of MedlinePlus as an online medical library for the public represents but one instance of how public access is influencing the organization of scholarly resources. More recently, in February 2000, the National Institutes of Health, other Federal agencies,

---

4. For users who do not belong to a life sciences research library, only the abstract of most articles is available without cost through PubMed, although PubMed provides links to purchase the full text of the article from the article's publisher or to locate a library with a subscription to the journal. PubMed offers online tutorials related to the article's content, as well as health consumer information (through MedlinePlus), supplementary genetic data, and author profiles. Initial studies of "information prescriptions" have found that they can increase the use of the high-quality information sources, as well as the sharing of sources with family and others (D'Alessandro et al. 2004).

and the pharmaceutical industry launched ClinicalTrials.gov. The Web site currently lists 11,400 clinical studies, many of which qualified people can elect to participate in, and others of which serve to inform the public about the state of ongoing investigations. The site involves studies in ninety countries, although most are taking place in the United States and Canada, and it receives approximately 16,000 visitors a day. For example, the listing for one study, "Early Characteristics of Autism," at the University of Washington, announces that the study is "currently recruiting subjects" while describing the eligibility and procedures, as well as providing a link to MedlinePlus information on autism.

Following on the growing public and professional expectation of access to clinical trials, the American Medical Association has appealed to the U.S. government to keep a mandatory public registry of all clinical drug trials, in light of the fact that negative or inconclusive results from such trials often do not see the light of day, whether as a result of suppression by the sponsoring pharmaceutical company or implicit journal policies against publishing these types or results. Without waiting for the government to act, a newly formed International Committee of Medical Journal Editors, made up of the editors of a dozen leading journals, including the *New England Journal of Medicine* and the *Lancet*, has announced that the journals the committee represents will not publish the results of a clinical trial that has not been initially registered in a public database (Meier 2004). However, as John Abrahamson (2004) wisely points out, the results of clinical trials, even when publicly available, are not always going to attract sufficient attention or be sufficiently scrutinized, given the massive promotional budgets of the pharmaceutical industry. Abrahamson provides startling instances of research results' being buried beneath marketing efforts, including the fact that $15 billion worth of the arthritis drugs Celebrex and Vioxx has been prescribed by doctors, despite studies publicly available, through a Food and Drug Administration Web site, that show that these medications increase the risk of heart attacks. (Vioxx's manufacturer, Merck & Co., subsequently withdrew Vioxx from the market on September 31, 2004.) He recommends the establishment of an oversight board, modeled on the National Institute of Clinical Excellence in Britain, to review the research and make recommendations.

Certainly I am not claiming that making research freely available will protect public interests in and of itself, especially when contrary forces are at work, such as the pharmaceutical marketing machine.[5] And yet that machine, too, is responding to the new sense of informed empowerment on the part of the public by shifting the way the drug companies pitch their advertising. Instead of the once-typical "nine out of ten doctors recommend" type of advertisement, they are moving to reports on the latest (supportive) research studies, or as a recent full-page advertisement placed by Merck in the *New York Times* proclaimed: "BE INFORMED. The largest clinical study of its kind including the largest number of people with diabetes: It could have an impact on millions" (June 4, 2004, A9).

The Swiss pharmaceutical Novartis announced that it had awarded $4 million in grants on diabetes research to Harvard and MIT, in what *Nature* termed "a rare public-private partnership that will require it to place a mass of genetic data in the public domain" (Knight 2004). Alan D. Cherrington, president of the American Diabetes Association, commented on the change that this arrangement signified: "Often, when the pharmaceutical industry gets into relationships with academia, they do it in a proprietary way, so they fund the lab and in return they have access to insider information. This [the Novartis arrangement with Harvard and MIT] seems extraordinary" (quoted in Krasner 2004).

While ClinicalTrials.gov and the Novartis research agreement with Harvard and MIT are not about open access publishing, they do reflect a new open and public sensibility regarding issues of access to scientific information. Similar sorts of registries of ongoing research could work just as well, one imagines, for educational, anthropological, sociological, and other sorts of research involving people, while incorporating a broader range of research methods than is represented by medical research's gold standard of the clinical trial.

Increased public expectations in regard to the right to know are contributing to changes among what might be called the subscription-based sector of journal publishing. As mentioned in chapter 1, the *New England Journal of Medicine* decided in 2001 to grant free access to its

---

5. See, for example, Marcia Angell's (2004) *The Truth about the Drug Companies: How They Deceive Us and What to Do about It.*

content six months after it is published and made available to subscribers, while offering immediate free online access to 117 of the world's poorest nations. As a result, more than 250,000 people are visiting the journal's Web site each week, three-quarters of whom are not subscribers and over half of whom come from outside of North America. When the journal first announced this new policy of offering delayed open access, the editors spoke in terms of a future that offered complete, if not immediate, access to the research literature: "It should be possible someday to establish a single, searchable archive of biomedical-research reports in a way that does not threaten the peer-reviewed journals that help create the literature We believe our commitment to providing the full texts of past research articles without charge is a step toward a useful central way to search the biomedical literature" (Campion, Anderson, and Drazen 2001). This book argues, of course, that when it comes to what "should be possible someday," that day has arrived. Were the spirit willing, the technology is ready.

The media are also playing a role in the increased access to health information, turning reports on research into a regular news-you-can-use service. Many newspapers now have weekly health sections that present stories on research covering not only the implications for readers, but the reversals and revisions, challenges and controversies surrounding the latest research. In 2003, for example, the *New York Times Magazine* devoted its entire March 16 issue to the theme "Half of What Doctors Know Is Wrong." The articles in this issue included details about sample sizes, risk probabilities, and research design flaws in the studies discussed, which were taken from the *British Medical Journal* and elsewhere. True, the *New York Times* is not everyone's newspaper, but the public's exposure to research reversals (such as that regarding hormone replacement therapy) and design flaws (such as those surrounding mammograms) are also found in the tabloids and on television news. And the greater understanding of research fallibility and contention that results from this increased media scrutiny and exposure has not led to any sort of outcry against continuing public support for medical research. Rather, it has arguably fed public support for this research, judging by how government funding has continued to grow (to well over $28 billion annually) in the United States while funding for other areas of research has remained relatively static.

While interest and access increase, the public's engagement with research will remain a matter of personal interests, pressing public issues, and passing curiosities. Environmentalist groups provide a good example of personal-public interests in research that go beyond concerns with personal health issues. In his study of environmentalists, political scientist Frank Fischer was impressed with how interested these nonscientists were in research results regarding environmental issues, especially if the data were "presented and discussed in an open democratic process" (2000, 130). More than that, these same "ordinary" citizens have in recent times become actively involved in the research process itself, giving rise to, for example, "popular epidemiology," in which the public helps to track the distribution of diseases, especially as this distribution might be related to environmental factors (151–157). To have a researcher-public alliance forming around environmental issues suggests one way in which both local and expert knowledge can play a critical part in what amounts to a deliberative process over what is to be done, for example, to reduce pollution. "Instead of questioning the citizen's ability to participate, we must ask," Fischer insists, "how can we interconnect and coordinate the different but inherently interdependent discourses of citizens and experts" (45). He calls for a reconstructed concept of professional practice among researchers whose task would then be about "authorizing space for critical discourse among competing knowledges, both theoretical and local, formal and informal" (27).

Just how far this public engagement can go in working for both the public and scientific good has been brought home by AIDS activists during the 1980s and 1990s. As Steven Epstein (1996) tells it in *Impure Science*, these activists successfully struggled for public participation in medical knowledge, managing to bring otherwise overlooked research into the limelight and change the conduct of clinical trials related to the disease. Scientists found themselves moved by these activists in both an intellectual and an ethical sense, and activists, as Epstein puts it, "imbibed and appropriated the languages and cultures of biomedical sciences," acquiring their own forms of credibility in public and scientific deliberations over how to respond to AIDS by "yoking together moral (or political) arguments and methodological (epistemological) arguments" (335–356). The AIDS struggle established the need for, in the words of ACT-UP (AIDS Coalition to Unleash Power) activist Mark

Harrington, "a lasting culture of information, advocacy, intervention, and resistance" (quoted in Epstein 1996, 350). One lesson that might be drawn from this chapter in the fight against this tragic pandemic, which is no less with us today, is that enabling people to play a greater part in the research that directly affects their own lives can lead to better science.

Up to this point, I have focused on the public value of research in a very practical or instrumental sense with health and environmental issues. However, public access to research and scholarship is also about knowing for its own sake. It is a way of supporting people's disinterested pursuit of knowledge, following in the historical tradition, as I noted, of the public library, mutual-improvement societies, mechanics institutes, and extension courses. In the opening decades of the nineteenth century, working men could be found joining botanical societies in England that, in the case of the Lancashire area, met each month in a local pub, according to the historian Anne Secord (1994), where they identified new specimens to be added to their herbarium and exchanged books from their small collections. By the turn of the nineteenth century, there was a thriving industry of working-class science periodicals that became a mainstay of mutual-improvement and cooperative societies, in which fees for subscriptions to these periodicals could be shared among the members (McLaughlin-Jenkins 2003, 150). As the historian Erin McLaughlin-Jenkins sums up this earlier era of increased access, "the penny press, cheap reprints of scientific texts, free libraries, the secularist and political lecture circuit, middle-class popular science and working-class educational initiatives created greater opportunities for contact with scientific ideas ... [and] as a result, intellectuals and hobbyists were increasingly part of a collective pursuit of knowledge" (2003, 161).

Jonathan Rose (2001) is another historian who, in his *The Intellectual Life of the British Working Class*, has done much to capture the voices of those during the course of the last two centuries who, having been otherwise prevented from attending college, strived to engage with its particular realm of ideas. Rose offers the instance of Ewan MacColl, who came of age in the 1930s and tells of his father, an iron founder by trade and a communist by belief, who, in MacColl's words, "belonged to the generation who believed that books were tools that open a lock which would free people. He really did believe it" (quoted in Rose

2001, 316). And in many ways so did MacColl: "For me to go at the age of fourteen, to drop into the library and discover a book like Kant's *Critique of Pure Reason* or *The Mistaken Subtlety of the Four-Side Figure* ... the titles alone produced a kind of happiness in me.... I can remember the marvelous sensation of sitting in the library and opening the volume, and going into that world of Akaky Akakievich Bashmachkin in *The Overcoat* or *The Nose*, or *The Madman's Diary*" (quoted in Rose 2001, 316).

Now it may well have been that "books were a kind of fantasy life," as MacColl reflects back on it, and a "refuge from the horrors of the life around us" during the Great Depression (quoted in Rose 2001, 316). Yet the era's impressive spirit of autodidactism and self-improvement, which MacColl represents so well and which led many to enrolling in extension courses, was to make this particular realm of ideas part of these working-class lives. And if the golden, heroic era of an independent working-class intellectual life is now long past—with Rose pointing to both state-sponsored educational opportunities and increased entertainment options as causes of its decline—that is no reason to deny public access to current discussions of Kant or Gogol in the scholarly literature, when that public access can be so readily provided. Certainly, many if not most journal articles will remain technically impenetrable for all but a small circle of scholars and students, but there are also pieces that might well engender that "marvelous sensation" MacColl speaks of that comes from seeing how others have managed to make greater sense of the human condition.

Then there is the more contemporary instance of Timothy Ferris's (2002) *Seeing in the Dark: How Backyard Stargazers Are Probing Deep Space and Guarding Earth from Interplanetary Peril*. Ferris not only celebrates in this book the considerable accomplishments of amateur astronomers today, he points to the "flourishing of amateur-professional collaborations" among astronomers in various regions of the world. Columbia University's Center for Backyard Astrophysics coordinates a number of projects involving such collaborations, which sometimes include middle and high school students and have led to amateur access to major telescopes, including the Hubble Space Telescope (51–53). The amateurs, of which there are ten times as many as professional astronomers, are able to generate a considerable body of observational data—

often making significant discoveries in the process—which serves the professionals' theorizing and follow-up.[6]

The results of these collaborations make their way into the astronomy journals, on occasion, although not always with due credit to the amateurs, according to some whom Ferris interviewed. Yet the shared interest and commitment to learning more about the heavens remains the driving force of their part-time engagement with astronomy. The personal computer and the Internet are what makes this amateur contribution and collaboration possible. These technologies enable amateurs to record and measure activities in the heavens and connect with other astronomers globally. They are also able to consult the considerable array of open access astronomical research papers, through arXiv.org E-Print Archive, and databases, such as the many-terabyte National Virtual Observatory, which is collecting and coordinating images from dozens of ground- and space-based telescopes around the world (Schecter 2003). A similar level of amateur involvement in linguistics, lexicography, and botany also has a long history, with the work of amateur naturalists proving of great benefit, for example, to Newton's work on tides in the seventeenth century and Darwin's studies in the nineteenth century. And today, noted physicist Freeman J. Dyson (2002) asks, "which other science is now ripe for a revolution giving opportunities for the next generation of amateurs to make important discoveries?" (4).[7]

6. In its analysis of the tragic re-entry breakup of the shuttle Columbia on February 1, 2003, the National Aeronautics and Space Administration (NASA) benefited from having access to 12,000 videos and images collected largely from amateurs, even if not all items collected proved to be reliable records of the breakup (Schwartz 2003, D1).

7. This quote comes from Dyson's review of Ferris's book, in which he points to botany and zoology as ready for great amateur gains: "We may hope that amateurs in the coming century, using new tools that modern technology is placing in their hands, will invade and rejuvenate all sciences" (2002, 8). I have dealt elsewhere (Willinsky 1994) with public participation during the nineteenth and twentieth centuries in the collection of citations for the editing of the *Oxford English Dictionary* (*OED*). For a well-told chapter in this amateur participation in the *OED*, see Winchester 1998. Finally, on the promise of amateur contributions to the study of history, especially through history Web sites, see Rosenzweig 2001.

By way of a final instance of the way access to research might support public interests in knowledge—before dealing in the next chapter with the political import of this access—I turn to the sweeping digitization of collections and artifacts now underway in many of the world's museums. It offers both a parallel open access development and a further argument for opening the research literature. The American Museum of Natural History, for example, now has 400,000 images and catalog entries online, covering portions of its vertebrate and invertebrate fossils, pickled frogs and snake skins, field journals and scientific sketches. On visiting the museum's Web site, one can take in a period photograph of Mrs. M. Brown posing with a shovel at the Jurassic Bone Cabin Quarry in Wyoming in 1897 or turn to the catalogued images of the fossils that she and the others found. The museum's declared goal is to make its entire collection of perhaps thirty million items available to the public online, and its efforts are multiplied across museums the world over. "We're all heading," the librarian of the Field Museum in Chicago observes, "toward a kind of digital global museum," which will amount, adds *New York Times* reporter James Gorman, to "a catalog of the world" (2002, A1).

As museum collections find their way online, some are being helpfully pulled together in thematic portals, such as the University of California's MaNIS (the Mammal Networked Information System). This portal, supported by the National Science Foundation, opens a door on seventeen museums' collections, enabling people to search across the geographical regions and historical eras represented by these collections. Private foundations, as well as federal agencies such as the U.S. National Endowment for the Humanities, see this new level of access as possessing both scholarly and public potential for making much better use of the treasures in these museums' collections. Although many of these sites are providing free access to their online collections, some are turning to subscription services like ARTstor to manage their online collections. ARTstor currently offers access to nine collections, including that of the Department of Architecture and Design at the Museum of Modern Art in New York, and is following, with Mellon Foundation support, in the footsteps of JSTOR as a "not-for-profit, public utility" (Mirapul 2003).

Subscription services such as ARTstor may encourage museums to place their collections online as well as assist them in doing so, but even with very reasonable fee structures, they will leave the museum field divided between open and closed online collections, much like the journal literature. In comparison to the journals, the museums have always had a public mandate, and one would hope that they will make as much of their collections as possible as open as possible to the public. Still, something is missing from these museum initiatives to digitize their collections. For to find oneself absorbed by a work of art or a natural-history artifact is an experience that could well be enriched by being able to learn more about these images and objects from the scholars and researchers who are studying them with such care. Access to the literature that documents these studies could bring related materials to light, situate fragments within wholes, reveal connections, provide contexts, and pose hypotheses about form and function, origin and evolution. By visiting selective museum Web sites, people are increasingly able to find their way into vast publicly sponsored storehouses of information, whether on paleontology or space travel, ceramic glazes or early typewriters, which they have not otherwise been able to view, even in the museums themselves, which have always faced constraints imposed by limited display space. Yet at the same time that the museums are opening their collections to online visits, the public is being excluded from no less a publicly sponsored effort at making greater sense of these holdings through related scholarship, which is also being rendered digitally in research journals.

At stake in this divide is, for example, an ability to move readily from museum catalogs on amphibians to the scientific analysis of increased mutations among these creatures, where there is some uncertainty about the contribution of pollution, ultraviolet radiation, or the most likely culprit, parasites. Even to begin to create common indexes that, in this example, link museum collections with open access abstracts in *Ecology Letters* or *Conservation Biology* would be a move in the right direction.[8] The educational and scientific potential of connecting artifact with anal-

8. Closely related work is already underway, fortunately, on linking "scientific data from museum specimen databases and library catalogs of scientific literature" at the Florida Museum of Natural History; see Caplan and Haas 2004.

ysis is about gaining an understanding that goes well beyond the level that can be obtained from viewing the typical museum exhibit. To create open access to museum collections and to the related research literature would facilitate linking digitized artifact to study and digitized study to artifact. The benefits for each would surely be reciprocal.

Now despite the weight that I am giving public access to research in this book, I understand that the common reader's downloading of the latest article on trilobites from the *Journal of Paleontology* is unlikely to be the number-one argument in convincing researchers, scholarly associations, and journal editors that the circulation of knowledge would be better served by open access to the journal literature. Although I have tried to present evidence from medical research and astronomy of the public's stake and interest in research, it is hard to determine in advance what the public will make of the growing access to all fields of scholarly endeavor. Yet I would argue that proving that the public has sufficient interest in, or capacity to understand, the results of scholarly research is not the issue. The public's right of access to this knowledge is not something that people have to earn. It is grounded in a basic right to know. As online technologies appear capable of extending that right to a greater portion of research and scholarship, it falls to the scholarly community to experiment and test just how far such access can be pursued with new publishing models.

Some will still object that the public already has too much information to deal with and that it is very unlikely to be interested in finding the virtual doors of the university libraries of the world suddenly opened to it. Will public exposure of this academese only further obfuscate the common sense and public knowledge that is democracy's great hope? Well, open access is certainly not about simply dumping shelf-loads of journals into people's laps or laptops. It falls to the scholarly community to keep its work in an orderly and well-indexed form, so that precisely what is needed on a given topic can be brought to bear on it. Having access to indexes that enable one to identify what work deals precisely with the topic of one's interest, following the model of PubMed in the life sciences, complete with user supports that enable further precision in searching, could minimize the dangers of the public's being overwhelmed or overloaded by the amount of available research. Access to high-quality indexing of the scholarly literature needs to go along with open access to the literature itself, as I go on to describe in chapter 12.

All of this is only to say that public access to research literature should not be dismissed as an incidental side-effect of the open access movement. Although it may seem that a vast, rich world of information is now within a click or two of most connected computers, the toll gates that surround the carefully reviewed and well-financed information constituted by scholarly research have grown more expensive and restrictive, even as many pockets of open access have emerged. Whether one considers how dependent research is on public support and good will, or the broader educational goals that could be served by making research more widely available, public access needs to figure in both the case for open access and, as I go on to explore, in the very design of electronic journals for readers. But before I take up the questions raised by the reading and indexing of research, I want to pursue the democratic and human-rights side of public access research and scholarship.

9

Politics

As if the *digital divide* did not pose enough of a challenge to extending the benefits of the Internet to a wider population, Pippa Norris, a political scientist at Harvard's Kennedy School of Government, contends that a *democratic divide* is being created by current government efforts to place more and more information online (2001). It is all well and good, Norris notes, that "government Web pages serve as a new channel for transparency and accountability," but in the absence of other sources of information, government postings can amount to "a form of state propaganda" (237). Her concern is that even as nations place information and policies online, "saving paper, postage and ink," they "rarely launch deliberative consultative exercises through un-moderated chat rooms" or other forms of consultation and deliberation (237). The theme of helping citizens take advantage of new information sources to further their democratic participation lies at the heart of the political case, as I see it, for open access to research and scholarship.

After all, where is a citizen, or a journalist for that matter, to turn to corroborate and check the standing of the new wealth of government information made available by the government's efforts to increase the availability of information online? It would seem, at first blush, that if citizen and journalist were to have ready access to the relevant research literature on any given political issue, they would be better equipped to participate in policy debates and make substantial contributions to what Norris terms "deliberative consultative exercises." Here, we arrive at the political import of the access principle. Politicians and bureaucrats, interest groups and activists are already using the Internet as a political information medium, and *digital democracy* is taking a wide variety of forms, from online voting to cyberactivism.[1] Greater public access to research and scholarship has the potential to raise the level of discourse for this emerging democratic form. It could turn a citizen's online forum from a sounding board into a far more informative review of government policies and practices. It could provide a check and balance to the one-sided representations of interest groups, political parties, and governments. Such, at least, are the potential political implications of open access.

Now, my own slight experiments with digital democracy have made it clear to me just how difficult the ideals of informed deliberation are to achieve. During the late 1990s, a team at the University of British Columbia of which I was a member established the Public Knowledge Policy Forum, in cooperation with the Ministry of Education in British Columbia and the British Columbia Teachers Federation. Our modest efforts to narrow the democratic divide consisted of creating a Web site with the Ministry of Education's newly proposed policy on the educational uses of technology for the province's schools, which we linked to related background documents from the government. The Web site also featured a public online forum or bulletin board in which people were invited to comment on the policy proposal. Finally, we added a carefully organized and annotated set of links to relevant research, related policies in other jurisdictions, media coverage, and other pertinent sources for citizens to consider in judging the policy proposal and to inform their deliberations.

During the few weeks that we had to prepare the site, in advance of the ministry's "period of public consultation," we scrambled to find

1. See, for example, the Web site of the Center for Deliberative Polling ⟨http://www.la.utexas.edu/research/delpol/⟩ and the U.S. ⟨http://www.e-democracy.org/us/⟩ and U.K. ⟨e-democracy.gov.uk⟩ Web sites of e-democracy (especially the report on e-democracy and inclusion prepared by Creative Research [2002]); in terms of the literature, see Alexander and Pal 1998, Hague and Loader 1999, Heeks 1999, and Wilhelm 2000. Although a U.S. Office of Electronic Government was created by the E-Government Act of 2002 (Raney 2002), see Clymer 2003 on the unprecedented restrictions that the Bush administration is placing on the public release of information. On the use of the Internet for the mobilization of resistance through the Zapatista movement, see Garrido and Halavais 2003.

freely available research papers and other materials online (government policies, media reports, classroom practices, etc.) that spoke directly to the different parts of the government's proposed policy. We were careful to identify for users the type of information that each document link offered (research, policy, etc.). The idea was to provide readers with a basis for assessing the government's proposed policy from a number of different types of resources. They could then discuss their position online with others or propose changes to the policy for the ministry to review.

During the ten weeks in 1999 in which the Public Knowledge Policy Forum Web site ran, close to 100 people participated in the site's policy discussion forum, most of them teachers, with a few parents and students adding to the range of perspectives presented.[2] It was not many, admittedly, but then this was still a novel approach to policy consultation at the time, and we did not have the experience or resources to promote it widely within the province. A further problem was that while ministry officials checked the forum frequently, they decided against participating in the discussion. A number of the forum participants later told Shula Klinger (2001), who conducted interviews with participants in the forum, that the government's reticence made it a little like talking into a dead telephone. The people clearly felt that the lack of a sign that the government was listening did not encourage a sense of consultation.

Some who participated in the forum, we later learned, did take the time to read related materials on the site—with one stalwart teacher telling us that he had reviewed all of the studies and other documents that we had assembled—but no one made direct reference in the discussion forum to what he or she had read. This I found sobering. The idea of drawing on this range of sources to substantiate, modify, or extend one's position was not how the participants understood what it meant to participate in such a forum. Learning how to bring a recent study of children and computers or a school technology policy to bear on policy deliberations, through the lens of one's own experiences and interests, represents a skill in itself. It takes experience to develop, even as it holds

2. An archive of the Public Knowledge Policy Forum, which no longer serves as an active forum, can be viewed at the Web site of the Public Knowledge Project ⟨http://pkp.ubc.ca⟩.

the promise of increasing the value of consultation for all involved. Enter open access. For well-organized access to research studies on an ongoing basis, at no or very low cost, could provide people with experience critical to informed consultation, especially as it fosters a public expectation that university research has something to contribute to these deliberations.

In building our policy forum site, we had been stymied by an inability to provide the public with ready access to the research that bore directly on the issues at hand. The research was in journals that, if they were even online, required subscriptions to consult. The occasional professor had posted a copy of his or her article on his or her Web site, in an early instance of self-archiving. The Stanford Institute for the Quantitative Study of Society made available its reports on the use of the Internet. Teachers had Web sites that posted their classroom work with computers. But by and large the knowledge gleaned by the university was restricted to the university community.

It struck me as more than a little odd. With social scientists experimenting with ways of improving citizen consultation, the very knowledge and background information that the university had to offer to this process was largely locked up and inaccessible. Should we not get our own virtual house in order first, or at least concurrently, with the development of online consultation and deliberation structures? But then that academic house of ours has long been struggling with the economics of its own access to the larger body of research. The situation speaks to a need and an opportunity for reforming journal publishing in ways that would, among other things, increase the public presence and contribution of research in the marketplace of ideas that is critical to democratic life.

The open access movement's potential contribution to democratic life is well illustrated by Amy Gutmann and Dennis Thompson's (1996) *Democracy and Disagreement*. In this book, these two political philosophers deal with the thorny issue of how people can, in democratic states, work through, and ultimately live with, fundamental disagreements by "seeking moral agreement when they can, and maintaining mutual respect when they cannot" (346). The focus of these two philosophers on *deliberation*—on people working though issues and giving thoughtful consideration to different positions in seeking a way forward—is what makes this political philosophy especially suitable for guiding our educational efforts to prepare the young for greater participation in democratic life. It is also a democratic model that strongly suggests the value of ensuring that intellectual resources are publicly available to support and further the kind of deliberation it advocates.[3]

Although Gutmann and Thompson do not consider the state of public access to research in their book, their approach certainly points to the contribution that increased access to social science research, as well as research on a range of scientific issues, might make to civic life. Greater public circulation of this knowledge might well encourage people to explore issues of interest in more depth, checking out the facts for themselves, asking questions and pushing for more work on a topic, rather than simply leaving such work to pundits and panels of experts.

Research could, on occasion, play a critical role in the "economy of moral disagreement" that constitutes, for Gutmann and Thompson, "a permanent condition of democratic politics" (1996, 3, 9). If the airing of the moral disagreements Gutmann and Thompson refer to is going to be based, as they hold, on appeals "to reasons that are shared or could come to be shared by our fellow citizens," then the use of research findings to illustrate one's reasoning would help to clarify people's positions, even as disagreements over basic values might well persist (14). Improved access to such findings and the research behind them would also make it easier to establish, in another of Gutmann and Thompson's deliberative requirements, that the "empirical claims that

3. Gutmann and Thompson contrast deliberative democracy to prevailing theories of procedural and constitutional democracy, neither of which is *as* concerned with creating citizen opportunities for dialogue as procedural democracy is with ensuring democratic processes and constitutional democracy is with adhering to constitutional rights. The impact of deliberative democracy has been tested empirically by James Fishkin, who has, with various collaborators, "conducted fourteen Deliberative Polls in different parts of the world with random samples of respondents, brought together face to face, to deliberate for a few days" (1999). The samples have been representative, and respondents' opinions have undergone large, statistically significant changes on many policy issues as a result of the deliberative process.

often accompany moral arguments ... [are] consistent with the most reliable methods of inquiry at our collective disposal" (14–15).[4]

The plurality reflected in "reliable methods of inquiry" raises an important issue about the diversity of the available scholarly literature. For example, a large-scale statistical assessment of reading achievement scores in schools produces one kind of understanding of the education children are receiving, whereas the close analysis of a program by following a few students' reading experiences as they grow comfortable in a second language leads to another. The point of making research public is not that any one study will simply resolve democratic disagreements, once and for all, although a single study may have that effect in rare cases. Rather, the value of access to this literature lies in how the body of research as a whole can serve as a public resource, helping people to articulate and understand the different positions being taken, as well as the points of disagreement. It can help people see a greater part of the picture, drawing their attention to what might be otherwise overlooked in, say, what it means to learn to read. The ready availability of relevant studies could well test people's assumptions, as well as enable them to see what can come of taking certain stances. And if people are not always ready to engage in the kind of critical reflection called for by such recourse to research, I suspect that others will be happy enough to point out the implications and consequences of different studies for their positions.

Gutmann and Thompson do suggest that people need to learn more about how "to justify one's own actions, to criticize the actions of one's fellow citizens, and to respond to their justifications and criticisms" (1996, 65). It would certainly assist people, in developing their ability to justify their actions and criticize the actions of others, to have greater ac-

4. There is an opposing view, presented by Noëlle McAfee (2004), for example, that holds that deliberative democracy's focus on giving *reasons* loses sight of a *public knowledge* based on how "people know things from their situated, partial, and interested perspectives," which McAfee sees as a form of collective intelligence, at a remove from both the expertise of scholarly work and the opinion of individual citizens (140). On the other hand, I believe the influence of scholarly expertise—itself situated, partial, and interested—to be already present in how "people know things," and I turn to open access as a way to make research's influence more transparent and readily available to more people, as well as to make rectifying the misapprehensions that much easier.

cess to relevant sources of information that they could consult and explore. Developing students' ability to draw effectively on such resources could, for example, become part of the standard high school program. Students would need to learn how readily accessible research can serve as both source and model for formulating arguments. One can see, then, how a public airing of the research relevant to particular policy or political decisions, itself open to revision in light of new information, could only increase the level of democratic accountability, enabling those who are significantly affected to substantiate their claims about the impact of those decisions.[5] In sum, these two advocates of deliberative democracy identify what I would hold up as one of the principal warrants for public access experiments with research: "Respect for [a citizen's] basic liberty to receive politically relevant information is an essential part of deliberative democracy" (126).

At issue here is not only democracy's deliberative qualities, but a more basic principle of access to information. To move academic research more thoroughly into the public domain is to create a substantial alternative source of public information. Modern democratic states have always depended on a free press to create an informed electorate, or as Thomas Jefferson put it in his famous 1787 letter to Edward Carrington: "The basis of our governments being the opinion of the people, the very first object should be to keep that right; and were it left to me to decide whether we should have a government without newspapers, or newspapers without a government, I should not hesitate a moment to prefer the latter. But I should mean that every man should receive those papers, and be capable of reading them" (Jefferson 1787/1997).

Receiving the newspapers Jefferson spoke of, as well as being capable of reading them, is one thing. Applying similar access principles to research is another. That said, the challenges posed by creating greater public access to research might well be moot, at least in a political sense, were the media doing all they could to inform democratic processes with the full range of available information. Unfortunately, this is not the

5. For Gutmann and Thompson, the scope of accountability for such a deliberative process includes a need to "address the claims of anyone who is significantly affected" by the issue at hand (1996, 129).

case, according to those who should know, the journalists themselves. Richard Reeves, syndicated columnist and professor of journalism, puts the sense of the press's lost value this way: "Once upon a time, reporters and editors [were] the national skeptics, sifting and evaluating news for readers and viewers; now, using the new technologies, the press [is] dumping information out by the ton and the readers and viewers [are] left to do the sifting, to sort it out for themselves" (1998, 122).

Ben H. Bagdikian, the former School of Journalism dean at the University of California at Berkeley, finds that the vital press of yesteryear has been reduced to "trivialized and self-serving commercialized news," largely through corporate concentration focused on profitability (2000, ix). Not only, he notes, do a handful of megacorporations control "the country's most widespread news, commentary and daily entertainment," but these conglomerates have "achieved alarming success in writing the media laws and regulations in favor of their own corporations and against the interests of the general public" (viii). Herbert Gans, a Columbia University sociologist, sees the journalists' hands as tied by current models of reporting: "If journalists had more of an opportunity to pursue the profession's democratic ideal, they would have to consider how to reorganize journalistic assembly lines so as to reduce the emphasis on top-down news and the publicizing of the powerful. They would have to discard the data-reduction methods they now use—or find new ones—that might make citizens more newsworthy" (2003, 67–68). This state of affairs is not what Jefferson had in mind, and the current state of corporate concentration in news media—with its parallels in scholarly publishing—does little to support a rich diversity of perspectives or particularly hard-hitting journalism, especially when it comes to economic issues of poverty and equity, as well as related needs for reform and change.[6]

6. Todd Gitlin, for example, expresses serious concerns over the press's particular focus on "the novel event, not the underlying, enduring condition; the person, not the group; the visible conflict, not the deep consensus; the face that advances the story, not the one that explains or enlarges it" (1980, 263). For other critiques of the press's declining democratic contribution, in addition to the inevitable, indispensable Chomsky 1997, see McChesney 1999, Cappella and Jamieson 1997, Iyengar 1991, Page 1996, and Schiller 1996.

This disenchantment with the press's democratic force is not about to be cured by open access to research and scholarship. Reform along those lines will have to come from within the press itself. Yet it does speak to how access to research might add some small measure to the democratic ideal of an informed citizenship. Those readers who are tempted here to throw up their hands and tell me, "Oh sure, just what the public needs and wants, gigabytes of unfathomable research on top of their barely read, quickly scanned newspaper," should recall the discussion in chapter 8 about the growing number of people going online for additional health information in a very focused, if not always discerning, way. And as far as the inevitable limits these people experience in making sense of what they come across, especially with health research, it hardly forms a compelling argument against experimenting with increasing their access to a wider body of research.[7]

Now that public access to research is proving itself a viable option for scholarly publishing, the question that bears testing is whether it might offer the public (and journalists) a further source of systematic inquiry and information. Given that the research literature benefits from press scrutiny—whether one thinks of tobacco industry research from decades ago or more recent pharmaceutical industry conflicts of interest in medical research—the benefits of increased access to information from such research could begin to flow to a greater degree both ways between journalism and research, in the classic system of checks and balances that Jefferson saw as critical to democracy's resistance to tyranny.

Although the press's coverage of research has certainly increased in recent years, more than a little wariness has crept into the relationship between the media and the research community. So one finds Christopher Forrest, a professor of pediatrics and health policy at Johns Hopkins University, accusing the press, in a *New York Times* article, of

---

7. In experimenting with a media supplement approach for access to scholarly research, the Public Knowledge Project ⟨http://pkp.ubc.ca⟩ ran a week-long research support Web site with a local newspaper, the *Vancouver Sun*, allowing readers to tap into a database of links to research studies related to a series the paper was running on technology and education and to join discussion forums with researchers and view pertinent teaching materials, policies, and organizations.

supporting public shortsightedness, in effect, or as Forrest puts it, "The public reads the bottom line. They act on that without putting the study into context. In politics, there is always a context. The same is true for science, but it doesn't get reported that way" (quoted in Stolberg 2001, WK3). As if to counter Forrest's concern, reporter Sheryl Gay Stolberg concludes the article by reminding readers that science today gives the impression that "we live in a dizzying world, where scientists produce a stream of research, and each new study seems to contradict the previous one" (WK3).

The larger scientific context that Forrest is referring to has to do with the situation of any given study in relation to related work. Yet it is hard for reporters and the public to locate such a context, in part because the research literature as a whole has been placed outside their reach. With open access e-print archives and journals, it is now easier for reporters and the public at least to begin to establish a basic context or background for the latest breakthrough study. Online journals now come with tools designed to help readers assemble a context; these tools usually consist of links to related materials for interpreting, evaluating, and utilizing the articles the readers are reading (as I discuss in chapter 11).

Just knowing that this body of research and scholarship is readily accessed by people could change the tone of public debate, adding a measure of caution over factual claims made in such forums. If not everyone has an equal capacity to engage in public deliberations—which is a common enough critique of deliberative democracy—greater access to research can still strengthen the role of underfunded advocacy groups that speak on behalf of those otherwise disenfranchised.[8] As I suggested in the previous chapter, such access could introduce into the doctor's office a greater level of deliberative democracy through shared decision making, as well as into other day-to-day relationships.

8. Although the right to the knowledge represented by this research has nothing to do with one's qualifications, the question of whether deliberative democracy favors, and thus will attract, those who already possess the capacity to deliberate (and read research) is addressed by Cohen and Rogers (2003, 244–246), who point to examples of interest and opportunity leading to wide participation in deliberation, as well as to the successful use of training programs with deliberative planning processes.

History contains numerous instances of literate classes' restricting opportunities for others to learn how to read and to access sacred or other powerful texts. Jonathan Rose sums up this politics of literacy as follows: "the exchange value of knowledge can be enhanced by creating artificial scarcities, monopolies and oligarchies" (2002, 334). He goes on to quote the anthropologist Mary Douglas to the effect that the "information class" is likely to, in Douglas's words, "erect barriers against entry, to consolidate control of opportunities, and to use techniques of exclusion" (quoted in Rose 2002, 394). Certainly, the Protestant Reformation, in conjunction with the invention of the printing press, inspired great concerns among many in power over the ready access these two events had provided to the Word, in the form of the vernacular Bible, just as it was clear to many that the printing press had led to a dangerous proliferation of secular and heretical texts. Then, centuries later, the democratic struggles of the nineteenth century over enfranchisement clearly followed on the spread of cheaply published papers and books. The prospect of increased public access to research and scholarship is not entirely removed from this earlier political history of reading and printing. Yet this time, it seems far less like the undoing of a clerisy, far less likely to threaten the position of the scholarly classes, except as it expands participation in the climb to the top ranks of professordom by offering access to those in the global academic community who are otherwise excluded from its journal culture.

Still, on hearing the case for open access, some have warned me that should we open the doors to the scholarly literature, the public will discover what many researchers already believe, which is that too much scholarly work represents poorly written exercises in career maintenance and advancement. Yet this overstated critique only raises the need for a more fundamental calling to account of higher education. If some substantial portion of the literature is indeed vacuous and bereft of value, then perhaps open access might foster, in some small measure, a correction, by making public impact and meaningfulness something worth striving for in conducting research. It could lead to greater coordination among research efforts to ensure that the cumulative value of a work is realized across a variety of settings and circumstances (Willinsky 1999).

My concern is that too many scholarly associations and publishers are building online publishing systems for their journals with little concern for how these publishing systems affect research's presence as a public good. More thought needs to be given to how these new systems might serve concerned and interested citizens, policymakers, and practitioners by enabling them to hone in on highly relevant research and scholarship, as well as establish a greater context for reading that work, in ways that could further democratic debate and deliberation.

This is not to deny the valiant efforts being made to breach the ivory tower on behalf of the public value of research. Portals such as the U.K. Centre for Evidence-Based Policy and the Web Resources for Social Workers, to name just two, do provide public access to an array of freely available research articles, conference papers, and other materials.[9] But these still represent an intermediary step in overcoming the isolation and inaccessibility of scholarly work. Open access scholarly publishing has the advantage of making the democratic contribution represented by such work widely available, without requiring an additional investment in reassembling the research and then serving it up in a public format.

The corporate sector's recent development of pay-per-view access to journal articles may seem to bring this knowledge within ready reach of the public. People no longer have to subscribe to the journals that publish studies relevant to their particular interest or find their way to a university library that subscribes to those journals but can locate and download the studies with the aid of a credit card. In the case of policymakers, however, what I have found, at least in a study of Canadian bureaucrats, is that to charge any price at all to view a relevant research article closes the door, in effect, to the policymaker's consultation of it (Willinsky 2003b). It is not a matter of setting a fairer price for reading a study online. The door to this knowledge is either freely open, as far as policymakers are concerned, or it is closed. And judging by

---

9. The Web site of the U.K. Centre for Evidence-Based Policy is available at ⟨http://www.evidencenetwork.org/home.asp⟩, and Web Resources for Social Workers can be accessed at ⟨http://www.nyu.edu/socialwork/wwwrsw/⟩.

those I worked with, they are very interested, it turns out, in having it open.[10]

Government officials still made it clear in this study that while exercising fiscal restraint, they were consulting more research than they had previously, and it was largely by tapping into open access resources. This ability to consult online research also broadened their policy perspectives, opening their eyes to a larger world of knowledge than they might otherwise garner from the circle of academic cronies they had tended in the past to turn to for ideas about policy issues. Still, however much these policymakers' research horizons had been expanded by the Web, they still faced a limited range of research resources because of the access issue. While those working with economic issues, for example, were able to draw on the very strong open access e-print archive Research Papers in Economics (RePEc) for working papers and published articles, and those concerned with ecological issues had open access journals such as *Conservation Ecology*, the options in agriculture, foreign policy, social welfare, and law were not nearly as strong.

As a final comment on the political impact of scholarly publishing, let me return to the U.S. Education Act, otherwise known as the No Child Left Behind Act of 2001, which I mentioned in the book's introduction. This law promotes "informed parental choice," as well as "innovative programs" that are "based on scientifically based research," as the act puts it.[11] One couldn't ask for a better entrée for research into public discourse than the legal and economic force of this act, which makes over one hundred references to "scientifically based research." Its focus on education research reflects a spillover, I suspect, from the public interest in medical research, leading to the government's narrow conception of what counts as research in school settings, namely, large-scale, randomly assigned control group studies, a definition that draws directly, if not

10. Michael M. D. Sutton provided invaluable assistance in the data gathering for this research study (Willinsky 2003b).

11. "To provide funding to enable State educational agencies and local educational agencies to implement promising educational reform programs and school improvement programs based on scientifically based research." Section 5101(a)(2), No Child Left Behind Act of 2001.

always appropriately, on the evidence-based medicine movement's "gold standard" for research (Willinsky 2001).[12]

The effect of the approach to education research promoted by the U.S. government's definition could well be to push the work of many no less committed and no less rigorous researchers to the very margins of legitimate or fundable research in education. Only a very small proportion of studies in education follow a clinical trials model, for reasons having to do, in part, with the human qualities and values at stake in schooling, which test scores do not always do well in capturing. This means that the vast majority of studies, many of them government-sponsored, and all of them published in peer-reviewed journals, are placed outside the government's new mandate for "scientifically based research." The current administration's partial and selective approach to the sciences on environmental and health issues has already led to damning reports by the Union of Concerned Scientists.[13] Its approach has been summed up by a

12. On evidence-based approaches to social issues, see the Web site of the Campbell Collaboration ⟨http://www.campbellcollaboration.org/⟩, which is an international evidence-based initiative "that aims to help people make well-informed decisions about the effects of interventions in the social, behavioral and educational arenas." Educational anthropologist Frederick Erickson presents an effective challenge to the act's approach to research by raising questions that are exemplary of certain types that are important in education but that are unlikely to be answered by randomized field trials: "What's happening and what do those happenings mean? What is it like to be a child in the bottom reading group in a particular first grade class? How does Miss Smith set up her kindergarten classroom so that students learn to listen closely to what each other says? What happened as the math department at Washington High School seriously tried to shift their teaching away from math as algorithms to math as reasoning? Why do the Black kids sit together in the lunchroom and should we as educators care about that?" (2003).

13. In 2004, the Union of Concerned Scientists issued a report, signed by sixty leading scientists, that accused the administration of George W. Bush of misusing science for political purposes. The first finding of the report is that "there is a well-established pattern of suppression and distortion of scientific findings by high-ranking Bush administration political appointees across numerous federal agencies. These actions have consequences for human health, public safety, and community well-being" (2004, 2). The examples that the report provides of this manipulation involve misuse of research on such subjects as air pollutants, heat-trapping emissions, reproductive health, drug-resistant bacteria, endangered species, forest health, and military intelligence.

New York Times editorial as "a purposeful confusion of scientific proto-cols in which 'sound science' becomes whatever the administration says it is" ("Junking Science" 2004).

In the case of education, the reliance on a singular approach to research implied by the administration's definition could just as easily narrow the range of innovative school programs to those that lend them-selves to large-scale assessments. One means of avoiding the sort of pro-gram distortion that would result from such a narrowing is to ensure that the full range of educational research is available to the teaching profession and the public. This would help people work out more of the implications of new and existing school programs in ways that could help them better gauge what those programs bring to the community.

Making itself available to be readily consulted by parents, teachers, elected officials, and administrators is precisely the role that relevant research should be playing for democratic governments. On the other hand, to have government policies appear to be driven, if not dictated, by "evidence-based" and "what-works" solutions, without ready access to pertinent educational research, only serves to undermine a democracy of autonomous citizens engaged in informed deliberation. If a single body of research determines what works and what does not work in the schools, then who among us, researcher or teacher, will dare to intro-duce educational innovations or call for a greater variety of educational experiences that risk falling beyond the measure of large-scale clinical trials?

No child left behind? It is a fine sentiment for an education act to up-hold. Yet perhaps the motto of researchers studying the schools should be "No body of hard-won ideas and findings left behind, when it comes to deliberations over schooling." What benefit is there in jettisoning rig-orously reviewed scholarship? If we have the technology to provide the public, teachers, and parents with broad access to the full range of re-search conducted in a field like education, then what a shame it would be to have the awakening public and policy interest in research go no farther than a strand of inquiry based solely on large-scale measures with achievement scores. Achievement in schools counts, by all means, but so should research on a child's experience with a book and a teach-er's efforts within a community, and the first step to making it count is to make it publicly available. The unrelenting focus on "what works" needs to be set within a larger and ongoing public dialogue over the nature of learning and the hopes of education.

The politics of open access to research is about the role that the knowledge represented by such research can play in the media, public discussions, and policymaking. Open access will add to the political stature and value of research in this way, as researchers see their work contributing more than it currently does to the weighing of facts, consequences, and alternatives in democratic processes. Initially, once access to such research is opened, the public is bound to experience shock and consternation over the level of disagreement and conflict that marks scholarly work, which goes well beyond the well-reported reversals over medical threats posed by coffee and salt. People will have to come to grips with how science and scholarship are rarely given to easy, straightforward, or definitive answers. But once they see how the pursuit of knowledge represented by scholarly inquiry can inform and deepen public understanding, openness about the results of such inquiry will carry lessons for both the public and researchers, even as both politics and research may well be changed by this public engagement with the work of the university.

10

Rights

I may be taking a step too far with this chapter by suggesting that the excessive increase in journal prices over the last two decades is a human-rights issue. It does seem a little odd to propose that annual subscription costs may be unjustifiably interfering with something vital to our humanity. On the other hand, I do think that the access principle represents something larger and more basic than current pricing policies. The right to know that is inherent in the access principle has a claim on our humanity that stands with other basic rights, whether to life, liberty, justice, or respect. More than that, access to knowledge is a human right that is closely associated with the ability to defend, as well as to advocate for, other rights.

To make the case for access as a right in this chapter, I turn to two recent works on the scholarly dimensions of human rights. The first is by the political scientist Richard Pierre Claude and deals with science's service to human rights. The second is by the philosopher Jacques Derrida, who defends a right to philosophy as critical to the future of the humanities in the university. In the case of both the sciences and the humanities, Claude and Derrida address the access-to-knowledge question in an abstract and somewhat ethereal way, as if people come into contact with ideas and information much as the proverbial fish swims through water, without giving it a second thought. Yet Claude's and Derrida's treatments of human rights have everything to do with what they otherwise take for granted, namely, having ready access to the knowledge at issue in their discussions. My interests are, then, in how the circulation of research and scholarship should figure explicitly in human-rights discussions of knowledge. At issue is who has a right of access to what is known.

Richard Pierre Claude (2002) begins *Science in the Service of Human Rights* with the uncomfortable side of science and human rights, by holding up the record of science in Nazi Germany. He points out that it was the very real prospect of science again being abused in the way that it was during the Third Reich that set the context for science finding a place in the Universal Declaration of Human Rights, which was adopted by the United Nations in 1948. The declaration holds that access to science is a matter of shared benefits: "Everyone has the right freely to participate in the cultural life of the community, to enjoy the arts and to share in scientific advancement and its benefits" (Article 27, Section 1).

The distinction made in the declaration—between sharing in the "advancement" of science and sharing in the "benefits" of that advancing science—is an important one for this project. It makes it clear that the human right at issue is not only about enjoying the fruits of scientific progress, whether through new medicines or modified strains of rice. It is also a right to science as a form of knowledge and understanding. It is a right of access to science. This right to know does not imply that research and scholarship should be distributed without charge to any interested reader. Rather, it suggests only that there be no unwarranted impediment to that access. The open access movement seeks to establish just how unwarranted some of the current access costs to research are, over and above the basic price of entry with online publishing, which is access to the Internet.

This right of access to the advancement of science is, for Claude (2002, 45), about being able to draw on the knowledge gained through such advancement to advance other human rights by making, for example, pertinent forms of information more widely available to those who might use it to represent their interests. He describes how Tenagantia, a women's group in Malaysia, had its research on the abuse of migrant workers suppressed by the Malaysian government, in part by charging the local founder of the organization, Irene Fernandez, with, in effect, libeling the state by publishing this research. What might have happened if Fernandez's research endeavors had been part of a larger body of publicly available research that linked community and academic research activities on a global scale? Would more open access to social science research, especially as it deals with the situation in Malaysia, help the women of Tenagantia form partnerships and alliances, as well as strengthen their advocacy role?[1]

Claude (2002, 144–145) repeatedly identifies the vital role that access to information has in the ongoing struggle for human rights. He advocates "scientists going to the mat" on behalf of disadvantaged groups, as well as working partnerships between scientists and health professionals, engineers, and educators in the service of human rights. He cites the heroic accomplishments of grassroots research activism found in the Loka Institute's Community Research Network, as well as the Dutch and Danish "science shops," in which scientists and students take on projects in the service of activists (162–177). He also calls on nongovernmental organizations (NGOs) to be more systematic in their research, and he commends the American Association for the Advancement of Science for producing the helpful guide *Making the Case: Investigating Large Scale Human Rights Violations Using Information Systems and Data Analysis* (Ball, Spirer, and Spirer 2000).

Claude does see promise in the ability of new Internet technologies to increase access to information: "By delivering cheap access to information, and by producing forums for debate in countries where the media are monopolized, the Internet offers the disenfranchised an opportunity to participate in responding to their own misery" (2002, 103). He relates "open Internet access" to the idea of a free press, pointing to the anti-censorship Global Internet Liberty Campaign, and he quotes the Survey of Press Freedom, conducted by Freedom House (founded by Eleanor Roosevelt and others in the 1940s) in 2001, which found that Internet freedom exceeded the degree of press freedom in most of the 190 countries it surveyed (104). He also gives serious consideration to the role that statistics and other scientific data can play in human-rights advocacy, while cautioning human-rights agencies about using reliable and

---

1. A similar mandate to Tenagantia's is found with the Women's Learning Connection, run out of Bethesda, Maryland, which seeks, according to its Web site ⟨http://www.learningpartnership.org/⟩, to "provide women with the technological tools and training that empower as well as educate" out of a recognition that "information has become a valuable world commodity; those with the greatest ability to generate and distribute information have the greatest power."

standardized methods for gathering data, lest they "miss opportunities to analyze trends over time" or "to analyze comparable data showing convincingly how abuses represent policies and just ad hoc aberrations" (115).

Yet for all that Claude does to link science and human rights, he does not consider the sharp contrast between the very public advocacy work of NGOs and the closed cloisters of scholarship. He does not calculate what greater access to relevant research might do for the NGOs that cannot otherwise lay their hands on the information it presents, as well as how increasing the public quality of the knowledge to be gleaned from this research might affect the whole climate around certain issues. He does not weigh how social scientists and others might alter how they go about setting research agendas, as well as conducting and writing up their work, if they knew that they would not have to make a choice between doing research for the use of an NGO and doing research for publication in a scholarly journal.

It is hard to imagine that researchers actively engaged in work that bears on human-rights issues would want anything but the widest possible public presence for their findings. Their work is work that might serve as background and context; it might be used by those who are skilled in turning it into practical advice, policy initiatives, legal suits, and political campaigns, if not always in ways that the researchers can foresee or would approve of. It might be directed at preventing and addressing immediate situations, a number of which Claude focuses his work on, including the Union Carbide disaster in Bhopal and the lack of informed consent in AIDS research in Africa.[2]

However, I want to reiterate that a *right to know* is not solely about having access to knowledge that will prevent harm or reduce suffering. Rather, the right to know, to reiterate this book's theme, is about having fair and equitable access to a public good. It is about the responsibility of researchers and scholars to ensure that there are no unwarranted impediments to the widest possible circulation of the ideas and information with which they work.

2. For a critical discussion of the U.S. government's handling of the post-Bhopal right-to-know legislation with regard to environmental issues and "empowerment as access," see Galusky 2003.

For all of the attention that I have brought in this book to increasing access to the sciences and social sciences, the case for access to the humanities also needs to be acknowledged, especially as it has been made with uncharacteristic clarity by Jacques Derrida (2002), under the rubric of *the right to philosophy*. Derrida speaks of this right to philosophy in three important senses by playing, as is his wont, on the very grammar of that phrase. He is concerned with a fundamental right *to* philosophy, with an ability to *go right to* philosophy, and with *who has the right* to philosophy (3).

For Derrida, this three-way right falls within the very spirit of philosophy: "Philosophy is the most easily shared thing in the world. No one can forbid access to it. The moment one has the desire or will for it, one has the right to it. The right is inscribed in philosophy itself" (2002, 23). For scholars working in the humanities, the right to philosophy is protected by the university's independence, or in Derrida's words, by "an *unconditional* freedom to question and assert, or even the right to say publicly all that is required by research, knowledge, and thought concerning the truth" (2001, 233, emphasis in original).

This is where I am tempted to interject a question on whether Derrida's defense of the "right to say everything" means much of anything for a member of the academic community if the "right to say it publicly, to publish it" is not closely related to the right of others to see what has been said in the name of philosophy (2001, 236). If this right is to be more than an abstract principle protecting the privilege of some scholars to exercise an unconditional academic freedom, then something more needs to be done about what it means to say things publicly. In the first instance, it would seem to fall to this academic community to do all that it can to ensure that this right to philosophy is within reach of the global scholarly community. This community needs to assist less fortunate colleagues in participating in the critical freedom that is so vital to the humanities. It must look for ways of furthering the exchange and circulation of the knowledge that is the happy result of this freedom.

It is one thing for the free-thinking humanities scholar to challenge "everything that concerns the question and the history of truth," as Derrida advocates, and to challenge it "in its relation to the question of man, of what is proper to man, of human rights, of crimes against humanity and so forth ... above all *in* the Humanities" (2001, 234, emphasis in original). Yet it makes something of a mockery of the humanities' independent questioning to have the resulting knowledge placed safely out of harm's way, hidden behind passwords and closed research library doors. How do those who are interested in seeing the university resist the powers of the state or the economy imagine that such resistance can take place as long as they are so little interested in making available the sound and compelling basis of that resistance to anyone who lives and works outside of the small circle of well-endowed universities? If the independent university is to profess an "unlimited commitment to the truth," as Derrida puts it, it must at some point be concerned with an unimpeded right of access to that truth (234). It is in just this sense that the open access movement in e-print archives and journal publishing has something to offer to Derrida's "right to philosophy."

For Derrida, the right of access to philosophy comes down, at its most basic material level, to a right to take courses in philosophy. He may speak of philosophy as that which is most easily shared, but he is just as quick to insist that the right to philosophy depends, in fact, on access to training: "To have access *effectively*, in effect, to these discursive procedures and thus to have the right to the *philosophical such as it is spoken*, for philosophical democracy, democracy in philosophy, to be possible (and there is no democracy in general without that, and democracy, the democracy that remains still to come, is also a philosophical concept), one must be trained in these procedures" (2002, 29, emphasis in original). And this right to training is not simply something that Derrida holds to in principle. Some thirty years ago, Derrida worked with other philosophers and students to realize and protect "the right to philosophy" through GREPH (Groupe de Recherches sur l'Enseignement Philosophique), a group that defended the then-current practice of teaching philosophy in the schools. They then went on to establish the Collège International de Philosophie, which offered philosophy courses along similar lines to those of Britain's Open University (36). "Right of access (to whatever, teaching, philosophy, and so forth) assumes the access to right," as Derrida puts it, "which assumes the capacity to read and interpret, in short, instruction" (36).

More than that, Derrida holds—rather surprisingly given his philosophy's reputation for opacity, if not outright obscurity—that a philosophy worthy of the name must itself be readily teachable. Derrida emphasizes the point by quoting Kant's insistence "that every philosophical teaching be capable of being made *popular* (that is, of being made sufficiently clear to the sense to be communicated to everyone), if the teacher is not to be suspected of being muddled in his own concepts" (quoted in Derrida 2002, 44–45, emphasis in original).

Setting aside one's amazement at Derrida's stance—given that muddling concepts seemed his very method at times—it is worth pausing over Kant's views on *teaching* philosophy. Kant saw the Enlightenment as all about independent thinking and, in effect, overcoming one's student-like dependence on others. Enlightenment comes sometime after class time. Kant made this clear and public when he addressed the question "What is Enlightenment?" in the pages of the newspaper *Berlinische Monatsschrift* in 1784. In his op-ed piece on that topic, Kant offered a phrase from Horace that might well have stood as a motto for Enlightenment carriage bumper stickers: "*Sapere aude!* Have the courage to use your *own* understanding!" (1970, 54, emphasis in original).

For Kant, people need the "freedom to make *public use* of [their] reason in all matters," that is, "without outside guidance" (1970, 55, 58, emphasis in original). Enlightenment, then, is about moving people out from under the tutelage of others. Enlightenment is furthered by a good education system, by all means, but it can only be sustained and made vital, I would dare to conclude from Kant's and Derrida's positions, by finding ways of increasing people's access to intellectual resources that would support the public reasoning and freedom Kant speaks of.

The current age of information, if not always enlightening, has seen access to university instruction extended by the Internet, with the open universities among the first to use new technologies to improve distance education. In addition, MIT has proven a beacon of educational access through its Open Knowledge Initiative, which is setting standards for learning technologies worldwide. MIT's OpenCourseWare is designed to "provide free, searchable, coherent access to MIT's course materials for educators in the non-profit sector, students, and individual learners around the world," as its Web site puts it.³ MIT, a private institution, is making these educational resources freely available "to advance knowledge and education to best serve the nation and the world." MIT's Open Knowledge efforts are obviously complemented by open access initiatives with e-print archives and journals, which can provide a similar public access to the necessary reading materials and content for these courses.⁴

Still, a distinction needs to be made here between open access to course syllabi and lectures and open access to scholarly journals and archives. That is, I want to argue, contra Derrida and in the spirit of Kant, that the right to philosophy goes beyond supporting instruction and extending opportunities to enroll in courses. As I would cast it, this right appeals to a broader sense of philosophy, one that persists outside of the classroom and ensures "that the right to philosophy never end," in Derrida's phrase (2002, 40). One does not desist from questioning or doubting, from seeing ironies or practicing *epochē* (suspending judgment). Open access self-archiving and publishing could be taken as extending the right of readers to have philosophical encounters, following on Derrida's hope of "ensuring each citizen the chance of encountering one of those things that are called philosophy at least once in his or her life" (2002, 39).

What might a citizen's philosophical encounters look like in a world of open access to the journal literature? Well, let me use the first two articles in a recent issue of *Critical Inquiry*, a journal in which Derrida's work has often appeared. A citizen granted access to this journal, if he or she happened to have seen any of David Cronenberg's films or to be a

3. For example, Sally Haslanger at MIT has her first-year Problems of Philosophy course in OpenCourseWare. It includes her 2001 lecture notes and the list of readings from Dostoevsky to Nietzsche (although the texts are not available online), as well as a practice exam (which asks whether it would be praiseworthy and morally permissible for Bill Gates to give all of his money to famine relief in order to achieve a Nobel Prize, with the further instruction "Explain and justify your answer in light of the moral theories we've considered.") The OpenCourseWare Web site can be accessed at ⟨http://ocw.mit.edu⟩.

4. In support of open access to these materials, the ever-resourceful MIT has created the open source DSpace software, which universities can freely download, for setting up an e-print archive into which faculty members can deposit their publications, as discussed in chapter 6.

fan of science fiction, might linger over Teresa de Lauretis's (2003) analysis of Cronenberg's 1999 film *eXistenZ*. In her article, "Becoming Inorganic," de Lauretis treats the film as "a reflection of the new technologies of postmodernity—information, communication, and biotechnologies and the new interactive media," challenging readers to see its larger social implications (547). Or a second citizen-reader, having been intrigued by Stephen Hawking's book *A Brief History of Time*, might pause over the next article in *Critical Inquiry*, "Reading Hawking's Presence: An Interview with a Self-Effacing Man." In this piece, Hélène Mialet (2003) deals with the specific mind-body dilemmas of a scientific "genius" that arose out of her interview of Hawking. Our hypothetical readers might read only a few pages or browse through the articles (more on improving the common reader's engagement with research in the next chapter). Yet it would be a philosophical encounter, in Derrida's sense, that would add to their understanding of what the humanities do—and humanities scholars must not be afraid of that—just as it would add to people's sense of having a right to know, a right to philosophy. And what they might encounter with these two particular articles bears, as it turns out, on the human-rights issues of cloning and biotechnologies, which were raised by Richard Pierre Claude (2002) in *Science in the Service of Human Rights*, which I discussed in the first part of this chapter.

If these instances from *Critical Inquiry* strike you as the most unlikely of online encounters, remember that public interest in access to medical research and astronomy has demonstrated that we do not yet know the extent of the public's capacity to pursue pressing or even passing interests, when the opportunity presents itself. The specter of learning at issue here, then, is about what is *self-taught* and the persuasive power of autodidactism. Autodidacticism has always been the after-hours tutor, the lifelong learner's best instructor. And as many teachers know, more than a few of the best moments in teaching come from just being there in the classroom, at that moment when the student is figuring things out for himself or herself—which is only to say that open access is the open university of autodidactism.

Yet in claiming that the public right to philosophy forms part of the case for open access, I am not asking scholars to begin catering to a vastly expanded readership for their work. Of course, some quick-witted writers are already profitably hitting up philosophy's public readership, judging by the rash of guides, from *Plato for Beginners* (Cavalier 1990) to *Kant in 90 Minutes* (Strathern 1996), to be found in most bookstores today. The apparent success of these guides takes nothing away from the argument for opening access to the journal literature, in which the ideas of philosophical figures such as Plato and Kant are fully alive and can be critically engaged in, say, ninety minutes. Quickie guidebooks aside, the value of the journal literature will remain in its scholarly depth of analysis, which need not be compromised by opening up access to this literature, for all that it might yet provide to that wider public and professional audience (e.g., policymakers, teachers, lawyers). The right of access at issue here is the right to see how ideas are being worked out among scholars, given that this right of access is realizable on a much greater scale—although by no means on a universal basis—through new journal-publishing technologies.[5]

Now, it may happen that opening the scholarly literature to the larger public audience will gradually alter its tone, as writers do tend to find their work unconsciously affected by having new sorts of attention paid to it. That said, open access is certainly not about abandoning the distinctive qualities of the scholarly project. Rather, it reasserts the basic value of knowledge's circulating as widely as possible. As I noted earlier, the quality and extent of that circulation is vital to scholarship's very legitimacy as knowledge. On the other hand, a continuing decline in that circulation, brought on by the increasing expense of keeping up with the journal literature, does not bode well for the future of the university and what it would make of knowledge, especially as the academic community continues to expand on a worldwide basis. If supply always exceeds demand for much of the work that scholars do, it is well to remember how the academic knowledge economy depends on surplus. What can

5. Derrida similarly holds to the continuing independence of philosophy, even after the state has enabled a right to philosophy to be realized: "Once the state is obligated to ensure the technical, material, professional, institutional, and so on, conditions of a right to philosophy, no contract would bind philosophy itself and institute this philosophy as a reciprocal and responsible partner of the state" (2002, 41). He also recognizes that increasing the right to philosophy does make it "more accessible to ideological misappropriations or to its dissolution in nonphilosophical disciplines" (112).

seem like an excessive number of studies—which produce nonsignificant results, or serve as pilots for larger studies, or prove blind alleys or false leads—have their way of contributing to the knowledge in a field. There is no way of predicting what will at some point spark another researcher, what will add a missing piece to another's work. Research is as much about exhausting possibilities as it is about ascertaining relationships.

It may well be that the very independence of scholarship, which adds greatly to its value in the struggle for human rights, has rested for too long on its relative inaccessibility. But academic freedom needs to be based on more than the fact that so few have access to what is being done in freedom's name. Derrida's notion, then, of the "weakness and vulnerability of the university" is in this case about the university's failure to take any form of responsibility for supporting the larger academic community that has developed on a global basis (2001, 236). How are we to ensure the university's contribution to a fairer world, if access to the research it produces about the world is itself a source of inequality, if for no other reason than faculty indifference over access rights, as they vainly pursue the glory of appearing in the top titles in the field?[6]

The critique that Derrida expects of the humanities—"in which nothing is beyond question" (2001, 235)—must begin, much like charity, in the intellectual homes of the humanities. Scholars working in this area need to see how readily they have allowed their scholarship to become subject to corporate interests in a knowledge economy of publisher mergers and acquisitions, as well as journal licensing surveillance and enforcement.[7] Universities may now be at risk, as Derrida warns, of

6. Among those advancing the public right to know in the humanities is Roy Rosenzweig, a historian who speaks directly to that profession's responsibilities for online access: "We need to put our energies into maintaining and enlarging the astonishingly rich public historical Web that has emerged in the past five years" (2001).

7. At the Indian Institute of Science in Bangalore, it was explained to me in 2003 that the institute's contract with Elsevier Science forbade those who "walked in" to the institute's library (as opposed to being members of the institution)—never mind that they might have traveled for two days to do their research at that library—to print out or otherwise "save" journal articles available in the library. Also, see Gibbs 2003 on restrictions for "walk-ins" in American research libraries.

"becoming a branch office of conglomerates and corporations" (237). Yet the knowledge that the universities produce already stands, in too many cases, as corporate assets for Blackwell, Springer, and Elsevier, as well as for university-affiliated publishers. If the rightly celebrated independence of the university has a higher purpose, it surely includes creating knowledge that will stand as a beacon for the right to know, as well as for knowledge that is useful in the struggle for human rights. The open access movement has done no more than demonstrate how the right to know can be more fully realized by more people, if scholars and researchers seize hold of current opportunities.

11

Reading

In the early years of the twenty-first century, it seems safe to say, most readers of research who come upon an article of interest on the Internet move their cursor to the print icon and click. I say "most" because a small number of readers have begun to resist the temptation to click-and-print. They are finding real advantages in reading online. Without getting up from their computers, this new breed of online readers can often check how fairly an author has treated a cited work (if it is also on-line) by clicking on that work in the reference list. This would seem to increase their critical engagement with the article (that is, if they aren't led to read the work cited instead, leaving the original article behind unfinished). This ability to check sources would also seem to place additional pressure on authors to take that much more care in referencing a work.[1] Reading online may yet prove to be a significant extension of the scholarly apparatus, comparable in some ways to the introduction of the scholarly footnote many centuries before, which also encouraged readers to consider the source of the work they were reading.[2]

1. This ability to check citations may yet prove a check on excessive citing, which appears to follow on the ease of electronic citation handling. The ISI Web of Science reveals a 30 percent increase in the average number of times articles in the top twenty medical journals were cited between 1998 and 2003. Some credit for this may go to bibliographic programs, such as EndNote's Cite as You Write feature, which, at a click, punctuate one's research papers with relevant citations gathered from the library over the Internet.

2. On the footnote, see Grafton 1994: "The footnote in its modern form seems to have been devised in the seventeenth century.... The historical footnote emerges not as a simple trademark guaranteeing quality nor as a uniform piece of scholarly technology, but rather as the product of long collective struggles and individual efforts to devise a visibly critical form of historical writing" (53).

The benefits of reading research articles online do not end with the handy reference link. In a number of disciplines, the advantages of online reading include having articles illustrated by far more color figures, providing richer detail and definition than the typical smattering of black-and-white illustrations favored by cost-conscious print journals. Online readers are also finding that in some fields they can consult the complete set of data or the research instruments on which the research article was based, as print's space limitations no longer hold. This supports the reanalysis of data, as well as the design of new studies that work with existing data and instruments. Online readers can compare studies related to the one they are currently exploring, consult other works by the author, contact the author, and post comments at the end of the article, all with a mouse click. They are also able to search through the last few years of the journal in which a particular article appears to track changes in the use of a single concept or research method. In the life sciences, they are able to refer to specific sections of medical textbooks that deal with the clinical, biochemical, or disease-specific contexts of the topic they are reading about. And if the article they are reading strikes them as a major breakthrough or as reflecting a serious lapse in the author's judgment, they have the option of asking to be notified by e-mail when the article is cited, enabling them to see what others have made of it.[3]

Now some aspects of this upgraded reading experience—such as the increase in color illustrations—simply come with the technology that makes online reading possible at all. Others, including the e-mail link to the author and the links to the works cited, expedite what has always been intended with the journal literature, namely, that sources can be consulted and authors contacted. Then there is the rather futuristic

3. See the Web sites of HighWire Press ⟨http://highwire.stanford.edu⟩ and PubMed ⟨http://www.ncbi.nlm.nih.gov/PubMed/⟩ and McKiernan 2001. Tenopir has found that, as of 2003, the majority of readers of research still relied on printouts, but among those reading online, hyperlinking was "rated as the most useful value added feature (63% like linking to scientific databases; 61% like linking to an author's e-mail address; 52% like linking to an author's Web sites; and 45% like linking to video-animated graphics)" (2003, 15).

when-it-is-cited notification, which integrates the function of a citation index and a thoughtful colleague.[4]

Now, these new features for readers do not, of themselves, constitute an open access issue. They are found in online versions of articles in journals that offer open access and those that do not. What is at issue with open access, however, is whether and how the new publishing environment engendered by these extended features can support a much wider range of readers. First of all, open access is opening the literature to a world full of students and instructors who may have had precious little experience with the research literature prior to this online access. And then, open access also provides a way into this online scholarship for the "common reader," to use Samuel Johnson's eighteenth-century phrase.

With this chapter, I shift my case for open access. If open access is a public good, as I have argued, the question here is, How can journals do more to help people enjoy that good? This entails improving the design of the reading environment that online journals create for the articles they publish. Any such improvements have to be made, however, without adding significantly to the journal's costs or the editor's workload—given the exigencies of open access publishing and archiving—and without getting in the way of the primary readership of the journal, the researchers themselves. Such are the challenges to be met with this chapter.

In seeking to improve the reading environment for scholarly literature, I have turned to the research on learning how to read, which has already had a profound impact on the design of textbooks used in schools and colleges. These books typically do a far better job of assisting students in their learning than they did when I went to school. For example, the typical textbook now uses an *advance organizer* at the beginning of each chapter that presents the chapter's key ideas in relation to each other, as well as new concepts or vocabulary. The book also has strategically placed questions, hint boxes, and concept maps at other

---

4. Two of the technologies critical to reference linking are OpenURL (Van de Sompel and Beit-Arie 2001) and CrossRef (Brand 2001).

points, to name just a few of the developments in modern textbook presentation.[5]

However, our knowledge of how online texts can be structured to improve learning is not nearly as well advanced: "We are already years behind," according to Patricia A. Alexander and Tamara L. Jetton, two leaders in literacy research, "in our understanding of learning under such non-traditional and nonlinear conditions" as readers in cyberspace encounter (2000, 303). While little enough is known about reading online texts, it is safe to assume that the way a text is structured and supported will have an impact on what readers learn from it.

Scholarly publishing is not starting from scratch, fortunately, when it comes to helpful structures. An article's *abstract* makes a great "advance organizer." It prepares readers for what is to follow and enables them to assess, from the outset, how the article's claims are being supported. Equally so, the standard subtitles and sections used by research articles in the sciences—"Methodology," "Results," "Discussion"—are intended to further guide readers, enabling them to concentrate on the logic of argument and standards of practice in each aspect of the research.

Alexander, who is at the University of Maryland, has done extensive work on "reading in the subject areas" that provides an excellent starting point for thinking about how to improve the reading environment for the research article. She has determined how high school students "acclimatize" to the challenges of reading in areas such as history and biology. She has found that *personal interest* and *background knowledge* are key to the quality of student learning. Consider the research on personal interest to start with: "Interest, particularly one's personal investment in the topic or domain, stimulates the depth of processing in the

---

5. David Ausubel (1968) is the source of the "advance organizer" concept. Sorrells and Britton, who have analyzed efforts "to improve the learnability of textbooks," conclude that "the overwhelming majority of those methods, when empirically tested, have been found effective" (1998, 95). While some methods require large efforts for small gains, simply identifying "the point of a text" for the reader can make a significant difference. On how improvements in textbook design are especially effective for novice readers, see Alexander and Jetton 2000 (302).

content and, thus, enhances subject-matter learning" (Alexander, Kuliko-wich, and Jetton 1994, 217).[6] Now, in the world of open access reading, personal interest forms a bond, at a basic level, between inexperienced readers and expert readers of research: The concerned parents of an ill child, for example, and medical researchers working in the area of that child's illness are both well-motivated readers. Yet they differ radically in their background knowledge, and "one's knowledge base," Alexander points out, "is a scaffold that supports the construction of all future learning" (1996, 89).

The parents in my example can bring little in the way of a context for positioning the research article within what they already know. *Context*, with its Latin roots in connection and weaving together, provides an-other guiding principle here. In this case, context is about how every re-search article—no less than every text—finds its meaning grow within the weave of related texts. How scholars contextualize the texts they are reading has been the subject of Sam Wineburg's (2001, 2003) research comparing historians' and students' responses to historical documents. As Wineburg, a Stanford University education professor, describes it, when historians first look at a document, "they glance momentarily at the first few words at the top of the page, but then their eyes dart to the bottom, zooming in on the document's provenance: Its author, the date, and location of its creation, the time and distance separating it from the event it reports, and, if possible, how the document came into their hands" (2003, B20). Then they read into the document itself, identifying what it is exactly, whether a diary entry, proclamation, or perhaps a pamphlet.

This is not what happens with students, at least not with the students in Wineburg's research. When confronted by the same historical docu-ments that the historians had been asked to examine, the students tended to start at the top and read to the bottom, while giving no indication, to Wineburg at least, of having called to mind a historical context that

---

6. Alexander strikes a similar note on the importance of reading research to the one I make for open access, namely, that people without benefit of access to texts for want of reading skills "remain the slaves to others' interpretation of what has been written, and they will never experience the exhilaration that can come from the pursuit of knowledge or the quest for expertise" (1998, 280).

would assist their interpretation. They paid little or no attention to the document's provenance. The difference, for Wineburg, is that students simply want information from the document that they can then convey on an exam, whereas the historians' reading habits reflect the "contours of a shared disciplinary culture" (2003, B20). I fear that Wineburg is being a little hard on the students; they have nowhere to turn to find that enriching historical context that historians bring to work every day like a worn briefcase, and that in itself, I would suggest, should form one of the design principles for open access journals.

Although Wineburg's research is concerned specifically with how historians read, I think of it as describing scholars more generally working within their own literature.[7] When experienced readers of research in any field come across an article in one of the journals in their field, they are bound to be conscious of the journal's status in the field, as well as its conservative or cutting-edge tendencies. These readers are often already aware of the authors' reputation and certainly the status of their institutions. They may read a sentence or two of the abstract before flipping to the article's references to see on whose work it draws (if they are not first checking for their own names). All of these pre- and mid-reading strategies are critical to making sense of the article, for locating and evaluating its contribution. These steps help such experienced readers decide exactly what parts, and how much, of the article to read and whether to save it for further use. This is close to what the historians who read for Wineburg did, even as they told him that they did not think these habits remarkable or worth teaching in their classes.

For Wineburg, the educational issue is, How do we then teach the unconscious reading habits of historians to students of history? On the other hand, the issue for open access journals and archives is somewhat different. It is about placing at an inexperienced reader's fingertips the

7. In holding that his research is specifically about how historians read, Wineburg (2003) uses the example of a literature professor who, on reading a historical diary entry out loud at one of his workshops, observed much about the language but failed to check on its historical context until coming upon the diarist's name and position at the end of the text. The historians at the workshop were appalled, but then, I imagine, so would many literature professors have been.

resources and background information on which an experienced reader readily draws. Now, the research article has always offered certain advantages over other kinds of texts, when it comes to providing readers with a context for interpreting what is before them. That is, the research article carries a good part of its context on its back, as it were, like a snail. The citations, footnotes, and references make visible what and who has informed the work being read. The author sets out the sources and provides a path back through the formation of the ideas at issue. This scholarly tradition of naming one's sources has received a great boost, as I mentioned at the outset of this chapter, from the electronic journal's ability to link an article's references to at least any that are from online sources. The ability to view the source of a particular reference, however, often depends on whether the reader belongs to a research library that subscribes to the cited source, unless the source happens to be available in an open access journal or archive.

However, the ability to check a reference directly may still leave the common reader at something of a loss. A way needs to be found to compensate for that missing "knowledge base," to return to Alexander's research, that "is a scaffold that supports the construction of all future learning" (1996, 89). The journal needs to afford these readers a *context* for interpreting the article that goes beyond the author's list of references, especially as the reader may have very limited access to the texts cited. How do we marshal open access resources that can constitute such a context and place them within ready reach of the reader? The journal needs to offer readers a way of examining related studies, of checking on how others have used key concepts, and of determining the definitions of specialized vocabulary. The reader needs to see that, to borrow from the scholarly poet John Donne, no study is an island of itself, with each a part of the main.

Reading certain types of articles, such as, for example, a study of welfare reforms or global warming, might also be enhanced by linking the article to relevant policy measures or legislation, of the sort now increasingly made available on government Web sites. The reading might also be furthered by consulting recent media coverage of the issue explored in the article, which would update and bring home current responses to it. It might be helpful to readers to consult online discussions of the quality and use of the data in the article. Links to some of these types of resources are, of course, provided by the author within the course of writing the article, but the journal itself might provide a ready set of links for searching those research, government, and media databases that often make themselves freely available, so that readers can assess the contemporaneous context for an article that might be a number of years old. Providing links to this wider context not only might serve inexperienced readers of the research article but could also help an expert in the area confirm his or her hunches about it.

There is a long textual tradition of providing readers with an immediate context of supporting commentary for enriching their reading. To draw on my own background, Jewish scholars began writing down the oral rabbinic commentary on the Torah, known as *midrash*, at least as early as the second century BCE, when Rabbi Judah HaNasi edited the oral legal commentaries. The rabbis were providing links from this sacred text to various interpretations that introduced mythic elements, related biblical verses ("As it is said . . ."), and related materials.[8] Midrash (from the Hebrew root for *to seek out* or *to inquire*) surrounds, in effect, a core text in a continuing spiral of context and connection.[9] When midrash came to be printed in book form, the text of the Talmud was placed at the center of the page, where it is surrounded by blocks of Hebrew text that are made up of further commentaries, literal interpretations, logical reasoning, disagreements, and cross-references, whether by rab-

8. See Hartman and Budick on midrash influence on reading in the West: "For some time now, it has been understood that many profoundly ingrained habits of Western reading ('typology' in its many varieties and quite possibly the expectations of 'closure' itself) are historical derivatives of midrash—some by way of emulation, sometimes as aggressive inversions" (1986, x).

9. To view a page of the Talmud online, complete with such commentary, see "A Page from the Babylonian Talmud," prepared by Eliezer Segal ⟨http://www .ucalgary.ca/~elsegal/TalmudPage.html⟩. Jonathan Rosen has written on the Talmud and the Internet: "When I look at a page of the Talmud and see all those texts tucked intimately and intrusively onto the same page, like immigrant children sharing a single bed, I do think of the interrupting, jumbled culture of the Internet" (2000, 10). While it is tempting to reach for the metaphor of hypertext with midrash, *hypertext* suggests frenetically active texts, heading heaven-knows-where, which diminishes the thoughtfulness and care with which the connections are made in midrash and on most Web sites.

binic luminaries of ancient times or more modern figures. One important effect of the way midrash is staged, as an approach to text and reading, is that although any one commentary is at once authoritative in its declarations on the page, it sits within a rich context of vying commentaries, inviting only further interpretation and judgment. Readings are layered on readings, suggesting provisional senses of meaning within possibilities of further contextualization.[10] In the very way that midrash is laid out on the page, it makes clear how knowledge—in the form of understandings, interpretations, and connections—moves among minds and how various forms of knowledge work on each other. It is a cogent reminder of how knowledge is shaped by the very layout or design of the page, and this strikes me as worth keeping in mind in thinking about the design of publishing environments for online journals.

To jump ahead, then, from page to screen, one need only imagine how readers might be assisted by having two or three texts available in overlapping browser windows, each one called up by the reader from the margins of the journal article that is being read. The windows would provide additional context—in the form of a related study or an online forum—for interpreting the article at hand. Of course, readers are always in danger of being overwhelmed by an excess of supplementary texts that virtually bury the original article being consulted. It falls to the reader to decide what constitutes a helpful context for his or her reading of the article. Is it to consult related studies, commentaries, forums? Is it to be able to look up the meaning of certain words, get some background information on the authors or their other works? Or is to

10. Frank Kermode's literary reflections on midrash bring it directly back to context: "Our minds are not very well adapted to the perception of texts in themselves; we necessarily provide them with contexts, some of them imposed by authority and tradition, some by the need to make sense of them in a different world" (1986, 192). Other examples of texts with commentaries include early printed Bibles with the Latin Vulgate text bolstered by parallel columns on either side of the original Hebrew and Greek. The Geneva Bible of 1560, which was the first complete translation into English from the original Hebrew and Greek, begins each book with an "argument" summary, and a continuous stream of marginal notes on both sides of the page and along the bottom comment on the logic and meaning of passages and words, if somewhat cryptically ("That is, whatever has been at any time, is, or shall be").

see how the work at hand has been indexed? Would it be more helpful to see the same ideas at work outside of the research context, perhaps through press coverage of a related event?

Such was the thinking behind our efforts at the Public Knowledge Project to create a supportive reading environment for articles appearing in journals that use our Open Journal Systems. We set out to build on the excellent models for readers' links established by HighWire Press, PubMed, and others, by extending the typical set of links provided for journal articles, with the aim of creating a richer context for reading them. HighWire journals, for example, provide support for expert readers, whether with links to related articles in the same journal or to articles by the same authors. We set out to build Reading Tools, as we call them, that would assist the wider range of readers who will follow on the heels of open access.[11] These Reading Tools sit just beyond the margins of the article, looking much like a traditional paper bookmark. The set of Reading Tools that appear in each journal is based on relevant resources for the field or discipline in which the journal publishes. Each set typically provides readers with ten to fifteen links to other open access sites and databases, depending on what is available in the journal's field, in addition to media, government, and other public sites. The journal's editors can reconfigure the Reading Tools to direct readers to further relevant sources.

Although testing the Reading Tools with a wide range of readers is just getting under way at this point, I outline here how the tools work (Willinsky 2004). Imagine that one is reading an article online in a scholarly journal and glances over to the left-hand margin of the browser and notices a neatly stacked column of links entitled *Reading Tools.* At the top of the tools is an answer to a question that troubles many readers of information online, as it identifies whether the article being read is *peer-reviewed* or not, with a link to an explanation of what the peer review

11. For a working version of the current Reading Tools, integrated into our conference and journal publishing systems, see the Web site of the Public Knowledge Project ⟨http://pkp.ubc.ca⟩. (Note that the design of the Reading Tools on the Web site may differ from the Reading Tools described here, as testing on them is now underway.)

process is about.[12] Also close to the top of the Reading Tools is a link that reads *View item's metadata*, which leads to the study's indexing information, including its discipline, keywords, coverage, method, and sponsor. Although it may take some time for readers to get a feel for what the tools offer, the metadata too may help less experienced readers of research identify the key concepts in the pieces they are reading, as this has proven to be something inexperienced readers have trouble doing (Alexander, Kulikowich, and Jetton 1994). The metadata also provides experienced readers with a quick overview, right down to the funding source for the research. Vocabulary is another obvious challenge for less experienced readers, and one tool can take any word in the article, once the reader double-clicks on it, and sends it to an online dictionary of the reader's choice for a definition.

The Reading Tools also allow readers to establish a context for the article they are reading by providing access to relevant materials that they may not have considered, or know the existence of, or otherwise be able to locate. These Reading Tools are also organized to the side of the article, grouped under the heading of "Find related items among ...," and include *Research Studies, Authors' Other Works, Dissertations and Theses, Government Web Sites, Press and Media Reports*, and *Instructional Sites*. Readers who are curious, for example, about whether the findings of a study they are reading are supported by similar sorts of studies would click on *Research Studies*. A Reading Tool window comes up, entitled Research Studies, that contains two keywords from the article, which have been provided by the authors, and a list of relevant open access databases for, in this case, related research studies. Readers can learn more about any of the databases by clicking on a link, or they can use the search button beside one of the databases to send the authors' two keywords in a Boolean search of the selected database. The results of this search come up in another window, in a list of related research

12. On the uncertain status of research on the Web, see Okamura, Bernstein, and Fidler 2002, who found, in a study of infertility Web sites, that half of the 197 relevant sites did not provide information for determining whether the article met even one of the four "core accountability standards"—authorship, attribution, disclosure, and currency—that they posit for judging the status of the information provided.

studies that were found in the database. Readers are then able to review any of the related studies (or in some cases only the abstracts of those studies, since they are largely drawn from open access databases, not all of which link to full texts). In this way, readers are learning more about the studies they are reading but are also acquiring good research-reading habits.

The other Reading Tools work in a similar way, with each drawing on a different group of databases. For example, *Authors' Other Works* uses the authors' names instead of their keywords to search for other studies that the authors may have conducted; *Discussions and Forums* enables readers to search online discussions for the topics identified by the authors' keywords; and *Government Web Sites* uses the author's keywords to search, in the case of the United States, the FirstGov.gov Web site for related policy and government documents. The journal's editors are able to add other Web sites for readers to choose from, such as the Web sites for other governments. In addition, readers are able to change the search terms that are sent to the databases, so that they can, if they choose, shift the focus of the search to what interests them most about the article they are reading.[13] Still, even with the additions of the journal's editors, the Reading Tools will remain limited in the databases that they can present to the reader, especially for an international readership. In light of those limits, it is hoped that readers will catch on to the example provided by the Reading Tools, then go outside the journal and its tools to use the article's keywords to search, say, their own government's Web sites or a local newspaper's site to see how the study they are reading relates to matters closer to home.

To offer a brief and hypothetical example of how the Reading Tools might be used by those from outside the research community: Imagine a few parents and teachers chatting one evening at a school get-together and realizing that they share a common concern over how *The Merchant of Venice* is the only literary work taught in grades 9 and 10 in their children's school that mentions Jews. In such a discussion, the appropriateness of teaching about the Holocaust as an addition to the students'

13. On the value of demonstrating to readers the effect of using multiple search terms (i.e., a Boolean search), see Vine 2001.

literature program might well come up. If one or two of them were to look online for more information on the topic, they might come across the article "Understanding in the Absence of Meaning: Coming of Age Narratives of the Holocaust," by my colleague Theresa Rogers (2001), as she has obtained permission from the journal that published it to post it online in an open access site.

Our imaginary readers of this study might find its contribution to teaching the Holocaust helpful, although they might initially be left wondering about its recommendations for providing "new forms of witnessing" and "narrative strategies" to counter the mythology of victimization. How would this best be introduced into the curriculum? Indeed, what about the meaning and use of this word *Holocaust* itself, which might come up in asking teachers to teach about this topic? The Reading Tools, which sit in the margins of Rogers's study, would enable them, for example, to explore the meaning of *Holocaust*, leading them to see how the word has been defined in various reference works, as both exclusively reserved for the extermination of the Jews during the Second World War and as possessing a wider usage in the English language. They could learn by searching under *Research Studies* that, in a study concerned with the teaching of German, the very difficulties of teaching the Holocaust have been made part of the curriculum taught to students (Schulz 1998).

In trying to evaluate how realistic it is to expect schools to include the Holocaust in the curriculum, these readers would find, using the Reading Tools, an editorial in the open access peer-reviewed journal *Reading Online* that points out that Anita Lobel's *No Pretty Pictures*, a Holocaust memoir, is listed by the California Department of Education as "recommended literature" for the teaching of history (Grisham 2002). They might also discover, through the *Press and Media Reports* link, that seven states have passed laws that provide for Holocaust education in public schools, and ten states have developed Holocaust curriculum units (Brabham 1997). The links that they could find under *Instructional Sites* would lead them to a number of teaching units that are freely available through, for example, MarcoPolo (a nonprofit consortium of educational organizations offering access to classroom content), so that they could offer teachers actual examples of how to teach this topic.

Finally, under *Discussions and Forums*, they might come across an on-line discussion on H-Net, a huge and multifaceted humanities forum operated out of Michigan State University, with David Klevan (1997), from the U.S. Holocaust Memorial Museum, talking about why some people object to the teaching of *The Diary of Anne Frank*, as it keeps students from considering the more common experience of European Jews during the Holocaust.

After each hyperlinked excursion into these publicly available re-sources that lie just outside the margins of Rogers's study, I imagine readers as returning to what she has written, finding greater cogency in her arguments for providing students with a historical framework for learning about the Holocaust. The Reading Tools provide readers with a context, then, for interpreting, evaluating and utilizing Rogers's study. They are able to enter databases and resources and select studies and documents that they would not have otherwise known about. They can find highly related materials because the tools use the author's own key-words to guide their search. They are learning, in the process, the stan-dard critical reading practices of looking at related studies, exploring the meaning of key terms, and considering implications for practice. Readers who use the tools have acquired a context around which to begin expanding the English curriculum's representation of difference, which will go well beyond teaching *The Merchant of Venice*. They may, as a result, also see a need to do more than portray the victimization of the *other* in teaching the young about prejudice and racism. They may also feel prepared to sit down with other educators and community members to begin to discuss how literature's representation of difference, whether in Shakespeare's plays or Anne Frank's diary, can become a focal point of great educational value for English classes, as well as for their own reading. Or so I would like to imagine at this point, as we begin to test the Reading Tools' ability to contribute to the reading of parents and teachers, as well as researchers and scholars.

I am all too aware that this example of mine may exaggerate the co-herence of the online reading experience. Our imaginary readers are just as likely to wander off, turning contexts into stepping stones, leading them far from Rogers's article. The Reading Tools do not follow the Ikea easy-assembly furniture model. However cleverly engineered, the tools let readers make their own way and assemble their own version of the reading experience. And if the reading that they do as a result of using the tools is far more fragmented than it was when they merely came across a single article in a print magazine, and more than a little unstable in its interpretation of the topic as a result of their online encounter with a variety of sources, what then? Well, I would argue that the lack of apparent coherence in not having stayed with a single text is made up for in a greater awareness of how scholarship works in just such partial and tenuous ways. It's true that some, both inside and outside of the research community, believe that science serves the public best by delivering assured and singular answers to the public's questions, preferably translated into the layperson's language. On the other hand, I see no reason why the public should not have access to the whole of what research has to offer. This does not prevent them from turning to summaries and syntheses and expert opinions, but it does acknowledge their right to see for themselves the original materials on which those summaries, syntheses, and opinions are based.

As readers grow comfortable with the new information environment constituted by the Web, they are likely to grow increasingly comfortable moving from text to text, abstract to abstract, lighting and gleaning where they will. Readers will go only as far as interest and meaning holds for them; but they will also find that the sense of things builds up over various encounters, leading them to go farther and farther. One subtle shift may be that the readers' commitment in the type of reading environment described here will be less to a given text or even to giving a particular author his or her due. Reading may instead be more about finding one's own way and sense in pursuit of knowledge: about the pleasure of exercising one's right to know.

By a strange turn, this opening of the research literature to a wider public may bring us back to the very idea of a common reader, at least as set out by Virginia Woolf, in her own borrowing of the term from Samuel Johnson. Woolf sets the common reader apart "from the critic and the scholar," and the common act of reading that she describes seems no less suited to an age of information than it was for Johnson's age, as Woolf makes clear. The common reader, according to Woolf, reads for his own pleasure rather than to impart knowledge or correct the opinions of others. Above all, he is guided by an instinct to create for himself, out of whatever odds and ends he can come by, some kind of whole—a portrait of a man, a sketch of an age, a theory of the art of writing. He never ceases, as he reads, to run up some rickety and ramshackle fabric which shall give him the temporary satisfaction of looking sufficiently like the real object to allow of affection, laughter, and argument. Hasty, inaccurate, and superficial, snatching now this poem, now that scrap of old furniture, without caring where he finds it or of what nature it may be so long as it serves his purpose and rounds his structure. (1925, 1–2)

In her own modest way, Woolf saw herself as a common reader. This common pattern of reading—"hasty, inaccurate, and superficial" (superficial like a Woolf, perhaps)—with its instinct to create, its sense of purposes served, needs to be explored within the new information environment created by online reading and access to aids like the Reading Tools. The point is not to compare the common reader's experience to that of the scholar's in terms of depth or reach. It is to ask whether the knowledge generated by scholarly endeavor has become a greater part of human experience as a result of the move to a new, promising medium and whether scholars have done all that they can, as authors of the work presenting this knowledge, to ensure that it is as open, and as well-designed in that openness, as possible.

As for scholarly readers, the proximity and precision of context proposed in this chapter strikes me, at least, as hardly detrimental to their reading. Although the scholarly community has only begun to read research online, members of that community have already expressed an interest, according to at least one study, in seeing more in the way of "deep archives" to support their reading (Tenopir, 2003, 15). They want e-journals that offer them more "tools and services that support seamless navigation across different landscapes," and they want it made very clear what links are available when they are reading (15). I would only add that the importance of creating open access to these different landscapes and links will certainly be a boon for those faculty and students who do not otherwise have access to journals or indexes.

The Reading Tools of Open Journal Systems (and other, similar online-reading aids) are one way of providing faculty and students with improved access to the wider literature, as these tools provide links to open access resources, including open access archives (for work otherwise published in subscription fee journals). This may well inspire in these readers the interest, excitement, and confidence that comes from working on a topic in a good library (although not too good a library just yet, in the case of this online "cybrary" known as the Web, for most of the literature remains restricted to subscribing institutions, and faculty members are just beginning to place their work in e-print archives). As a result, these tools and the general approach they facilitate do not provide anything like the whole picture. What they offer is a way of organizing the current and growing access in ways that support greater critical engagement, as well as more basic comprehension and utilization of the research literature; they do so in a way that can richly supplement an article's reference list and improve the quality of access for a much greater number of readers. The development of such devices for enriching the reading environment in which journals publish constitutes another means of honoring the access principle.

12

Indexing

The question of journal indexing and open access begins, for me, with a tale of two libraries. The first of these is the library at the University of British Columbia in Vancouver, where I work. In 2003, it subscribed to 125 index and abstract services to guide its 30,000 students and 2,500 faculty to the world of serial literature. The members of this academic community can search these indexes online from office, home, or anywhere in the world, really. The library, which was ranked twenty-fourth in size in North America by the Association of Research Libraries in 2003, spends roughly $750,000 annually for online indexing services against the $5 million it spends on subscriptions to 40,000 print and electronic serials.[1] In addition to traditional indexes, like the ISI Web of Science and *Chemical Abstracts*, the library offers full-text access to thousands of journals through the search engines of a journal aggregator, such as EBSCO, or a publisher, such as Elsevier, with its 1,700-title ScienceDirect. Finally, the library offers links to a small number of open access indexes, most notably PubMed in the life sciences and ERIC (the Education Resources Information Clearinghouse), both sponsored by the U.S. government. Despite this considerable array of indexes and portals, earnest scholars and students still have to wend their way through overlaps, gaps, and partiality in the coverage of the research literature that the indexes provide, even as the university librarians struggle against the corrosive effects of cost increases for both indexes and journals that continue to exceed the growth of the library's budget.

1. The Association of Research Libraries has reported that its average member library spent $600,000 on "electronic indexes and reference tools" in 2000–2001 (Young, Kyrillidou, and Blixrud 2003, 10).

Halfway around the world from Vancouver stands the University of Bangalore, which is the largest university in India, with more than 300,000 students enrolled across 430 colleges. Its main library subscribed at one time to thirty-seven abstracting and indexing services, including *Physics Abstracts, Journal of Economic Abstracts*, and *Biological Abstracts*. It had acquired bound volumes of *Chemical Abstracts*, for example, back to 1916. However, its most recent volume of *Chemical Abstracts* is dated 1981. It can no longer afford to subscribe to any commercially available indexes in the sciences, economics, or most other disciplines. It continues to receive only four current indexes in print: one each in library science, psychology, sociology, and statistics.[2] The loss of indexes only further reduces the scholarly value of the university's serials collection, which has shrunk over the last decade from over 500 titles to 225. The situation at the University of Bangalore is not an unusual one for Indian universities, N. V. Sathyanarayana, chair of Informatics Inc., a company that provides online access to journals in India, explained to me during my visit to Bangalore in 2003. By Sathyanarayana's estimation, perhaps 90 percent of Indian universities run their libraries without serial indexes. This makes it more than a little difficult for their faculty and students to take advantage of interlibrary loan services, as well as to explore the small set of serial titles that these universities subscribe to. They are, however, able to visit the National Centre for Science Information at the Indian Institute of Science in Bangalore, which offers an online search service that receives perhaps four or five visitors a day from across India, with just as many inquiries coming in by mail. For 150 rupees, about the equivalent of a modest restaurant meal in India, a member of the Centre will work personally with visiting researchers (as well as respond to their mail inquiries).[3]

2. A study of 129 university libraries in India, published in 1992, found that fifty-eight libraries subscribed to *Chemical Abstracts*, fifty-six subscribed to *Biological Abstracts*, and forty subscribed to *Physics Abstracts* (Patel and Kumar 2001, 59).

3. The visiting scholar is typically provided with a list of five to fifty bibliographic records, drawn from the major abstracting and indexing databases, many of which are available at the library of the Indian Institute of Science where the Centre is located. The Centre also has a document delivery service that covers the institute's print journals and a portion of its electronic journals, for as I noted

Yet the situation has begun to change for students and faculty at the University of Bangalore, as well as at other Indian institutions, thanks to a small but growing number of computer terminals appearing in the university libraries. The change reflects an expanded notion of what it means to provide a guide to the research literature, a guide that now takes a form that goes well beyond traditional notions of a serials index. Students and faculty at Bangalore can turn to open access indexes such as PubMed (life sciences), ERIC (education), CiteSeer.IST (computer science), and the NASA Astrophysics Data System; they can search the databases at arXiv.org E-Print Archive (physics) and HighWire Press (biomedical), in which they will find hundreds of thousands of papers in the sciences freely available. They can browse the abstracts of pay-per-view and subscription sites such as ScienceDirect, that of the IEEE (engineering), and Ingenta (general).[4] There is also a new generation of search engines cum indexes that are devoted to serving up open access scholarly resources, such as the University of Michigan's OAIster, whose name puns on the OAI (Open Archives Initiative) indexing information (or metadata) that it harvests from hundreds of registered e-print archives, and the *Directory of Open Access Journals* (Lund University Libraries 2004) at the University of Lund, which offers a growing listing of over a thousand journal titles and links, with full-text searching for some.

While there's no question that considerable differences persist for those who carry on research at the University of British Columbia compared to the University of Bangalore, the stark contrast is at least somewhat reduced today when it comes to finding a guide to the literature in a number of specific areas, such as physics, engineering, education, astronomy and others. Although there are still many substantial gaps in access to indexes, whether in chemistry, sociology, and a dozen other

---

earlier, Elsevier does not permit articles to be printed out by nonmembers of the institute or "walk-ins" to the library. The Centre also refers researchers to similar services at the British Library and the Australian National Library.

4. For example, HighWire Press currently offers over 830,000 open access articles from among the nearly 800 journals it hosts. Of PubMed's roughly 15 million citation entries, roughly 500,000 link to open access articles. PubMed attracts 60,000 unique visitors each day.

areas, certainly things are better at Bangalore than they would have been had they continued on the track on which they had been headed with print indexes and journals over the last few decades. The importance of these developments lies in the opening of indexing resources—from government, university, and commercial sources—and these resources are just as important to ensuring equality of access to scholarly knowledge as is access to the journals themselves. The increased online access to indexes, databases, and search engines reflects the convergence of publishing and indexing functions of search engines, databases, and portals. It is a convergence that holds out prospects for more immediate and comprehensive coverage of the literature, in what could well be a far less labor-intensive (and thus far less expensive) indexing process than the print era offered. That much is encouraging. Yet what adds incentive, if not urgency, to a rethinking of indexing in this new online medium are the continuing gaps and overlaps in the coverage of current indexes that interfere with the most basic step in getting a scholarly project underway, namely, a review of all the pertinent literature on a topic. These gaps and overlaps also complicate the always-difficult budgeting decisions of librarians in purchasing indexing services.

With this chapter, then, I do not want simply to present the case for open access indexing, although as I noted earlier, such indexing is just as important to the principle of access as open access e-print archives and journals. Given the current situation, I believe far more is to be gained by considering how journal publishers—both commercial and nonprofit—can work toward creating a far more comprehensive, integrated, and automated indexing of the scholarly literature, an indexing that would be as available to the University of Bangalore as to the University of British Columbia, as well as to public libraries in Bangalore and Vancouver.

Historically, the value of compiling a guide or index to written works appears to have occurred to readers and writers not long after the first few inscribed tablets had been completed. The first record of texts' being indexed goes back to at least 2000 BCE. The archaeological records of Mesopotamia include the Nippur tablets, which present lists of Sumerian works of literature by title (Casson 2001, 4). Some seven centuries later, around 1300 BCE, individual documents in Mesopotamia were inscribed with what we now refer to, in the digital context, as *metadata* or indexing information, describing the works. The metadata of the ancient world included, for example, the title of the work (which was typically a description of its use within the community or its first line) and possibly its proper place within a sequence of tablets. Such an index might also identify the scribe, by position and genealogy, the state of repair of the tablet, and on occasion the penalty faced by anyone who defaced or stole the tablets, in a self-enforcing copyright notice: "May Ashur and Ninlil, angered and grim, cast him down, erase his name, his seed, in the land" (12).

To leap ahead to the seventeenth century, which is where the story of the academic journal begins, Henry Oldenburg did not waste any time in ensuring that the first English-language scientific periodical, *Philosophical Transactions*, was properly indexed. The initial index of *Transactions* appeared at the end of the first volume in 1666. In this index, the year's worth of twenty-two issues, as editor Oldenburg explained, "was abbreviated into an Alphabetical Table, and also afterwards Digested into a more Natural Method" ("Philosophical Transactions" 1666, 399). The alphabetical table offered a detailed subject index for the journal, by issue and page, with many entries offering a protoabstract: "Air. The weight of it in all changes, by wind, weather, or whatever other influence observable by a standing *Mercurial Balance*, call'd a *Baroscope*, hinted in reference to M. *Hooks* Micrography, n. 2. p. 31" (399). The brief index entries were often no less intriguing: "*Rainbows* strangely posited, 13. 219" (403). Authors whose books were mentioned in the *Transactions* were indexed under "Books abbreviated or recited," creating something on the order of a citation index. And as for the "more Natural Method" advertised in the index's title, it consisted of a three-part division of articles, with the first section including all of those that fell under "A Natural History of all Countries and Places, is the foundation for solid Philosophy" (405).

Some 425 years later, to mercifully attenuate this indexing history, the Internet realized the scholar's dream of having every single word in every single work across an entire virtual library indexed by full-text search engines. Now, Google may not look like an index. Yet the ability of Google and the other major search engines to scan for any given word or phrase among the billions of pages of the Web and produce a list of every use in a matter of seconds can only count as an instance of extreme indexing. Full-text searching is clearly a boon to information seekers. In the hands of a skilled user, Google can turn up the needle of a missing reference (on what page does David Rusin's *Astrophysical Journal* article start?) or pin down the exact wording, context, and location of a famous phrase ("For 'tis the sport to have the engineer/*Hoist with his own petard*"; *Hamlet*, III.iv.221–222).

Under the old adage "Be careful what you wish for," Google is increasingly demonstrating the limits of full-text searching within an endless sea of texts, as it produces tens of thousands of hits for almost any term searched. At the same time, Google and other search engines have induced a "full-text fixation" among undergraduate students, according to Stephen J. Bell, library director at Philadephia University, resulting in their use of virtually any full text in which the term of interest appears (quoted in Carlson 2003; see also OCLC 2002). "The mind-set is that all the information is out there," Bell complains of the students he observes in the library, "and that they just need to plug in a few words to find it." The recent introduction of Google Scholar does offer the advantage to a student writing, say, a history essay on imperialism of being able to identify Edward Said's *Culture and Imperialism* as the most-cited work within the Google Scholar corpus, at least among that use "imperialism" in their title. That is to say, Google still lacks the basic features of a good subject index.

Fortunately for the future of scholarship, not only does the Internet lend itself to indiscriminate full-text search, but it can also facilitate new levels of precision, detail, and comprehensiveness in indexing the scholarly literature. Through emerging standards for affixing metadata to digital documents, journal articles can be indexed, not only by author and title, but by its discipline, topic, research method, research subjects, peer review status, publisher, and research sponsor. This level of indexing enables readers to cut through the information overload that otherwise abounds. With the detailed indexing afforded by adherence to these metadata standards, one can quickly narrow one's focus to work that is related, perhaps not in regard to topic, but in the method used, or the sample studied, or the historical period examined.

However, before stepping any further into the promising future of scholarly indexing, let us consider the current state of overlap in the indexing of serials. In chapter 4, I pointed out how readers could make their way to David Rusin's (2002) "The Expected Properties of Dark Lenses" in the *Astrophysical Journal* through a number of different open access and subscription fee routes. Because of the current merging of indexing and publishing functions, Rusin's article is also indexed by both open access and licensed indexing services. Among open access sources, arXiv.org E-Print Archive provides indexing by title, author, date, abstract, and journal in its database of well over 200,000 articles (including Rusin's), largely in high-energy physics. Rusin's article is also listed in the open access NASA Astrophysics Data System (ADS), which uses an indexing system similar to that of arXiv.org, although in the case of Rusin's paper, it directs readers to the University of Chicago site for the journal, which is restricted to subscribers to the *Astrophysical Journal*, as well as to the arXiv.org version, which ADS identifies as a "preprint," presumably to avoid undermining its link to the subscription copy.[5]

On the commercial side of indexing, the ISI Web of Science sets the standard for citation indexes. It provides both an indexed guide to a researcher's publications and a measure of each work's status, by calculating how many times it has been cited. The ISI entry for Rusin's paper includes its abstract and a list of works that Rusin cites in his paper, with most of these works linked to their own entries in the ISI

---

5. ADS provides a striking example of the power of open access indexing. It "maintains four bibliographic databases containing more than 4.0 million records: Astronomy and Astrophysics, Instrumentation, Physics and Geophysics," according to its Web site in 2004 ⟨http://adswww.harvard.edu/⟩. Michael J. Kurtz and his colleagues describe it as "the most sophisticated discipline centered bibliographic system ever developed" (2005). Kurtz and company present evidence associating the use of ADS with an increase in "the total readership and use of technical astronomical literature by a factor of three." They describe how ADS connects the literature and the cited research databases, "with many of the data-sets being brought together for the first time." The result is that "simple queries, such as 'show me the most cited papers containing the phrase "redshift survey"'' [that] were not possible before the ADS merged the text and citation databases" are now possible through ADS.

Web of Science. As for the paper's contribution to science, as of October 2004, the ISI listed seven articles that had cited it, which places it above the average for the *Astrophysical Journal*, in which it appears, a journal that is ranked second in its field, according to its impact factor, by the ISI Web of Science.[6] The citation indexing and ranking of journals—bibliometrics, in a word—has become career critical to faculty members in many fields, and this makes the Web of Science an invaluable scholarly tool.

Information on Rusin's paper is available across a range of indexes, just as the paper is available as a full-text from more than one site, and this variety speaks to very different types of indexing services that are emerging, from free archives to contracted databases, which in the case of the ISI Web of Science can cost a university the equivalent of two or three faculty salaries annually. The road from costly to open access in indexing is paved by integrating the indexing into the publishing process (leaving aside government-run indexes like PubMed), rather than having a third party undertake the indexing once the literature is published, along the lines of the ISI Web of Science.

Because of its central role across the disciplines and considerable expense, it is worth considering the scope of the ISI Web of Science for a moment. It currently indexes roughly 8,500 journals from around the world in the sciences, social sciences, and the humanities. Although the index's coverage is clearly extensive, James Testa, a senior manager with ISI, has made it clear that "ISI's editorial staff reviews nearly 2,000 new journal titles annually, but only 10–12 percent of the journals evaluated are selected" for inclusion in the index (1998). The ISI accepted its first electronic journal for indexing in 1994 and is continuing, according to Testa, to "monitor the growing body of journals published in electronic form," suggesting the cautiousness of ISI's approach. Apart from containing its costs, in making the transition from what was largely a

6. In 2003, *Astrophysical Journal* was ranked second among those in its field with an impact factor of 6.604, which, as noted in chapter 2, the ISI Web of Science bases on the average number of times articles in the journal have been cited over the previous two years. It has an immediacy factor of 1.593, which is a measure of how frequently a journal's articles are cited during the first twelve months after they have been published.

hand-indexed operation, ISI has limited the number of journals it indexes because of the evidence that researchers tend to rely on a small circle of journals in their work. Testa points out that "as few as 150 journals account for half of what is cited and one quarter of what is published," and "a core of approximately 2,000 journals now account for about 85 percent of published articles and 95 percent of cited articles." The concentration of citation within a narrow set of journals may reflect researchers' judgments about where articles of scientific merit are published. Yet to index 8,500 journals among perhaps 50,000 titles prevents this rationale from being fully and fairly tested. The inability of so many journals to be part of the citation index only adds to their struggle to garner submissions and citations, a problem that affects the circulation of knowledge across the developing world in particular.[7] Compounding the problem is the pressure scholars feel to publish in journals indexed in the ISI Web of Science. In South Africa, for example, the government compensates authors and their departments for each "ISI journal" article published, and this only adds to the struggle of South African scholars to develop a local journal culture.

Yet efforts are underway to create a more inclusive open access citation index with two experimental systems, Citebase and CiteSeer.IST, which automate processes that tap into the online availability of published materials.[8] With the prospect of even citation indexing's becoming an

7. For example, physicist Ana María Cetto, of the National Autonomous University of Mexico, has demonstrated the underrepresentation of African scholarly journals in the ISI Web (2000, 148). In response to this situation, Cetto has worked on the construction of LATINDEX ⟨http://www.latindex.unam.mx/⟩, which is an open access electronic information system on and for scientific journals that covers some 7,000 journals from Latin America and the Caribbean, Spain, and Portugal. Also see the Web site for SciELO (Scientific Electronic Library Online) ⟨http://www.scielo.org⟩, an open access cooperative for electronic publishing of scientific journals on the Internet among South American, Latin American and Caribbean countries, which as such provides a portal and search service.

8. Citebase ⟨http://citebase.eprints.org/⟩, a project of the Open Citation Project at the University of Southampton, provides for each article a list of the papers it cites and those that have cited it, as well as a graph of the paper's "hits" and cites over time. Citebase allows readers to search for the most-cited work in a given area, as well as for works that are co-cited with a given article. On Citebase, see

open access resource, the possibilities of building an integrated and open system of indexing across commercial and nonprofit, subscription and open access publishers seems that much more feasible. The ISI Web of Science has also been exploring the indexing of open access materials, which would add to the status of these works while increasing the value of the ISI index. What seems important here is to end the all-or-nothing economics of access to indexing, which is what I saw at work in Bangalore as many Indian universities were forced to give up the hope of having current indexes in the 1980s while at the same time minimizing disparities between two tiers of access: the well-endowed research library version and the open access economy class.

After all, the move to online indexes has opened new possibilities that could benefit all those who are in search of research and scholarship. When indexes were issued, like journals, in print volumes not so very long ago, the scholarly dream of being able to conduct a search across multiple indexes—as a way to compensate for the unevenness and overlap of coverage among the indexes—would have been unlikely even to occur to anyone besides a philosopher-librarian such as Leibniz (see Willinsky 1999, 87–98). Now, with all the indexes and related engines appearing online and virtually only a window away from each other, it seems a small step to bring them together. The One Great Scholarly Search Engine has become something of the Holy Grail of indexing,

---

Hitchcock et al. 2002. CiteSeer.IST is another important open access citation index, developed by Steve Lawrence, C. Lee Giles, and Kurt Bollacker (1999) at the NEC Research Institute. CiteSeer.IST and Thomson ISI have recently announced plans to collaborate on a multidisciplinary citation index for Web-based materials that brings the indexing of open access materials within the scope of the ISI Web of Science ("ISI Web" 2004). Stevan Harnad presents an excellent summary of where impact measures are headed with open access: "Citation counts for article, author, and journal; download counts for article, author and journal; co-citation counts (who is jointly cited with whom?); eventually co-download counts (what is being downloaded with what?); analogs of Google's 'page-rank' algorithm (recursively weighting citations by the weight of the citing work); 'hub/ authority' analysis (much-cited vs. much-citing works); co-text 'semantic' analysis (what—and whose—text patterns resemble the cited work?); early-days download/citation correlations … (downloads today predict citations in two years …; time-series analyses; and much more" (2004c). Also see Hitchcock et al. 2002.

according to a Library of Congress survey of librarians and reference personnel (Larson and Arret 2001). As one librarian summed up the problem that many of them were perceiving: "Having one place to search that would include relevant resources would make research less fragmented" (2001).

Just how fragmented the indexes currently are can be seen by turning to appendix E, in which I have presented, with the assistance of Larry Wolfson and Alnoor Gova, a comparison of the coverage of common serial indexes in the sciences and social sciences. One finds that the two major indexes in a field like the study of education each cover roughly 60 percent of the journal holdings in my university library, with perhaps 20 percent of the available education titles (albeit loosely defined) not included in either of the leading indexes. While it is not surprising to find that no one index provides complete coverage of a single discipline, the greater concern is with journals that are overlooked by multiple indexes. And determining which journals are missing from the indexes is not easily done. Of course, no scholar or student should live by the results of a single index—even an index dedicated to the field of study under investigation—as that is to risk working with an incomplete picture of the research literature.

The comparisons presented in appendix E also point to how, in certain fields, the coverage of open access indexes has come to rival that of commercial services. It all points to the advantages of working toward a universal and integrated system. From a librarian's perspective, if there is a near-perfect overlap between two indexes, it makes it easy for libraries to decide to subscribe to one or the other, perhaps on the basis of interface or search capacities. A partial overlap, however, makes such decisions difficult, and libraries often end up subscribing to a number of overlapping indexes, ostensibly covering the same fields. This means paying to have some journals indexed a number of times, only to find their contents also covered by an open access site. It also means that scholars must learn which indexes to consult for a given topic, playing the odds on having reviewed all of the relevant literature. It is like having to first guess, when looking for a book in the library stacks, in which of several often overlapping databases it might be listed, rather than turning to a single library catalogue. Scholars have obviously learned to live with the current state of serial indexes by checking multiple indexes, as well as the bibliographies of relevant articles, just as they have learned to work around the "crisis in scholarly publishing" by utilizing interlibrary loans, online pay-per-view services, e-print archives, and other means.

But there is another way, one that moves along that somewhat utopian path toward integrated, comprehensive indexing.[9] It involves using the emergent indexing or metadata standard set by the Open Archives Initiative and calls for building the indexing process directly into journal management systems, which are used to handle submissions, reviews, and publication. With such a system, authors enter detailed metadata on their articles when they upload them to the journal (including not only keywords, but the study's coverage, method, and sponsor), with further metadata (such as the study's bibliographic information and peer review status) generated by the journal management system. When the article is published, this metadata can be harvested by a search engine that complies with the Open Archives Initiative protocol, creating an instant and detailed index for all of the content from sources registered with the search engine. This journal-based indexing can be done whether or not the journal is open access (appendix F).

The Open Archives Initiative issues a standard for preparing metadata for an article so that it can be harvested and searched, and this OAI standard is also used by e-print archives, research databases, thesis repositories, and other scholarly journals. There are a number of OAI search engines, perhaps most notably OAIster, mentioned earlier in the chapter. The Public Knowledge Project software uses the author, with support from the management system, to index the contents of journals and conferences. The project has also created software, PKP Harvester, that goes out and collects this indexing information from the journals and conferences that register with the Harvester, creating an open access index within a community of users, whether in an institution or across a disci-

---

9. This idea owes a debt not only, as noted, to Leibniz, but to Robert Cameron, a Simon Fraser University computer science professor, who proposed a "universal, Internet-based, bibliographic and citation database [that] would link every scholarly work ever written—no matter how published—to every work that it cites and every work that cites it" (1997).

pline. The journals and conferences that register with the Harvester are also typically harvested by a compatible system, such as OAIster, which is creating a global index of research resources.

Although most publishers have not been using OAI with their journals up to this point, it would be easy enough for them to do so, with index entries leading readers back to the journals' Web sites, which could be entered only by subscription (or a credit card payment).[10] Commercial publishers could treat the development costs of becoming OAI compliant as marketing expenses (as OAI creates a virtual catalogue of their work). The implementation of an indexing system on this scale could be coordinated by the leading libraries and publishers on a cooperative basis, as I describe in chapter 6. This would also mean that the libraries would cover the open access journals' share of the cost for indexing back issues, for example, as the libraries are the chief financial beneficiaries of open access publishing and indexing.

Such a system would greatly increase the likelihood that material published in less-well-known journals would turn up in the limited results of the detailed searches that this OAI approach affords readers. It would level the research playing field somewhat and yet would not prevent readers from being selective in their searches about the quality of the journals in which material appears. For the same automated systems would eventually include citation rankings for article and journal, which could be used to assess impact without necessarily excluding the otherwise unrecognized gem. The big difference between indexing via this approach and that offered by the commercial indexing services is that the former is open to all journals, allowing the potential contribution of an article to overcome the fate of the journal in which it is published, which might not be indexed in a highly selective commercial index like the ISI Web of Science.

The key to making automated and open access indexing systems work is drawing authors further into the publishing and positioning of their

10. The best example of this sort of cooperation among libraries and different types of publishers is found with CrossRef ⟨http://www.crossref.org⟩, which provides a standard and system for linking the references in an article to their original source texts. Membership in CrossRef includes the entire range of publishers, from large corporate ones to small nonprofits.

work. The new academic saw might read, "As authors index, so they will be known (found, read, and cited)." Now, of course, asking authors to do their own indexing has its risks, especially as I am also promoting the idea that detailed and precise indexing offers the best weapon against information overload. To assist with indexing, some disciplines (such as mathematics and physics) have established subject classification systems or a subject-specific thesaurus (which ERIC, for example, provides in education). Some disciplines or journals may opt for what is called a "controlled vocabulary" to classify articles, providing authors with a list of terms with which to index their articles. The upside of author indexing is that it will require authors to think more about how their work is positioned and identified in relation to what others are doing or calling what they are doing.

Still, in a letter challenging my earlier work on indexing (Willinsky and Wolfson 2001), on which this chapter draws, Dan Duncan, executive director of the National Federation of Science Abstracting and Indexing Services (the "premiere trade organization representing the interests of information aggregators," according to its Web site), rightly cautioned me that "scholar-authors within a narrow field may not properly recognize the value of their work to those outside their own immediate niche. Even more to the point, scholars are not always properly equipped to recognize how others outside their immediate environment may be approaching a search or wording a query—an increasingly important consideration in interdisciplinary research."

Undoubtedly, professional indexers would do a better job than authors of creating accurate, useful metadata. Yet if ensuring the degree of greater indexing accuracy Duncan is advocating is going to mean the difference between letting people everywhere use the index and keeping most scholars and students at bay, because their library lacks a sufficient indexing budget to afford the superior indexes that would result from the use of professional indexers, then I am inclined to favor authors' learning more about how others are "approaching a search or wording a query." And if they are working in interdisciplinary research, that is all the more reason for their being conscious of this, as it can only help their work. After all, authors have been providing abstracts and keywords for their journal articles for some time now, and this, too, was once the work of professionals. This is not the classic move of automation leading to a deskilling, but a continuing shift of skills to authors as they take control over the process. Still, Duncan does invite the testing of "new economic models" in information's marketplace, and I ask for no more than for the exploring of new models to continue, with an eye to furthering the access principle at the heart of this book.

At this point, viable alternatives to traditional commercial models have been established for both running journals and providing indexing services have been established in ways that greatly increase access. In particular, a new generation of open indexing services has developed in the United States, including those indexes supported by government agencies (PubMed, ERIC, arXiv.org, ADS, and others), information technology industries (CiteSeer.IST), corporate publishers (Elsevier's ScienceDirect), and university libraries (HighWire Press). These new systems hold out the hope that research libraries the world over—too many of which have otherwise seen cuts in their indexing services—can now begin to reclaim that vital and necessary bibliographic access to the scholarly literature. Yet there is clearly more to be done.

The current state of serial indexing presents a particularly good reason for research libraries and professional associations, as well as individual researchers and journal editors, to work together on developing compatible distributed systems that greatly improve the comprehensiveness of indexing and promote universal access to research by placing at least this initial, discovery phase of scholarship squarely within the public sector of the knowledge economy. Comprehensive indexing may be an area in which commercial and open access interests can coexist peacefully, complement one another, and even thrive and serve one another, as the future of scholarly publishing sorts itself out within this new digital medium. This indexing initiative may be just the sort of project to be overseen by the publishing and archiving cooperative that I introduced in chapter 6. We certainly need to press ahead with ways of improving the quality of scholarly indexing, as the realm of digital publishing promises considerable benefits over print publishing, even as the amount of information in need of indexing grows exponentially. To rethink these indexing overlaps and gaps is to rethink the access principle. It speaks to the right to know what is known. It addresses, by first making it possible to identify and locate the knowledge that research generates, how research can serve as a greater public good on a global scale. Rather than simply being a result of publishing reforms, improvements in the quality and comprehensiveness of indexing could well become the driving force behind those reforms.

13
History

When the historian Elizabeth Eisenstein (1979) published her landmark study on the introduction of print in Europe, *The Printing Press as an Agent of Social Change*, she entitled the opening chapter "The Unacknowledged Revolution." Although some five centuries had passed since Johannes Gutenberg began to pull inked sheets of vellum and paper off his makeshift press in Mainz, Eisenstein believed that this invention had yet to receive its due as a cultural force. Insufficient credit had been given, she held, to all that the production of uniform, standard, and multiple-copy editions of books had contributed to the spread of science and learning generally.[1] And to her credit, at least in part, the historical study of the book, and print culture more generally, has taken off since Eisenstein's book was published, with the result that there is now little doubt about the revolutionary impact of the printing press.

Today, it is easy to imagine that we are in the hands of a similar agent of social change. Only this time, there is no shortage of people ready to cry "revolution" as they surf their way into the post-Gutenberg era of a

1. In terms of precursors, Eisenstein is leery of giving the "mischievous" Marshall McLuhan his due for the *Gutenberg Galaxy* (1962), which certainly did acknowledge the revolution, although she does credit this prophetic "anti-book" for inspiring her work (1979, x, 40). It is also worth noting that Eisenstein's book reads like a last hurrah for print as the unchallenged medium of ideas and information; she saw it as a "runaway technology which was leading to a sense of cultural crisis," with "data impinging on us from so many directions and with such speed that our capacity to provide order and coherence was being strained to the breaking point (or had it already snapped?)" (1979, x).

digital age.[2] Whether this readily acknowledged revolution will have an impact comparable to that of the printing press, only future generations can judge. Yet if it is prudent to avoid pronouncing on the revolutions of one's own times, it still makes sense to look at print's revolutionary contribution to scientific communication in thinking about the future of scholarly publishing. I have saved the historical case for the penultimate chapter of the book, as opposed to placing an introductory history at the beginning of the book, because I did not want to suggest that open access is simply another chapter in the unfolding story of scientific communication. Rather, I want to draw attention to a few distinct parallels between the introduction of the scientific journal in the culture of print and the critical decisions now faced in moving the journal online.

Open access obviously represents a break with the past in a number of ways. Yet it also speaks to the spirit of that past, to the long-term aspects of the access principle, which is the point of this chapter. The story of Oldenburg, Newton, and the beginnings of the *Philosophical Transactions* offers insights into the choices that people have made about a new way of publishing scientific work in light of their consequences. We are not yet able to gain the same sense of consequence with, say, the decision to open access to the contents of the *New England Journal of Medicine* six months after the publication of an issue, which is to say that what is necessarily speculative about the future of open access publishing is well met by instances from the past, our view of which is not entirely free of speculation either. This chapter makes its case for open access to research and scholarship in the form, then, of back-to-the-future. It reaffirms how open access is ultimately about people deciding that there may be a way to extend the circulation of knowledge, even as the history of the *Transactions* reveals how the risks and apprehensions that intro-

2. Consider the revolution that is, and will be, as reflected in the "message from the founders" on the launch of the open access journal *PloS Biology*: "Communication among scientists has undergone a revolution in the last decade with the movement of scientific publication to a digital medium and the emergence of the Internet as the primary means of distributing information.... Our aim is to catalyze a revolution in scientific publishing by providing a compelling demonstration of the value and feasibility of open access publication" (Brown, Eisen, and Varmus 2003, 1).

ducing a new form of scholarly communication can invoke in the academic community are still with us.

Amid the wealth of insights that Eisenstein presents on what print did for scholarship, one of particular relevance to the theme of this book concerns the gradual loss of contact between scholar and printer. During the early years of the print revolution, the learned could often be found hanging around printing shops, seeing their own work through publication, picking up the latest works of others, and generally keeping a hand in the book industry. Such was the inky life of the early modern knowledge worker. It was only with the increasing industrialization of printing and publishing that this relationship between scholar and printer was lost, leading Eisenstein to ask whether "this growing distance from printing plants has affected the attitudes of men of knowledge" (1979, 18).

The alienation of mental labor suggested here bears as well on the current move from print to digital publishing among scholarly interests. Online publishing technologies are drawing women and men of knowledge back to the (digital) typeface. These women and men are not only turning their thoughts to fonts and layout, but to economies of distribution and access. With open access publishing, some university faculty members are working again with the rude mechanics of publication, and it may well afford these scholars a stronger sense of how their work is situated in the world, as well as how it connects with that world. And this may, perhaps, with time, affect how they write for that world. These faculty members are setting up twenty-first century "printing shops," consisting of computer terminals and high-speed Internet connections, in laboratories and offices, in an effort to take back control of scientific and scholarly publishing.[3] They are bringing the publishing process home with their laptops, as if to throw a cable across the divide between workplace and domicile that Max Weber (1930) identified as a necessary feature of capitalism.[4]

3. As noted already, "declaring independence" is the theme of a campaign of the Association of Research Libraries' Scholarly Publishing and Academic Resources Coalition, which is intended to reduce journal dependence on corporate publishers by supporting editors who pursue other models (SPARC 2001).

4. I owe this point to Adrian Johns (1998, 629), although I do not consider here whether this domestic movement is good for home and family (or merely a further intensification of work for the achieving classes).

The introduction of the printing press more than five centuries ago also managed to bridge boundaries between public and institutional approaches to learning. Stillman Drake, for example, holds the growth of printing responsible not only for the "restoration of classical mathematics in the sixteenth century," but for the widespread circulation of mathematical knowledge beyond the universities (1970, 44). This historian of science argues that the printing press had its greatest scientific impact on those working outside of the universities, rather than on the scholars within. The universities were not early champions of the printed book. Their faculty members were happy enough to continue, at least initially, with the known world of manuscripts and medieval thinking. On the other hand, the European public, at least of a certain class and gender, clearly relished the sudden access to a much larger world of learning that the printing press provided. By increasing access to works on natural history, mathematics, and other areas of scholarly interest, the printing press managed to put a vast range of ideas into the hands of many more people, and this led to, in Drake's terms, "the independent origin of a totally different set of inquiries outside the universities," largely by adding "self-educated men and talented amateurs of liberal education to the ranks of those who made substantial contributions to science" (46, 48).

In making this point, Drake offers the example of the self-educated Niccolò Tartaglia, born into a poor family in Brescia, Italy, in 1500, who went on to translate Euclid and related mathematical commentaries into Italian (such translations were not, Drake notes, the sort of thing a professor would do in the Latinate universities). These translations, according to Drake, "enormously widened the access of Italian readers in every walk of life to mathematics and its applications to practical problems" (1970, 52). And if Drake's "every walk of life" overstates the interest and application of Euclidean geometry, the larger issue should not be overlooked. The new communication technology represented by the printing press was initially used to undermine "the tyranny of an authority other than those of mathematics and of nature herself" represented by medieval scientific thinking in the universities during the fifteenth and sixteenth centuries, which was otherwise inhibiting the growth of mathematics and the related sciences (52).

If that was the story for scientific books in a print culture, what then of our principal concern here, namely, the journal? Well, Eisenstein tends to play down the breakthrough quality of the journal's introduction in 1652. It arrived, after all, some two hundred years after the invention of the printing press. She points out that long before the *Philosophical Transactions* was launched in 1665, and as early as 1500, the printing press was supporting the serial publication of scientific materials, the preservation and circulation of data, and the celebrated move from scientific secrecy to public disclosure through publication (1979, 462). She does allow that the journal "did contribute significantly to the sharper definition of the professional scientist, to new divisions of intellectual labor, and to the creation of the 'referee system'" (462). Yet even here the credit needs tempering. Sending someone's scientific ideas out for a second and third opinion had been unceremoniously and informally instituted in the republic of letters some time before the first issue of a scientific journal was published. Prior to launching the *Philosophical Transactions*, the journal's founder, editor, author, and publisher, Henry Oldenburg, had been tirelessly recopying, annotating, translating, and recirculating for review the letters that were sent to him as corresponding secretary for the Royal Society of London.[5] The initial vehicle for peer review was the letter. The early journal reflected the results and sometimes the very course of review-related correspondence.

What the introduction of the journal did do for science, however, was to considerably increase the reach of ideas beyond those who were likely to get hold of scientific books.[6] The journal offered a far more affordable, portable, and engaging medium than the book. The *Philosophical Transactions* was initially a sixteen-page pamphlet of miscellaneous

5. See Guédon 2001 for additional reflections on the shadow cast by Oldenburg over the current state of journal publishing.

6. In considering an earlier instance of this public reach, Falk Eisermann discusses how sensational natural phenomena—such as meteorites and conjoined twins, complete with woodcut illustrations—were reported on printed broadsides toward the end of the fifteenth century, with these incidents interpreted in political terms. Eisermann argues against the idea that these materials reached a wide audience, in favor of a more realistic sense of a readership of "humanist friends and colleagues of the authors and thus members of the ... erudite in-groups" (2003, 172).

(and sometimes fantastical) information. It supplemented—as well as reviewed and promoted—the scientific book. "There is in the Press, a New *Treatise*," Oldenburg announced in the first issue of the *Transactions* about a forthcoming work ("in the Press") by his friend and employer, "entitled, *New Observations and Experiments in order to an Experimental History of Cold*, begun by that Noble Philosopher, Mr. *Robert Boyle*" ("An Experimental History" 1664/1665).[7] The *Transactions* was part newsbook—as newspapers were originally known—part gazette and miscellany (Sommerville 1996). It was a *newspaper* for the learned, as the *Journal des sçavans* from Paris had it (after scooping the *Transactions* by only months in earning the honor of being the first scholarly journal).

Adrian Johns (2000, 163), in his own landmark study, *The Nature of the Book: Print and Knowledge in the Making*, outlines a number of reasons why printing shops began experimenting with new forms of periodical publication during the seventeenth century. Periodical publication promised a sustained print run, one issue after another, in an easily marketed form that could well build a loyal readership. But just as attractive to printing houses, given the tendency of books to be picked up and reprinted by unauthorized printers, was the periodical's seeming resistance to pirating by unscrupulous printers. Before these Robin Hoods of the reading public could print cut-rate unauthorized editions, often from outside the original publisher's country, a new issue of the original periodical would have been released. The very currency of a periodical made any copy of it that much more likely to be the real thing. A pirated version would have been so much yesterday's news. "Such rapid response strategies," as Johns puts it, "meant that the credibility of a periodical as well as its economic viability could be protected" (164).

In the case of England's first scientific journal, however, that credibility took the form of a sanctioned piracy all of its own. After all, the *Philosophical Transactions* was trafficking in the private correspondence

7. The split year, 1664/1665, reflects the dating practices at a time when England still started the new year in March, under the Julian Calendar, while the Continent started the year with January, following the Georgian Calendar. This meant that the March 6 issue of the *Philosophical Transactions* was published in 1664 in England and in 1665 on the Continent, and was marked March 6, 1664/1665, accordingly.

of the Royal Society, which had licensed the printing of the *Transactions* but offered no explicit Society sponsorship or endorsement of it (Hall 2002, 84). As its editor and publisher, in effect, Oldenburg was simply taking advantage of his position as secretary to the society to furnish this new periodical with items of scientific interest, as well as with questions for readers to respond to, lifted directly from the society's correspondence: "Inquiries for Guiny.... Whether the *Negroes* have such sharp sights, that they discover a Ship at Sea much farther off, than the *Europeans* can" (Hill 1667, 472). In its early days, the journal was a public posting of an otherwise private correspondence, signaling a further opening of science (David 2001). Oldenburg ran letters in the *Transactions* objecting to previously published letters and letters that attested to the honesty of their author: "Mr. Colepress ... assures in his Letter ... that the matter of fact was thorowly examined by himself, and that he was fully, and in all respects, satisfied of the truth thereof" ("A Relation" 1666, 380).

It must have been a common mistake to think that this journal served as the official *transactions* of the society, whereas I do have to allow that what set English-language journal publishing in motion was Oldenburg's entrepreneurial spirit, operating independently of the university and the academic community. In the first issue, published March 6, 1664/1665, Oldenburg makes no mention of the Royal Society, but instead simply explains, in his one-paragraph introduction to this new genre, that "communicating" is "necessary for promoting the improvement of Philosophical Matters" and that "it is therefore thought fit to employ the *Press*, as the most proper way to gratifie those, whose engagement in such Studies, and delight in the advancement of Learning and profitable Discoveries, doth entitle them to the knowledge of what this Kingdom, or other parts of the World, do, from time to time, afford" ("Introduction," 1664/1665, 1). This very idea of *entitlement* is, of course, critical to the question of access to such knowledge, and all the more so because it is inspired by "delight in the advancement of Learning," drawing on Bacon's sense of knowledge's belonging to the people, as William Eamon (1990, 356) has pointed out. When Oldenburg went on to dedicate the first complete volume of the *Transactions*, in 1666, to the Royal Society, he made it clear that the journal was but "the Gleanings of my *private* diversions in broken hours" ("To the Royal Society" 1665, emphasis in original).[8] It was so thoroughly Oldenburg's own diversion that the *Transactions* ceased publication for five years following his death in 1677.

By going public with the society's correspondence, the *Philosophical Transactions* provided, in effect, a middle ground for the circulation of scientific ideas between the prevailing scientific genres of published book and private letter. The journal offered something of the book's public and formal declaration of knowledge, matched by the far more immediate, dialogic, and tentative nature of the private letter. As the preface to issue 143 of the *Philosophical Transactions*, which signaled the end of the publishing hiatus that followed Oldenburg's death—an absence that was "much complained of" according to the preface—put it in 1683, the journal was already understood to be "a convenient *Register*, for the Bringing in, and Preserving many *Experiments* which, not enough for a Book, would else be lost" ("Preface" 1682/1683, 2). This register acted as an open invitation for public participation by featuring a new experimental science that was entirely a matter of seeing for oneself. It placed the scientific correspondence of the day, which reflected for Oldenburg the "friendship among learned men," into a larger public realm, making it a greater part of "the whole world of learning."[9] In creating this new middle ground, this third way, for communicating scientific ideas, the *Transactions* by no means eclipsed the vital role played by both printed book and personal letter in the circulation of knowledge.[10]

8. The only regular, though oblique, reference made to the Royal Society in the previous volumes had come at the bottom of the last page of the *Transactions*, which noted "Printed with Licence, For *John Martin* and *James Allistry*, Printers for the *Royal Society*."

9. Oldenburg wrote to Johannes Hevelius on February 18, 1662/1663: "Indeed, friendship among learned men is a great aid to investigation and elucidation of the truth; if such friendship could be spread through the whole world of learning and established among those whose minds are unfettered and above partisan zeal, because of their devotion to truth and human welfare, philosophy would be raised to its greatest heights" (Oldenburg 1966, 27).

10. See Rusnock on the continuing importance of the Society's correspondence well into the eighteenth century: "While publication and distribution of the *Philosophical Transactions* certainly contributed to the diffusion of knowledge, it did not provide for the flexibility, openness, maneuverability and relative rapidity of

Oldenburg arranged to have 1,000 copies of each issue of the *Transactions* printed, and its distribution throughout England was thought to spark the emergence of local societies in the provincial capitals, as well as serving as a book-buying guide for local readers and a focal point of coffeehouse discussions. Its ongoing invitations for readers to participate in scientific projects most notably resulted in "virtuosi," or amateur scientists, who were living close to the seashore, gathering the information about the tides in their area, as I noted earlier, that Newton needed for the *Principia* (Oldenburg 1966, 563; Hunter 1981).

That the interest in learning reflected in the society and the *Transactions* was situated outside of the universities was openly criticized by some, and others objected to the society's particular fascination with experiments, judging by Thomas Sprat's need, in his 1667 *History of the Royal Society of London, for the Improving of Natural Knowledge*, to reassure people that "Experimental Knowledge will not hinder Obedience ... to the Civil Government" (1722, 427).[11] If some objected to the society's effrontery in pursuing such knowledge outside of its proper home, a few academics were more than a little curious about the *Transactions* and what its "publick concernment" with the "private considerations" of those working on scientific questions would mean

---

interaction that correspondence did. In short, the Society's correspondence encouraged a more participatory science" (1999, 156). This desire within the Society for an open, participatory science was only to grow, leading Rusnock to conclude that "eighteenth-century correspondence networks ... set a precedent for the more fluid networks of professionals and amateurs of the more democratic nineteenth century" (169).

11. Michael Hunter holds that the universities were doing a better job of promoting science at this time than is otherwise recognized, while also crediting the contribution of scientific societies and periodicals: "In the long run the extension of science's audience could only benefit research by providing a growing body of enthusiasts and a rising tide of popular acceptance" (1981, 86). See also Shapin on how the natural history and experimental science societies that formed at the time differed from the universities: "The universities, after all, were important institutions in forming the character of the young.... The new societies aimed to provide a novel organizational form uniquely suited to the new practice; they made the production of new knowledge, rather than the just guardianship of and commentary on the old, central to their identity; and they aimed, with varying degrees of success, to link the progress of science to civic concerns rather than wholly scholarly or religious ones" (1996, 133).

for knowledge. At least that is how Isaac Newton framed the question in a letter that he sent Oldenburg on January 29, 1672, granting Oldenburg consent to publish in the *Philosophical Transactions* an earlier letter that Newton had sent him on his reflecting telescope (Newton 1959, 84).[12]

Just how the pull between public concernments and private considerations played out in the earliest days of this new periodical literature is made particularly vivid by the circumstances surrounding what might fairly be called Newton's one and only journal article. Newton, who had assumed the Lucasian Chair of Mathematics and Natural Philosophy at the University of Cambridge at the age of twenty-seven in 1670, was certainly not one to be readily drawn into public exchanges and remains to this day famous for his secretive nature. Yet he seems to have quickly realized the scientific value of the very public *Philosophical Transactions*, judging by the extensive notes he made on it beginning in its first few years of publication.[13] On January 2, 1671, Oldenburg wrote to Newton to convey that the members of the Royal Society had seen great merit in Newton's reflecting telescope, which had been demonstrated at a society meeting, and they were keen to help "secure" the invention for Newton by sending details of it to Christiaan Huygens in Paris (Newton 1959, 73). This expression of support and interest must have impressed Newton, for two weeks later, on January 18, he wrote to Oldenburg about presenting to the society "an accompt of a Philosophical discovery ... being in my Judgment the oddest if not the most considerable detection wch hath hitherto beene made in the operations of Nature" (82–83).

12. Newton wrote to Oldenburg (January 29, 1671/1672) that he was "willing to submit my private considerations in any thing that may bee thought of publick concernment" (1959, 84).

13. John Maynard Keynes's précis describes Newton as given to "a profound shrinking from the world, a paralyzing fear of exposing his thoughts, his beliefs, his discoveries in all nakedness to the inspection and criticism of the world" (1947, 28). Jan Golinski, writing on Newton's "secret life as an alchemist," notes that "the correspondence between Newton and John Locke that followed Robert Boyle's death in 1691 reveals that Newton and Boyle had entered into a pact to share knowledge about the mercury preparation, and not to communicate it to others" (1988, 155).

Newton's subsequent letter of February 6 on his optics experiments was read before the society, and when Oldenburg not surprisingly requested permission to publish the letter on optics, Newton's reply conveyed his support for this public exposure as both a duty and a privilege: "For believe me Sr I doe not onely esteem it a duty to concurre with them in ye promotion of reall knowledge, but a great privelege that instead of exposing discourses to a prejudic't & censorious multitude (by wch means many truths have been bafled & lost) I may with freedom apply my self to so judicious & impartiall an Assembly" (Newton 1959, 108–109).[14] When it came to Newton's estimation of his own work, he "thought it too straight & narrow for publick view," and yet he appears persuaded by how the "R.S. [Royal Society] have thought it fit to appear publickly" (109). This was again the journal offering a middle ground, enabling one to test an idea with an interested public without yet committing it to book form.[15] The letter was published less than two weeks later, taking up the first dozen pages of the February 19, 1671/1672, issue, no. 80 of the *Philosophical Transactions*.

Oldenburg introduces it as "*A Letter of Mr.* Isaac Newton, *Professor in the Mathematicks in the University of Cambridge; containing his New Theory about Light and Colors: sent by the Author to the Publisher from Cambridge, Febr. 6, 1671/72; in order to be communicated to the* R. Society" (Newton 1671/1672, 3075). The article then begins with a salutatory "SIR," as if Newton were indeed addressing a letter to Oldenburg, and in the same spirit, it opens with a reference to his previous

14. The letter was read to the society, after which Oldenburg wrote back to Newton that "they voted unanimously, that if you contradicted it not, this discourse should without delay be printed," with the point made that it was again to protect it from being "snatched from you" (Newton 1959, 107).

15. It may have been, as Charles Bazerman suggests, that Newton saw the *Transactions* as "an opportunity to present his own findings in preview of the book version of his lectures he was preparing," and certainly Oldenburg and others used the *Transactions* to advertise and promote scientific books, but given that Newton's *Opticks* did not appear for another thirty years, in 1704, it seems more likely that Newton felt the pull of the new journal medium and its prospects for promoting knowledge (1988, 88). Newton published *Opticks* a year after the death of Robert Hooke, who had raised a number of challenges to Newton's theories (Kuhn 1978, 37).

(unpublished) letter: "To perform my late promise to you, I shall without further ceremony acquaint you, that in the beginning ..." (3075). With Oldenburg going unnamed in this letter, the *you* in Newton's phrase "my late promise to you" might be read as addressing the reader, reflecting the otherwise unstated promise that authors and scientists commit to in making their work public. Yet it could also be said that Newton had made a promise to himself, which was to test the value of giving his idea this sort of public hearing.

If Newton's article in the *Philosophical Transactions* reads like a personal letter in its opening, he concludes it with a public invitation to the Royal Society membership and readers at large: "This, I conceive, is enough for an Introduction to Experiments of this kind, which if any of the *R. Society* shall be so curious as to prosecute, I should be very glad to be informed with what success: That, if any thing seem to be defective, or to thwart this relation, I may have an opportunity of giving further direction about it, or acknowledging my errors, if I have committed any." As it turns out, some did come forward with imagined defects in this relation, and Newton ended up responding to objections and questions raised by Robert Moray, Ignace Gaston Pardies, Robert Hooke, Christiaan Huygens, and Francis Linus, with much of the correspondence published in the *Transactions* over the subsequent four years.

Newton's published letter constituted the first substantial scientific article, according to Thomas Kuhn (1978, 27), to appear in the *Transactions*. Yet the publication of this letter proved to be a more open and immediate forum for his work than Newton was willing to bear, and he did not again use the journal to publish his experimental pursuits but relied exclusively on the unhurried book, most notably with the *Principia*, published fifteen years later in 1687.

Newton may have had little taste for clarifying his work, and *tedious* is a word that he uses more than once in discussing the level of detail he felt was necessary to help his critics see the light. Yet Oldenburg's publication of the challenges and responses that arose around Newton's theory of light demonstrated how crucial such public exchanges were to advancing knowledge that was at issue.[16] What transacted was at times no more than Newton delimiting what he had already written against the broader sense that his readers wanted to make of his work on optics: "I never intended to show," he wrote Oldenburg on April 3, 1673, in response to a letter from Huygens, "wherein consists the nature and difference of colors, but onely to show that *de facto* they are originall and immutable qualities of the rays wch exhibit them" (1959, 264).[17]

The public exchange over Newton's article led Oldenburg to consider a form of *blind* review to reduce the play of personalities in the judgment of scientific work. He wrote to Newton on May 2, 1672, asking whether "ye names of the objectors, especially if they desire it may be so, be omitted, and their objections only urged: since those of the R. Society ought to aime at nothing, but the discovery of truth, and ye improvemt of knowledge, and not at the prostituting of persons for their mis-apprehensions or mistakes" (Newton 1959, 151). On May 4, Newton responded that he was "not at all concerned whether Objections be printed with or without ye Objectors [*sic*] names" (154). Yet Newton may well have begun to question the value of the exchange itself, given that ten months later, he sought to withdraw from the Royal Society. His letter to Oldenburg on March 8, 1672/1673, conveys this desire: "for although I honor that body ... yet since I see that I shall neither profit them, nor (by reason of distance) can partake of the advantage of their Assemblies" (262). He was persuaded to remain, though he rarely attended the society's meetings, at least until he was elected president in 1703. For four years after the optics letter was published in 1671/1672, Newton continued to respond to the queries and challenges that were sent to him, via Oldenburg, until finally requesting that Oldenburg send no more letters on the matter. The exchange proved a formative experience in the public quality of science, as it led Newton to more explicit

16. All of the correspondence was directed through Oldenburg—in yet a further mix of private and public audiences—just as Oldenburg judged which letters to publish, omitting, for example, Hooke's respectful initial response to Newton, while publishing Newton's occasionally harsh replies in their entirety (see Kuhn 1978, 38–39). In a letter of April 13, 1672, Newton asked Oldenburg to edit his responses, "rendering any expressions more perspicuous or less ambiguous" before "you commit [my responses] to ye presse" (1959, 139).

17. Newton's (1673) letter was published in the *Philosophical Transactions* in July 1673, preceded by an extract of Huygens's letter.

descriptions of his experimental techniques and in formulating arguments for his work through a published exchange.[18]

As mentioned earlier in the chapter, following Oldenburg's death in 1677, the *Philosophical Transactions* ceased publication, until the Royal Society resuscitated it five years later, amid an established market for experimental science periodicals consisting of both new and pirated titles. When the *Transactions* reemerged in January of 1682/1683, it opened with a preface that again went some distance in disavowing the journal's official status with the Royal Society: "Although the Writing of these *Transactions*, is not to be looked upon as the *Business* of the *Royal Society* ..." ("Preface" 1682/1683, 2). The society did stand behind the publication, at a distance, as it did not wish to "seem now to Condemn a Work, they have formerly encouraged; or to neglect the just Expectations of Learned and Ingenious Men." The members of the society were clearly torn between embracing this newfound public interest in its work that Oldenburg had built up and keeping to its own internal business as a scholarly society for its members to present and hear ideas.

The society's equivocation over how involved it should become in publicizing its private activities was further asserted in volume 47 of the *Transactions*, for the years 1751 and 1752, with an "Advertisement," which was to remain a constant frontispiece for each subsequent volume published over the next two centuries ("Advertisement" 1753). It again distances the Royal Society from the journal, which was to be seen as

---

18. In Thomas Kuhn's estimation, this exchange marked a "novel pattern of public announcement, discussion, and ultimate achievement of professional consensus science [which] has advanced ever since" (1978, 28). He identifies the Royal Society and the *Philosophical Transactions* with "a new conception of science as a cooperative enterprise with utilitarian goals" in which "the experimental contribution to an ultimate reconstruction of a system of nature" became more important than the "construction of the system itself" and that lent itself to the experiment-reporting journal article over the system-building book (28). Charles Bazerman holds that as a result of Newton's confronting his critics, "Newton had now satisfactorily solved how to present his optical findings in a compelling manner within a critical forum of competing researchers" (1988, 116). For Steven Shapin, "the confrontation over Newton's optical work can stand as an emblem of the fragmented knowledge-making legacies of the seventeenth century" (1996, 117).

nothing more than "the single act of respective Secretaries." This needed to be clearly stated, the advertisement held, because too often the publication had been erroneously identified as the *Transactions of the Royal Society* by "several authors, both at home and abroad": "Whereas in truth the Society, as a body, never did interest themselves any further in their publication, than by occasionally recommending the revival of them to some of their secretaries...." What interest the society showed toward the *Transactions* had been, according to the advertisement, "with a view to satisfy the public, that their usual meetings were then continued for the improvement of knowledge, and benefit of mankind, the great ends of their first institution by the royal charters, and which they have ever since steadily pursued." The *Transactions* stood as a limited act of public accountability, while the society's real business of holding knowledge up to critical scrutiny and appreciation went on in "their usual meetings."[19]

The society appears to have been torn between serving, if not feeding, the "just expectations" of the "Learned and Ingenious" and its admirable desire not to abuse its own authority by accrediting experiments and accounts that it was reluctant to verify or authorize as a society. The society's proposed resolution of this dilemma, according to the 1752 advertisement, was to set up a committee, as the advertisement put it, "to reconsider the papers read before them, and select out of them such, as they should judge most proper for publication in the future *Transactions*." The selection of items was to be made on the basis of "the importance or singularity of their subjects, or the advantageous manner of treating them." The society made it clear that setting up an editorial committee for the *Transactions* was being undertaken "without pretending to answer for the certainty of the facts, or propriety of the reasonings" for such judgments. Nor should readers ever expect it to be so. After all, the "established rule" of the society, the advertisement reminded readers—"to which they will always adhere"—was "never to

19. One factor that may have contributed to the Royal Society's decision not to become more directly involved in the journal was John Hill's publication of a *Review of the Works of the Royal Society* in 1751, which attacked the *Philosophical Transactions* for its inclusion of "trivial and downright foolish articles" (quoted in Gross, Harmon, and Reidy 2002, 51).

give their opinion, as a body, upon any subject, either or nature or art, that comes before them."

This "established rule" not to give an opinion is presented without explanation. The advertisement does go on to refer to "the dishonour of the Society" that could be brought about by those who, having presented their "several projects, inventions, and curiosities of various kinds" to the society, went on to claim its endorsement "in the public newspapers." The Royal Society's good name was, it felt, being pilfered and pirated. This was a poor enough return on its efforts to enhance the circulation of knowledge, which the society had undertaken out of its belief that only through such circulation—in meetings, letters, and publications—could one hope to test and advance knowledge. For there would be no final recourse, in this republic of science, to a conclusive and final pronouncement from a single authoritative body.

The Royal Society was advertising, in effect, its belief in the tentative quality of knowledge, letting the public know that it placed its faith in the open circulation of ideas rather than in official forms of endorsement. Although human vanity would readily lead an author to believe that appearing before the society or in the *Philosophical Transactions* was a great endorsement of one's ideas, society members wished to temper such vanities—including the public's willingness to believe what they found in print—without giving up on the powerful means the *Transactions* afforded them of circulating the current state of knowledge. The advertisement served as an epistemic warning label. The society stopped running it only in the 1950s, presumably because by that point, although perhaps well before, scientific journals had taken on an entirely academic role, safely removed from public view, as if they were once more a members-only affair. Only in our own day has the Royal Society actively sought a greater public role for its scientific contribution, and it now issues its own "Media Releases," "Issues in the News," and other public pronouncements, which are made readily available to the public through its Web site.

What the printing press opened for science, with the gradual emergence of a periodical literature dedicated to experimental inquiry in the seventeenth century, was both a greater reach and a level of exchange that did this emerging field no end of good. It is as if the members of the society had come to realize that the larger circulation of their work was a risky but necessary business. Yes, the authority of the society could be easily misrepresented; it could be stolen or pirated away. Or more dangerously, more culpably, the society could be mistaken, within the pages of the *Philosophical Transactions*, for certifying or endorsing some final, permanent truth in what it circulated, and that would undermine a basic principle in science, which holds that knowledge lives through the scope of its circulation, and thus through its very susceptibility to contention and alteration.

Journal publication and what followed from it may have proved too tedious for Newton, but it must have been clear to the society's members that it was unquestionably good for science. Certainly, Oldenburg had been driven by economic opportunity and necessity in his tireless work on the *Transactions*. Yet his skillful handling of the interested if apprehensive Newton proved crucial to opening scientific discourse further to a larger community. The value of what Oldenburg and Newton did together in the early 1670s lies in the formation of a viable alternative to the very limited circulation of the society's correspondence and to the far less accessible or open book. Yet in those early years, it is good to remember, the journal's business model was never quite adequate, as Oldenburg would be the first to attest. Yet the journal quickly found a following. Its public sales gave rise to far more than a passing or passive reading, as this audience proved itself willing and able to participate in the advancement of knowledge. What was then a risky, untested form of publication challenged how the Royal Society, as well as the university community, went about doing science, leading them to see the value of greater openness and access to the work they were doing. If Newton had his doubts about whether the access principle was worth the price of having to explain oneself repeatedly, Oldenburg never let go of the principle. As a result, Oldenburg was part of a publishing revolution in the sciences, with the assistance of Newton's one big concession to the principle.

Today, open access to research and scholarship represents another kind of upheaval in scholarly publishing. It has already begun to make a radical difference for faculty and students in developing countries. It is attracting increasing support from governments and foundations. It is building on parallel developments that are opening scientific databases and creating clinical trial registries. This openness is inspiring amateur astronomers and historians to contribute to the study of the heavens and the past. It is feeding a growing public interest in health information that could well spread to other areas of people's lives. It is leading to a new sense of entitlement to knowledge, much as the printing press did with the Bible, more than five centuries ago.

For their part, more than a few scholars have begun to look up from their work and have taken the opportunities posed by this new publishing medium to further the public good that their work represents, whether by entering a paper into an e-print archive or by pushing the associations to which they belong to consider forms of open access publishing and data sharing. Open access is setting a new standard for the circulation of research and scholarship. It is changing what it means to contribute to the world of learning, to subject work to review and critique. It is showing every sign of being able to sustain a wide range of new economic models for scholarly associations and commercial publishers.

The case presented here, however, has not only been about the why and how of open access, but about the need to improve the quality and value of that access. The case for open access is multifaceted. It draws on the spirit of copyright law, the mandate of scholarly associations, the promise of global knowledge exchanges, the right to know, the prospect of enhanced reading and indexing, the improved economic efficiencies of publishing, and the history of the academic journal, which speaks to the courage—and risk—of new ventures at opening this world of learning.

In the process of making this case, I have drawn on my own experiences developing software that supports open access journals and complements the work done on open source archiving software, and I have proposed ways for scholarly associations and research libraries to play a greater role in managing and structuring access, whether through the formation of open access publishing and archiving cooperatives or by hosting open access journals and e-print archives. Yet I know that there is no way of predicting what will turn out to be the best means for increasing the circulation of knowledge in the years ahead. It could well take surprisingly new forms. But I can predict that only a steady stream of arguments, instances, and studies—each unequivocally demonstrating the value of open access—will make what is now the promise of increased access part of the research culture of the academy. For that to happen, something approaching this *principle of access* will need to become a greater part of what we talk about when we talk about the history and philosophy of science, or the contribution of the humanities, or the role of the social sciences.

How knowledge circulates has always been vital to the life of the mind, which all of us share, just as it is vital, ultimately, to the well-being of humanity. At this point, the access principle may still be far too caught up in the sheer mechanics and detailed economics of moving journal publishing into this new publishing medium. Grand principles can be lost amid emerging technical standards for automated systems, linking tools, and indexing protocols. The quandaries of detail will pass. New standards and conventions, as well as expectations of access, will take hold, as we come to understand the potential of the medium better. What will continue to guide this process in principle, I hope as a scholar, educator, and reader, is a right of access to the fruits of inquiry and study.

Appendixes

Appendix A

Ten Flavors of Open Access

Only by working with a loosely defined approach to open access archiving and publishing can one begin to capture the variety of and variation in the means that are now being used to increase access to scholarship and research. I have grouped the current variations into ten flavors or models, based largely on how they are financed and the nature of the access that they provide (table A.1). A number of these flavors place restrictions on access that contravene one or more of the well-worked-out definitions of *open access*, but all increase access to the journal literature over traditional models of scholarly publishing (see, for example, "Budapest Open Access Initiative" 2002; "Bethesda Statement" 2003).

1. Home page open access: Researchers first began to make their work freely available on the Internet by posting it on home pages, either their personal ones or those provided by their university departments. Kristin Antelman (2004) found, in a study of 2,000 papers published in 1999–2002 across four disciplines, that although an open access version could be found for 40 percent of the papers, half of those open access versions were found on the author's home page.[1] The principal distinction

1. In Antelman's (2004) study, 69 percent of the mathematics papers were available in open access versions (with 30 percent on personal Web sites and 60 percent in archives); 37 percent of the electrical and electronic engineering papers had open access versions (with 50 percent of those on personal Web sites and 18 percent in archives); 29 percent of the political science papers had open access versions (with 43 percent on personal Web sites and 6 percent in archives); and 17 percent of the philosophy papers had open access versions (with 72 percent on personal Web sites and 14 percent in archives).

Table A.1
Ten flavors of open access to journal articles

Type of open access	Economic models	Journal or portal example
Home page	University department maintains home pages for individual faculty members on which they place their papers and make them freely available.[a]	http://www.econ.ucsb.edu/~tedb/
E-print archive	An institution or academic subject area underwrites the hosting and maintenance of repository software, enabling members to self-archive published and unpublished materials.[a]	arXiv.org E-Print Archive
Author fee	Author fees support immediate and complete access to open access journals (or, in some cases, to the individual articles for which fees were paid), with institutional and national memberships available to cover author fees.[a]	BioMed Central
Subsidized	Subsidy from scholarly society, institution and/or government/foundation enables immediate and complete access to open access journal.[a]	*First Monday*
Dual-mode	Subscriptions are collected for print edition and used to sustain both print edition and online open access edition.[a]	*Journal of Postgraduate Medicine*
Delayed	Subscription fees are collected for print edition and immediate access to online edition, with open access provided to content after a period of time (e.g., six to twelve months).	*New England Journal of Medicine*
Partial	Open access is provided to a small selection of articles in each issue— serving as a marketing tool—whereas access to the rest of the issue requires subscription.	*Lancet*
Per capita	Open access is offered to scholars and students in developing countries as a charitable contribution, with expense limited to registering institutions in an access management system.	HINARI

Table A.1
(continued)

Type of open access	Economic models	Journal or portal example
Indexing	Open access to bibliographic information and abstracts is provided as a government service or, for publishers, a marketing tool, often with links to pay per view for the full text of articles.	ScienceDirect
Cooperative	Member institutions (e.g., libraries, scholarly associations) contribute to support of open access journals and development of publishing resources.[a]	German Academic Publishers

a. Supports "open access" as defined by the Budapest Open Access Initiative (2002) and Bethesda Statement on Open Access Publishing (2003), although some users may impose restrictions that fall outside these definitions (e.g., Bethesda Statement: "Grant(s) to all users a free, irrevocable, worldwide, perpetual right of access to, and a license to copy, use, distribute, transmit and display the work publicly and to make and distribute derivative works, in any digital medium for any responsible purpose, subject to proper attribution of authorship, as well as the right to make small numbers of printed copies for their personal use" [2003]). See also p. 27, n. 14.

between papers placed on personal home pages and those placed in an institutional or disciplinary e-print archive is the archive's indexing of the papers for a global research indexing system.

2. Open access e-print archive: Authors are increasingly permitted by the journals in which they publish to place a copy of their work, whether prior to publishing or after, in an open access e-print archive or institutional repository. The overwhelming majority of journals now enable authors to self-archive in this way.[2] An e-print archive may be

2. Elizabeth Gadd, Charles Oppenheim, and Steve Probets (2003) reported that in 2002, a little less than half the publishers in their study permitted both preprint and postprint self-archiving, with a third allowing postprint and 20 percent specifying preprint only. John Cox and Laura Cox (2003) found that in 2003, 60 percent of publishers permitted posting of the final published version of an article. As of February 2005, in a sample of 8,950 journals, 13 percent allowed preprints only to be posted and 79 percent allowed postprints, for a total of 92 percent of publishers permitting self-archiving ⟨http://romeo.eprints.org/stats.php⟩.

organized around a discipline—most notably that in high-energy physics by the arXiv.org E-Print Archive located at Cornell University (Ginsparg 2001)—or be run by a university for its faculty, as with DSpace at MIT. Open source or free software is available for setting up e-print archives, and the contents of these archives are indexed, following the global research standard set by the Open Archives Initiative. The e-print archive concept has grown out of the preprint circulation of manuscripts in some of the sciences, making it something of a foreign idea for the humanities and social sciences, where published articles often serve as a "preprint" for a subsequent book by the author. Nonetheless, Stevan Harnad (2003b) persuasively argues that the e-print archive offers a far more immediate path to open access than the prospect of converting the existing set of research journals to, or replacing them with, open access equivalents.[3]

3. Author fee open access: The most prominent form of immediate and unqualified open access to journals is currently found in the biomedical sciences and is based on charging authors a fee of somewhere between $500 and $3,000 for published articles. The leading corporate entry into the open access field, BioMed Central, uses author fees (in the area of $500) with its more than 100 journals, as does the Public Library of Science with *PloS Biology* and *PLoS Medicine* (at a rate of $1,500). Author fees can be covered by institutional (and even national) memberships. A further variation on the author fee version makes the purchase of open access optional. Springer's Open Choice program gives authors the option of purchasing, in effect, open access for their own article ($3,000), and *Florida Entomologist* and the journals of the Entomological Society of America provide a similar, if less expensive, service (Walker 2001).

4. Subsidized open access: A second form of immediate and unqualified access is made possible through a variety of subsidies that journals

3. It is worth noting that despite a sustained focus on self-archiving, Harnad holds to "the need to take both roads to open access," referring to self-archiving and open access journals (2003c). For open source e-print archiving software, see, among others, the Web sites for GNU Eprints Software ⟨http://software .eprints.org/⟩ and DSpace ⟨http://dspace.org⟩.

are able to secure for publishing, whether from scholarly societies, university departments, government agencies, or foundations. Journals that offer this type of open access charge neither author nor reader and typically publish only online. Of all the forms of open access, this one perhaps relies the most heavily on the volunteer labor of editors playing multiple roles, with journals such as *Education Policy Analysis Archives*, for example, running on a zero budget, apart from the editor's time and Internet bandwidth, both supported in this case by Arizona State University.

5. Dual-mode open access: Some journals that continue to publish in print through the sale of subscriptions have decided at the same time to publish an electronic edition that offers immediate and complete open access to the entire contents of the print edition. The *Journal of Postgraduate Medicine*, one of the oldest medical journals in India and a publication of the Staff Society of Seth G. S. Medical College and K. E. M. Hospital in Mumbai, publishes in this dual mode of open access.

6. Delayed open access: What might be thought of as a more conservative fiscal version of the dual mode is deployed by the *New England Journal of Medicine* and other journals, which continue to sell print editions and online access to subscribers, while offering open access to articles some period of time, typically six months, after initial publication. Whether the dual-mode and delayed versions of open access represent a transition to online-only publishing remains to be seen.

7. Partial open access: A further option for increasing access among subscription-based journals has been to make a small number of articles in each issue free to read. On registering with *Lancet* at no cost, for example, one is offered open access to designated articles, as well as other services. One variation of this approach is exemplified by the Institute of Physics, which publishes some forty journals and provides free access to the journals' contents for the first thirty days after an article's publication, while asking readers to adhere to "fair use" with this access.

8. Per capita open access: For those in developing countries, which have been hardest hit by journal price increases, a measure of relief has been established through programs such as the World Health Organization's HINARI project, which makes over 2,000 medical journals freely available online to qualifying institutions in countries with a gross national product per capita of less than $1,000. Another instance of this approach is found in the success of the International Network for the Availability of Scientific Publications in negotiating electronic access to a wide range of journals for developing countries in Africa (Smart 2003).

9. *Open access indexing*: Two major sources of open access or free indexes to the journal literature are the U.S. government–sponsored PubMed in the life sciences and ERIC in education. In addition, open access indexing is available through a number of publishers' portals that provide free access to journals' tables of contents, as well as the bibliographic information and abstracts of the articles they publish. For example, Reed Elsevier provides this type of access for its 1,800 journals through ScienceDirect, with links to a pay-per-view service for full-text access. Additional open access indexes for research resources include CiteSeer.IST, which is a citation index, and OAIster, which also indexes research databases.

10. *Open access cooperative*: The German Academic Publishers Project, run by the Universities of Hamburg, Karlsruhe, and Oldenburg, is a cooperative dedicated to making open access viable for German academic journals by centralizing the development of management and publishing systems and operating through membership, enabling the cooperative to "offer an organizational and technical infrastructure to partners interested in exploring new paths in academic electronic publishing," according to its Web site ⟨http://www.gap-portal.de⟩ (see also Braun 2003).

Appendix B

Scholarly Association Budgets

I gathered financial information from twenty-one American scholarly associations, distributed across a range of disciplines, using their publicly available tax filings (table B.1).[1] This sample does not include any societies that have a large professional, nonacademic component to their membership, such as the American Chemical Society (with a revenue exceeding $300 million). Although the associations' publishing expenses (and revenues) reported here also cover books and other materials, journal publishing appears to make up the majority of the costs and includes the support of the editors, the editorial offices, copyediting, composition, printing, and distribution. For the eleven associations in the sample that turn to commercial publishers and university presses to produce their journals, the associations' "publishing costs" refer to the amount paid to the publisher or press through a variety of arrangements. Among current arrangements, the publisher Taylor and Francis, for example, gives the International Association for Feminist Economics a 25 percent discount on copies of its journal *Feminist Economics* purchased for its members, in return for the right to sell subscriptions outside the association's membership. The American Psychological Society, on the other hand, pays Blackwell a flat fee of $20 per member for the publication of

1. Internal Revenue Service Form 990 (Return of Organization Exempt from Income Tax) states that it is "open to public inspection" and must be filed by nonprofit organizations with a revenue of over $25,000. The filed forms are available from the GuideStar Web site ⟨http://www.guidestar.org/⟩.

Table B.1
American scholarly associations' annual publication budgets in 2000

Scholarly associations	Total revenue[a]
Academy of Political Science[c]	$679,894
African Studies Association	382,240
American Anthropological Association[c]	4,680,764
American Astronomical Society[c]	8,683,893
American Education Research Association[c]	5,104,541
American Economic Association[c]	4,501,541
American Federation for Medical Research	842,744
American Historical Association[c]	3,350,835
American Political Science Association	6,524,835
American Psychological Society[c]	2,248,227
American Society for Cell Biology[c]	5,277,253
American Society for Information Science[c]	1,185,074
American Society of Human Genetics	3,319,369
American Studies Association[c]	651,251
Cognitive Science Society[c]	123,002
History of Science Society	99,825
International Association for Feminist Economics	143,156
Linguistic Society of America[c]	864,798
Microscopy Society of America	1,058,897
National Reading Conference	358,573
Radiation Research Society[c]	919,855
Averages	$2,428,594

Note: Data are drawn from Internal Revenue Service Form 990 for the year 2000, available from GuideStar.org. Parentheses indicate a negative amount.

a. Total revenue includes membership fees, whereas publication revenue does not.

b. Combines journal and conference expenses.

c. Association's journal(s) available online through the University of British Columbia Library.

d. Association's journal(s) published by university press or commercial publisher.

A Publication revenue	B Royalties	C Publication costs	(A + B) − C Revenue over costs
$12,128	$16,434	$265,878	($237,316)
37,715	0	344,826	(307,111)
637,950	6,679	790,133	(145,504)
6,404,038[d]	0	6,294,050	109,988
591,011	55,431	1,073,930	(204,783)
1,685,640	0	3,974,715	(2,289,075)
124,600[d]	11,869	268,253	(131,784)
725,514	22,464	1,406,567	(681,053)
84,397	129,819	840,616	(626,400)
211,648[d]	0	328,765	(117,117)
1,493,454[d]	121,767	1,208,136	428,264
259,889[d]	0	208,071	(51,818)
1,294,395[d]	82,025	1,072,869	303,551
211,684[d]	438	193,460	(8,662)
0[d]	2,434	104,490[b]	(102,056)
201,500[d]	0	141,007	60,493
0[d]	6,872	71,718	(64,846)
5,761	8,549	272,438	(258,128)
74,187[d]	0	94,314	(20,127)
10,010	17,790	44,429	(16,629)
497,085	0	347,595	149,490
$691,873	$22,918	$921,250	($206,459)

its two principal journals, *Psychological Science* and *Current Directions in Psychological Science*.[2]

2. Blackwell currently publishes the journals of some 500 societies. Also, the European Economics Association recently moved its journal, *European Economic Review*, from Elsevier (which was charging libraries $950 annually) to MIT Press ($325 annually), at which point Elsevier made it known that it had provided the association with more than $500,000 in profit sharing over the sixteen years of their association (Glenn 2003).

Appendix C

Journal Management Economies

The key to economic viability for open access is not simply to find an alternative revenue stream to cover the subscription income lost as a result of providing open access to journal contents. For some portion of that lost revenue can be recovered by reducing the costs of running the journal, archive, or index in making the move to an online medium. To illustrate the potential savings that can be realized using an online journal management system, I draw on the example of Open Journal Systems, which is open source (freely distributed) software developed by the Public Knowledge Project (table C.1).

Briefly, a system such as OJS sets up a Web site for a journal, and that Web site serves as an editorial office for not only editors, but reviewers, authors, copyeditors, and others as well. OJS also sees to the labeling, filing, and tracking of all submissions and guides the submission through each of the necessary steps, ensuring that it lands on the right desktop at the right time in the editorial process. So when it comes to calculating the savings from using such a system, one can begin with those associated not having to maintain an editorial office. The journal's virtual online editorial office is available, with complete records and materials, through the system, from any computer plugged into the Internet. On submitting a paper, authors are presented with a template to fill in that includes indexing categories (keywords, coverage, etc.) and relevant examples (provided by the journal's editors)—reducing the cost of indexing down the road—and in turn, authors can submit their work without the need to print out and make copies of the submission and mail them

Table C.1
E-journal management systems savings (in relation to print journals) based on Open Journal Systems

Stage	Agent	Automated and assisted journal management	Savings
Submission	Author	a. Manuscript, appendices, data, instruments, etc., uploaded to journal in a variety of file formats b. Templates provided to assist author in indexing work	Clerical time, copying, postage, courier, stationery, editor time
Submission	Editor	a. Author notified of submission receipt b. Submission dated and queued for review c. File readily modified (e.g., remove author's name)	
Peer review	Editor	a. Reviewer contacts, interests, and record maintained b. Reviewer contacted with title, abstract, date, etc. c. Review due date, with reminders, thanks, available d. Review progress tracked (and viewable by author)	
Peer review	Reviewer	Comments managed and editor contacted	
Editor review	Editor	a. Author notified with access provided to reviews (complete or excerpts) and marked copies b. Complete archival record of review process maintained	
Revisions	Editor	a. Back-and-forth with author and submission facilitated b. Paper recirculated among reviewers, as needed	
Editing	Copyeditor Proofreader	a. Link to editor and author, re: submission queries b. Link to Layout for proofreading changes	
Layout	Editor	Manages multiple formats (HTML, .pdf, PostScript) with previews	Printing services, time

Publishing	Editor	a. One-click scheduling and ordering of articles and sections b. Volume and number, special issue, assignment	
Distribution	Editor	Automated e-mail notification of contents to readers, authors, and editors	Postage, packaging, time
Indexing	Readers	a. Automated harvesting of article metadata by Open Archives Initiative engines, including citation indexes b. Articles linked to relevant items in open access databases, based on article's keywords	Third-party indexing services
Interchange	Readers Authors	Comments to articles posted and online forum maintained for continuing exchange on range of themes	Not otherwise available
Archiving	Host library or society	Server maintenance, backup, and content migration to new systems provided by Web host	Hosting and storage
Upgrading	Open Journal Systems	Continued system development provided by open source community	Software

to the journal, significant factors for those working in developing countries, if somewhat offset by the price of an Internet café, which many faculty members in these countries have to use to access an online journal submission system.

Online journal management systems are structured around the workflow required to review, edit, and publish submissions, with records maintained of who is doing what and when. Such a system typically uses a prepared set of e-mails to contact the necessary people at each step: authors, editors (managing, section, and layout), reviewers, copyeditors, and proofreaders. These e-mails, which are used to coordinate among these various participants in the process, contain the necessary information for each submission and can be edited in advance and on the fly. Now, such a journal management system needs to be hosted on a Web server. Most commercial journal management systems provide hosting as part of their centralized service, which adds to their cost for journals using their services. With an open source system, such as OJS, a local Web server is used, and many journals using OJS have it hosted on a university library or other institutional Web server.

To take an example of how a journal management system such as OJS works in action, consider the most common task of an editor, namely, assigning two or more reviewers to evaluate a manuscript for possible publication. The editor logs onto OJS through her Internet browser, whether at the office, home, or on the road (a cell phone version of the software has yet to created). On entering the journal's Web site, the editor first comes to a table indicating the current state of her assignments, with some submissions still waiting for receipt of an overdue review, and others that are brand new, requiring peer reviewers to be assigned to them. With the new submissions, the system has already notified the author with a standard e-mail indicating that the manuscript was successfully uploaded to the journal and provided the author with a user name and password for tracking its progress through the editorial process as well as participating in revisions, copyediting, and proofreading if it is accepted.

The editor goes to the Submission Review page for one of the new submissions and downloads the paper to see if it is suitable for the journal and ready for review. Once satisfied on these two points, the editor then clicks a Select Reviewer button. This takes the editor to a list of reviewers that indicates each reviewer's areas of interest and the date his or her last review was assigned and completed, as well as how many reviews he or she has completed, and possibly a rating of the reviewer for timeliness and quality of review, if the journal has chosen this feature. The editor scrolls or searches for a suitable reviewer, or decides to enter the name of a new reviewer, before clicking the Assign button. The Assign button causes a series of windows to appear, the first of which asks whether the requested review's due date should fall within the standard number of weeks for the journal or be modified. This window is followed by a second one, containing a prepared e-mail, addressed to the reviewer from the editor, which invites the review, presents the paper's title and abstract, and provides a password for the reviewer to use to visit the site and download the paper (or it attaches the paper to the e-mail, if the editor chooses that option in setting up the journal). The editor can personalize the e-mail or otherwise edit it before sending it to the reviewer. Once it is sent, the name of the reviewer, along with the date the invitation was made and the deadline date for the review, is recorded on the Submission Review page for that paper in association with the reviewer's name. All this can be accomplished in the time it might otherwise take the editor, in a print model, to instruct an editorial assistant to check when a certain colleague had last reviewed for the journal. The editor then moves on to select the second reviewer for that particular submission.[1]

1. According to Fytton Rowland's study (2003), the current average cost that journals attribute to the peer review process is $400 per published paper.

Appendix D

An Open Access Cooperative

The proposal for an *open access publishing and archiving cooperative* is intended to suggest a not-so-new economic model, given the long history of cooperatives, for increasing access to research on a sustainable basis. It would bring together research libraries, scholarly associations, and publishing bodies (such as university presses, publishers' research institutes, and groups of scholars), most of which have reason enough to collaborate on creating a wide-scale open access publishing model. The cooperative model is particularly suited to supporting journals in those academic disciplines, whether in the humanities, social sciences, or even the sciences, in which typical levels of grant funding cannot be reasonably expected to support an author fee approach to open access.

The basic economic principles underlying the cooperative are divided between those that affect libraries and those that pertain to publishers. For libraries, such a cooperative would provide a means of containing and reducing the costs of journal access, by utilizing existing capacities and expertise within many research libraries. For scholarly societies, university presses, or independent groups of scholars, it would allow a focus on scholarly quality with maximum readership (through open access), with predictable revenue lines and access to the information science and systems expertise of participating research libraries. For publishers, there may be opportunities for service and management contracts with the cooperative. The open access feature of the cooperative can help the libraries fulfill their public-service mandate and publishers achieve their common long-term goals of improving scholarly communication in an economically responsible manner.

To provide an example of the possible financial workings of such a cooperative, I have drawn on recent economic data gathered from Canadian social science and humanities journals. Although the social sciences and humanities account for a substantial proportion of the scholarly work on university campuses, they have not figured as prominently as the hard sciences in discussions of alternative models of academic publishing. It is true that their journals have much lower subscription costs. However, the potential value and contribution of open access in these fields is just as great as in the sciences, whether one thinks of the public, professionals, policymakers, or scholars and students at institutions that cannot otherwise afford even the lower-priced subscriptions of journals in the social sciences and humanities.

The budget figures presented here for journal revenues and expenses are average figures for a sample of sixty-one Canadian social science and humanities journals (table D.1). The projected business plan for this cooperative model assumes that the journals will move, if only gradually, to publishing only online, and drop their print editions. It also assumes that the cooperative will employ open source software systems for managing and publishing and that the journals will continue to qualify for current levels of grants and subsidies.[1] By publishing in an open access format, journals will lose revenue from individual subscriptions and other sales (e.g., reprint permissions). Institutional subscriptions will be replaced, at a lower level, by cooperative fees charged to member libraries.

However membership in the cooperative comes to be structured, whether nationally or internationally, a drop in the number of institutions participating in the cooperative seems inevitable, compared to the number of institutions that currently subscribe to the journals that are to be published by the cooperative. A second assumption is that the

1. The Social Sciences and Humanities Research Council of Canada's Aid to Research Journals provides up to $30,000 (Canadian) per year to peer-reviewed journals that qualify in terms of scholarly excellence and overall presentation (see "Aid to Research and Transfer Journals" ⟨http://www.sshrc.ca/web/apply/program_descriptions/journals_e.asp⟩).

Table D.1
Open access cooperative model based on 2003 average revenues and expenses for a sample of Canadian social science and humanities journals

Budget items	Current	Cooperative
Revenue		
Grants/donations	$22,876	$22,876
Subscriptions		
Institutional ($75/year)	18,662	9,331
Individual	12,775	N/A
Other sales	7,908	N/A
Total	$62,221	$32,207
Expenses		
Editing (copyediting/proofreading)	$12,256	$12,256
Marketing	1,814	1,814
Prepress[a]	4,207	2,104
Printing, paper, binding	14,253	N/A
Postage and handling	3,885	N/A
Subscription fulfillment	2,705	N/A
Administrative overhead[a]	17,231	8,616
Total	$56,620	$24,789
Operating surplus	$5,601	$7,418

Source: Lorimer, Lindsay, and Boismenu 2003.
Note: All figures in Canadian dollars. N = 61. N/A = not applicable.
a. Online management systems are used to reduce costs by 50 percent.

member libraries belonging to the cooperative should, in principle, pay less in membership fees to the cooperative than they paid, prior to its formation, in subscription fees for the journals now published by the cooperative. To cover those two assumptions in the projected cooperative budget presented here, based on the survey of Canadian journals, I have cut the institutional revenue in half from its subscription levels (table D.1).

Although the humanities journals that make up this sample have small circulations, with an average of 561 subscribers, they have still managed through their current subscription lists and grants to produce a surplus that is equivalent to close to 10 percent of their revenues. To be fair, the journals may well need this operating surplus, in light of the uncertainties associated with the number of subscribers and the size of the subsidizing grants. The publishing and archiving cooperative, while promising to greatly increase the journals' readership, also has the potential to increase their operating surpluses by dropping their print editions and utilizing online systems. These increased surpluses not only could cover unexpected declines in grants but could help defray the costs associated with managing the expected increase in submissions that appears to follow a move to open access publishing. And given the trend of declining individual subscriptions to academic journals, a loss of the income stream associated with those subscriptions has been a reality for some time (Tenopir and King 2001).

This leaves the question of whether a publishing and archiving cooperative makes as much economic sense as a proven cost recovery or nonprofit digital service for scholarly publications, such as JSTOR. As I have noted, the leadership and direction for JSTOR comes from the Andrew W. Mellon Foundation, the major philanthropic benefactor of scholarly communication. Although the Mellon Foundation has supported the development of open source software among universities, for projects such as courseware, when it comes to scholarly publishing, the foundation has focused in recent years on "creating sustainable not-for-profit enterprises" as a means "to accelerate the productive uses of information technologies for the benefit of higher education around the world," according to the mission statement of the recently formed Ithaka Harbours, Inc. Ithaka was established by the foundation, with Kevin M. Guthrie, former president of JSTOR, at its head, to support new not-for-profit enterprises in scholarly communication, principally those that have received Mellon support. If this not-for-profit enterprise model appears to build on the high-tech start-up wave of the 1990s, underwritten by venture capital (and Ithaka speaks of new enterprises as "incubated entities," in the lingo of that era), the Mellon Foundation has proven that the model works in the twenty-first century with JSTOR and ARTstor, both of which have increased access to important scholarly and cultural resources. The idea of a publishing and archiving cooperative that I am introducing here is something of a tendril of that demonstrated success, as it seeks to extend the Mellon idea of a community-based organization by situating that organization far more directly within the community, as a cooperative rather than a service enterprise.

To take advantage of Mellon's leadership in cost recovery publishing, as well as to follow its wise counsel to begin with a viable business plan, I offer JSTOR's budget as a rough benchmark in determining whether a cooperative among libraries, scholarly societies, and other publishing groups can succeed in advancing this common desire "to accelerate the productive uses of information technologies for the benefit of higher education around the world," to return to the Ithaka line (see table D.2). In 2002, the most recent year for which tax returns are available, JSTOR offered the back-issue sets for roughly 220 journals (according to

Table D.2
JSTOR revenue and expenses based on its 2002 IRS Form 990 return information[a]

Budget item	JSTOR
Revenue	
Subscription fees	$7,400,000
Capital fees[b]	6,400,000
Grants and donations	2,547,000
Other	626,000
Total	$16,973,000
Expenses	
President and trustees	$370,000
Other salaries	3,382,000
Scanning	1,267,000
Hardware and software	673,000
Occupancy	410,000
Travel	543,000
Professional fees	550,000
Meetings and presentations	1,433,000
Asset depreciation	689,000
Other	1,966,000
Total	$11,184,000
Operating surplus	$5,789,000
Net assets[c]	$28,607,000

Source: GuideStar ⟨http://guidestar.org⟩.
a. Tax-exempt organizations are required to file Form 990 with the U.S. Internal Revenue Service.
b. Paid by new member institutions to join JSTOR.
c. Principally investments and savings.

its March newsletter of that year) and added in the area of 90 new journal titles to its list (judging by its growth in titles to date).

The JSTOR figures suggest the scope and leeway that library and scholarly associations have in exploring the financial prospects of a cooperative model for supporting journal publishing and archiving. However, the larger question at hand is whether there are other ways of going about the business of scholarly communication, review, authorization, and reward and whether there are other ways of taking advantage of new technologies to benefit higher education and society on a global scale. The Mellon Foundation has done a great service with JSTOR in improving access to the back issues of journals and in demonstrating the viability of not-for-profit enterprises based on developing new digitized scholarly services. However, I don't imagine that anyone at the Mellon Foundation, or anyone associated with related projects, has it in mind that current initiatives should be the end of the conversation on ways and means of improving access to research and scholarship on a sustainable and long-term basis.

Appendix E

Indexing of the Serial Literature

To suggest the scope of overlap and gap in current serial indexes, I worked with Larry Wolfson and Alnoor Gova to analyze, within the context of the University of British Columbia serials collection, a sample of nine indexes, comprising traditional indexes, government- and industry-sponsored indexes, and a new generation of publisher portals (table E.1). Given our interest in open access approaches to scholarly publishing, we included five open access indexes in the sample. Two of these open access indexes are sponsored by the U.S. government: ERIC, which is a project of the National Library of Education, and PubMed, which is the work of the National Library of Medicine. Two are publisher portals that serve, in effect, as open access indexes: Elsevier's ScienceDirect and Stanford University Library's HighWire Press. And one is an experimental citation index, CiteSeer.IST, which was initially developed by the NEC Research Institute and is now also associated with Pennsylvania State University.

We compared the indexes' coverage of the research literature using two measures. The first was a measure of the index's coverage of fifty randomly selected journal titles, drawn from the relevant disciplines' journal sections of the University of British Columbia library. The second was a measure of the index's coverage of the top fifty journals in education, as ranked by the ISI Web of Science according to impact factor (which, as stated in chapter 2, is the ratio of citations to articles in the journal over the two previous years). Coverage measures of the type we used are admittedly crude, and the resulting tables are meant only to

Table E.1
Indexes used in the analysis

Commercial serial indexes
Education Index (New York: H. W. Wilson)
ISI Web of Science (Philadelphia: Thomson Institute of Scientific Information)
Serial aggregators (subscription management services)
Academic Search Elite (Chicago: EBSCO Information Services)
Publisher portals
Highwire Press (Palo Alto, CA: Stanford University Library)
Journals@Ovid (Amsterdam: Wolters Kluwer N.V.)
ScienceDirect (London: Reed Elsevier)
Open Access Indexes
ERIC: Education Resources Information Clearinghouse (Rockville, MD: U.S. Department of Education)
CiteSeer.IST (Princeton, NJ: NEC Research Institute; State College: Pennsylvania State University)
PubMed (Washington, DC: National Library of Medicine)

Note: The analysis of the databases and indexes was conducted in July 2003.

suggest the value of exploring alternative systems of comprehensive indexing.[1]

To begin with a comparison of indexes in education, among the fifty randomly selected education journals from the UBC library, seven of the titles found in the commercial *Education Index* do not appear in the much larger and open access ERIC, with 993 journal titles in 2003 (table E.2). The titles in this sample that were missing from the otherwise comprehensive ERIC index were *Journal of Curriculum Theorizing, Journal of the College and University Personal Association, Learning and Lead-*

---

1. On index coverage, also see Pillow 1999, which discovered many inconsistencies in the ways that print and electronic indexes cover Afro-American Studies. Gaps have also been noted in women's studies by Kristin H. Gerhard, Trudi E. Jacobsen, and Susan G. Williamson (1993), who examined the respected *Social Sciences Index, MLA Bibliography,* and *Humanities Index* (see also Krikos 1994). In comparing the *Education Index* and the *Current Index to Journals in Education,* M. Suzanne Brown, Jana S. Edwards, and Jeneen Lasee-Willemssen concluded that "researchers who prefer one index unknowingly miss key articles" (1999, 216). For additional studies on indexing comprehensiveness, see LaRose 1989 and Holt and Schmidt 1995.

Table E.2
Indexing coverage of education journals

	Commercial indexes		Open access index
	ISI Web of Science	Education Index	ERIC[a]
Total titles indexed	92	553	993
Random titles (N = 50)[b]	12	29	31
In ISI alone	1	N/A	N/A
In EI alone	N/A	7	N/A
In ERIC alone	N/A	N/A	9
ISI top-fifty titles[c]	50	38	46

Note: N/A = not applicable.
a. Abstract index (open access, with optional document delivery service).
b. From current journals in the University of British Columbia Education Library.
c. By impact factor in ISI Web of Science for education.

ing with Technology, School Arts, Science Scope, Teaching PreK–8, and *Journal of the National Association for the Education of Young Children.*

When it came to the ISI Web of Science's top fifty journals in education (as ranked by impact factor), both *Education Index* and ERIC provided, not surprisingly, excellent coverage, with the one exception missing from both indexes—*Journal of Computer Information Systems*—hardly a surprise. Still the fact that ERIC did not index four of the top fifty journals in its field—*Health Education Research, Journal of College Student Development, Minerva: A Review of Science, Learning and Policy,* and *Academic Psychiatry* (from the American Association of Directors of Psychiatric Residency Training and the Association for Academic Psychiatry)—again suggests the benefits of pursuing more comprehensive and coordinated coverage strategies in indexing. One obvious issue in this analysis is what counts as an *education* journal, given that research in professional schools, such as education, draws on a number of academic disciplines. What still comes through, though, is an overlap and gap among the indexes that might be addressed by building indexing into the journal-publishing process. ERIC provides public access

Table E.3
Indexing coverage of open access education journals

	Commercial indexes		Open access index
	ISI Web of Science	Education Index	ERIC
*E-journals (N = 135)*ᵃ	5	15	38
In ISI alone	0	N/A	N/A
In EI alone	N/A	1	N/A
In ERIC alone	N/A	N/A	26

a. From the Open Access Education E-journal List ⟨http://aera-cr.ed.asu.edu/links.html⟩.

to abstracts along with bibliographic information, and began in 2004 to add open access to a small number (so far) of journal articles. It makes the educational research literature, including unpublished materials, available to a wider public of parents, teachers, educational administrators, and policymakers.

To gain a sense of how open access journals are currently being indexed, we checked a list of 135 open access journals in education, using the complete list of such journals posted on the American Education Research Association (AERA) Web site. Many of these titles were new and available only in electronic form, although some had long-standing print editions, going back over a century in the case of *Teachers College Record* (table E.3). Only 39 of the 135 titles in this list were to be found in *Education Index* or ERIC. Clearly, open access journal editors should be seeking ways of having their journals indexed by implementing, for example, the Open Archives Initiative Metadata Harvesting Protocol, which enables online research resources to be automatically indexed in open access indexes or search services such as OAIster, with ERIC currently in the process of adopting such metadata standards to improve its service (see appendix F). Still, five of the open access journals on the AERA list—*Teachers College Record, Educational Psychological Review* (University of Texas), *Teaching Sociology, Journal of Extension,* and *Educational Theory*—are indexed in the highly selective ISI Web of Science.

Table E.4
Coverage of top-fifty science journals

	Commercial indexes			Open access indexes		
	Index	Portals[a]		Portals[b]		Index
	ISI Web of Science	Academic Search Elite	Ovid	Science-Direct	High-Wire	Pub-Med
Total titles	8,500	8,000	900	1,800	336	4,600
ISI top fifty[c]	50	24	5	12	10	47

a. Portals permit only subscribers to search, with full-text access to articles, although some portals delay that access to some time after articles appear on journal's Web site.
b. Portals permit free searches, with full-text access to articles restricted to subscribers or pay per view.
c. Ranked by impact factor in ISI Web of Science.

In the sciences, open access to serial indexing is growing on a number of fronts. For example, corporate journal publishers provide free access to abstracts and tables of contents as marketing devices, linking to pay-per-view access to the full articles, perhaps most notably with Elsevier's ScienceDirect, which provides a portal onto Elsevier's 1,800 journal titles. On the other hand, the HighWire Press portal, with close to 800 journals, offers both pay-per-view and "the largest repository of free full-text life science articles in the world," according to its Web site (table E.4). In the life sciences, the major commercial and open access indexes both provide a high degree of coverage, with the open access PubMed index doing somewhat better than the ISI Web of Science, although the Web of Science still managed to cover two journals in this area—*Journal of Biological Systems* and *Fisheries Oceanography*—that were not covered by PubMed (table E.5).

A detailed feature comparison among the science indexes in this sample—which includes examples of commercial, nonprofit, experimental, and government sites—reveals the richness and redundancy of current services (table E.6). At this point, however, the ISI Web of Science continues to provide indispensable citation-indexing and journal-ranking services. The still-experimental citation indexing systems, such as CiteSeer.IST and

Table E.5
Indexing coverage of life sciences journals

	Commercial index	Open access index
	ISI Web of Science	PubMed
Random titles (N = 50)[a]	40	45
In ISI only	2	N/A
In PubMed only	N/A	7

a. Drawn from current life science journals in University of British Columbia Library.

Citebase, have not begun to approach the reliability or systematic coverage of the ISI Web of Science. Nonetheless, the Web of Science's limited range of coverage and its subscription costs (which cannot be disclosed in the case of the University of British Columbia, according to its current licensing agreement) make the value of an open access citation index apparent, and efforts to develop prototypes of such an index in association with Open Archives Initiative metadata standards are likely to continue.

At this point, CiteSeer.IST does not index journals, per se, but only individual papers that have been posted on the Web, whether on home page Web sites, in e-print archives, or on other Web sites, such as those for conferences. Admittedly, improving the accuracy and completeness of the bibliographic information gathered by CiteSeer.IST's autonomous indexing is no small challenge (as it crawls the Web for science articles in .pdf format and parses those it finds, using a bibliographic algorithm that extracts, as best it can, given the irregularities of article formatting, the author, title, etc., as well as the works cited). Yet CiteSeer.IST has demonstrated how much can be done, even with what is essentially a disorganized array of online and open access publications, through automated systems that make free online indexes economically feasible.

PubMed, which represents a major investment in open access indexing by the U.S. National Library of Medicine, also goes a step further toward supporting greater "public" access by including multiple search functions for both scholars and clinicians, so that one can look specifically for studies that relate to "therapy," those that relate to "diagnosis,"

Table E.6
Comparison of services among five science indexes

| Feature | Commercial index | Open access indexes | | | |
| | | Publishers' portals | | Indexes | |
	ISI Web of Science	Science-Direct	HighWire Press	PubMed	CiteSeer.IST
Alert service	No	Yes	Yes	No	Yes
Category search	Yes	Yes	Yes	Yes	No
Citation graphs	No	No	No	No	Yes
Citation indexing	Yes	No	No	No	Yes
Citation statistics	Yes	No	No	No	Yes
Context for citations	No	No	No	No	Yes
Coverage	8.5 K journals 23 M records[a]	1.8 K journals 59 M records	550 K articles 1.4 M records	4.6 K journals 12 M records	300 K articles 10 M records
Document comparison[b]	No	No	No	No	Yes
Full-text articles	No	Yes	Some[c]	Some	Some
Match search terms with database terms	No	No	No	Yes	No
Order articles online	Yes	Yes	Yes	Yes	No
Practitioner search	No	No	No	Clinical studies	No
Ratings/comments	No	Yes	Yes	No	Yes
Reference library	No	Yes	No	Yes	No
Related article linking	Yes	Yes	Yes	Yes	Yes
Related resources	No	Yes	Yes	Yes	Yes
Save/edit searches	Yes	Yes	No	Yes	No
Scientific glossary	No	No	No	Yes	No
Sort parameters	Yes	Yes	No	No	Yes
User customizable	No	Yes	No	Yes	No
User tutorial/help	No	Yes	No	Yes	No

a. Science, Social Sciences, Arts and Humanities Citation Indexes.
b. Shows percentage of matching sentences between documents.
c. HighWire Press offers full-text articles, with the majority of journals offering pay per view, although a quarter of its titles offer open access, from immediately on publication to two years after.

and those that relate to "prognosis." There are links to the full text of articles, where publishers permit, as well as a medical glossary, a search terms thesaurus, and links to related documents, including medical textbooks.

The need for greater coordination among the variety of indexing services in existence should be readily apparent in light of continuing gaps and overlaps, and there are signs that efforts toward such coordination are underway. It is still too early to know if Google Scholar will prove the way forward, as it is too early to judge what will come of Thompson ISI's announcement of a joint initiative with NEC Laboratories America to build on CiteSeer.IST tools for autonomous searching of open access materials (Quint 2004).

Appendix F

Metadata for Journal Publishing

Online indexing for e-print archives and journals works like this (at the risk of things' getting a little complicated): In online settings and with digital formats, each published article in an archive or journal has what is called metadata (data about data) associated with it. This metadata typically consists of what we traditionally think of as indexing items, such as the author's name, the paper's title, the date it was published, and the journal's name. The Open Archives Initiative has established a protocol or standard for the metadata that enables this indexing information to be gathered or "harvested" from online e-print archives, journals and other research databases. This means that if a journal registers with an OAI harvester, such as OAIster at the University of Michigan, all of the metadata associated with the journal's articles will be harvested on a regular basis and contribute to a virtual index at the OAIster Web site, where it can be searched, along with metadata from all of the other registered journals, e-print archives, and other sorts of research databases, with links leading back to the indexed articles. At this point OAIster is harvesting materials from 400 institutions, and the OAI protocol is proving itself to be the emerging standard for indexing research resources.

The OAI protocol is used to index an article by employing a standard set of fifteen metadata or indexing elements. These elements, which are drawn from the Dublin Core Metadata Initiative, include the traditional indexing items such as Title, Author, Subject, Publisher, and Date, along with a number of other helpful categories, including Description, Contributor, Type, Format, Source, Identifier, Coverage, Relation, Language,

Table F.1
Use of the Dublin Core Metadata Element Set in the indexing of materials published in journals using Open Journal Systems

Dublin Core elements	Open Journal Systems indexing for scholarly journals
Title	Title of article, book review, item, etc.
Creator	Author's name, affiliation, and e-mail address
Creator	Biographical statement
Subject	Academic discipline
Subject	Topics, keywords, or disciplinary classification system, if available
Description	Abstract of article
Publisher	Publisher or sponsoring agency (name, city, country)[a]
Contributor	Agencies funding or contributing to the research
Date	When paper was submitted to journal[a]
Type	Peer-reviewed, non-peer-reviewed, invited; article, book, review, etc.[a]
Type	Research method or approach
Format	HTML, .pdf, PostScript (file formats)[a]
Identifier	Universal Resource Indicator[a]
Source	Journal title, volume (issue)[a]
Language	Language of article
Relation	Title and identifier for document's supplementary files (e.g., research data, instruments)[a]
Coverage	Geographical and historical coverage
Coverage	Research sample (by age, gender, ethnicity, class)
Rights	Author retains copyright, granting first publication rights to journal (default version)[a]

a. Items generated by Open Journal Systems; all other items entered by the author, on submission of article, and later reviewed as part of editorial process.

and Rights.[1] These elements can be further defined for specific purposes by the journal or archive that utilizes them. In addition, a metadata element can be used more than once, so that for example, a document can be indexed by Subject (academic discipline) and Subject (keyword). This allows for increasingly fine-grained indexing of the research literature

1. The Web site of the Open Archives Initiative can be accessed at ⟨http://openarchives.org⟩; that for the Dublin Core Project is available at ⟨http://purl.org/DC/index.htm⟩; also see Van de Sompel and Lagoze 2002.

and more accurate searching (as a countermeasure against what is otherwise the threat of information overload), and OAI harvesters can be set up to catch the distinctions introduced by, say, a set of journals and to allow readers to search on one or some combination of the elements, such as research methodology and funding agency.

To see how this can work in practice, consult table F.1, which sets out the indexing items that the Public Knowledge Project utilizes with its Open Journal Systems, an example of open source software designed to manage and publish journals online discussed in chapter 11. Each of these elements, such as Type (peer-reviewed) or Contributor (funding agency), can be used to refine and create greater precision in searching. With OJS, when the author submits a paper, he or she fills in not only Name and Title, but a range of other metadata elements, such as Discipline and Coverage, using a template that supplies him or her with relevant examples for each element (provided by the journal's editors). The author can be directed, as well, to consult more formal subject classifications, such as the American Mathematics Society's 2000 Mathematics Subject Classification, with its exhaustive set of 5,000 topics, although only a few disciplines have such a classification system. The information the author provides is combined with additional metadata that is generated by the publishing system, including Date (date submitted), Source (journal title, volume, issue), and Type (peer-reviewed status, etc.). The metadata submitted by the author can be reviewed as part of the journal's editorial process and is subject to copyediting, proofreading, or even review by a librarian with cataloguing expertise in the relevant area, if the journal happens to be, say, a member of a publishing and archiving cooperative of the sort outlined in chapter 6.

References

Abbasi, Kamran. 2004. Let's dump impact factors. *British Medical Journal* 329, doi:10.1136/bmj.329.7471.0-h (accessed October 23, 2004).

Abrahamson, John. 2004. Information is the best medicine. *New York Times*, September 18.

Acosta-Cazares, Benjamin, Edmund Browne, Ronald E. LaPorte, Dieter Neuvians, Kenneth Rochel de Camargo, Roberto Tapia-Conyer, and Yang Ze. 2000. Scientific colonialism and safari research. *Clinical Medicine and Health Research*, January 11. http://clinmed.netprints.org/cgi/content/full/2000010008v1 (accessed September 27, 2003).

Adebowale, Sulaiman. 2001. The scholarly journal in the production and dissemination of knowledge on Africa: Exploring some issues for the future. *Journal of Cultural Studies* 3(1): 26–42.

Adeya, Catherine Nyaki, and Banji Oyelaran-Oyeyinka. 2002. *The Internet in African universities: Case studies from Kenya and Nigeria.* Maastricht, The Netherlands: United Nations University. http://www.infonomics.nl/globalequality/reports/IDEaf.pdf (accessed September 16, 2003).

Advertisement. 1753. *Philosophical Transactions* 47: a.

Alexander, Cynthia J., and Leslie A. Pal, eds. 1998. *Digital democracy: Policy and politics in the wired world.* Toronto: Oxford University Press.

Alexander, Patricia A. 1996. The past, present and future of knowledge research: A reexamination of the role of knowledge in learning and instruction. *Educational Psychology* 31(3): 89–92.

Alexander, Patricia A. 1998. The nature or disciplinary and domain learning: The knowledge, interest, and strategic dimensions of learning from subject matter text. In *Learning from text across conceptual domains*, ed. C. R. Hynd, 263–287. Mahwah, NJ: Erlbaum.

Alexander, Patricia A., and Tamara L. Jetton. 2000. Learning from text: A multidimensional and developmental perspective. In *Handbook of reading research*, ed. M. L. Kamil, P. B. Mosenthal, P. D. Pearson, and R. Barr, 3: 285–309. Mahwah, NJ: Erlbaum.

Alexander, Patricia A., Jonna Kulikowich, and Tamara L. Jetton. 1994. The role of subject-matter knowledge and interest in the processing of linear and non-linear texts. *Review of Educational Research* 64(2): 201–252.

Alliance for Taxpayer Access. 2004. Birds-of-a-Feather Working for Taxpayer Access: An Open Letter to the U.S. Congress Signed by 25 Nobel Prize Winners. August 26. http://www.taxpayeraccess.org/bof.html (accessed January 12, 2005).

ALPSP. *See* Association of Learned and Professional Society Publishers.

Anderson, Deborah Lines, ed. 2004. *Digital scholarship in the tenure, promotion, and review process*. Armonk, NY: Sharpe.

Anderson, Kent, John Sack, Lisa Krauss, and Lori O'Keefe. 2001. Publishing online-only peer-reviewed biomedical literature: Three years of citation, author perception, and usage experience. *Journal of Electronic Publishing* 6(3). http://www.press.umich.edu/jep/06-03/anderson.html (accessed September 30, 2002).

Angell, Marcia. 2004. *The truth about the drug companies: How they deceive us and what to do about it*. New York: Random House.

Antelman, Kristin. 2004. Do open-access articles have a greater research impact? *College and Research Libraries* 65(5): 373–383.

Aristotle. 1958. *Aristotle's metaphysics*. Vol. 1. Trans. William David Ross. Oxford: Oxford University Press.

ARL. *See* Association of Research Libraries.

Aronson, Barbara. 2004. Improving online access to medical information for low-income countries. *New England Journal of Medicine* 350: 966–968.

Arunachalam, Subbiah. 2002. Information and knowledge in the age of electronic communication: A developing country perspective. *Journal of Information Science* 25(6): 465–476.

Arunachalam, Subbiah, and M. Jinandra Doss. 2000. Mapping international collaboration in science in Asia through coauthorship analysis. *Current Science* 79(5): 621–628.

Association of Learned and Professional Society Publishers. 2003. Who pays for the free lunch? *Scholarly Communication Report* 7(4): 13–16.

Association of Learned and Professional Society Publishers. 2004. *ALPSP principles of scholarship-friendly journal publishing practice*. London. http://www.alpsp.org/2004pdfs/SFpub210104.pdf (accessed April 1, 2004).

Association of Research Libraries. 2000. Principles for emerging systems of scholarly publishing. http://www.arl.org/scomm/tempe.html (accessed September 24, 2003).

Association of Research Libraries. 2004. Monograph and serial costs in ARL libraries, 1986–2003. In *ARL Statistics, 2002–03*. Washington, DC: Association of Research Libraries. http://www.arl.org/stats/arlstat/graphs/2003/monser03.pdf (accessed February 1, 2005).

Ausubel, David. 1968. *Educational psychology: A cognitive view*. New York: Holt, Rinehart & Winston.

Bachrach, Steven, R. Stephen Berry, Martin Blume, Thomas von Foerster, Alexander Fowler, Paul Ginsparg, Stephen Heller, Neil Kestner, Andrew Odlyzko, Ann Okerson, Ron Wigington, and Anne Moffat. 1998. Who should own scientific papers? *Science* 281(5382): 1459–1460. http://www.sciencemag .org/cgi/content/full/281/5382/1459 (accessed September 29, 2003).

Bagdikian, Ben H. 2000. *The media monopoly*. 6th ed. Boston: Beacon.

Ball, Patrick, Herbert F. Spirer, and Louise Spirer, eds. 2000. *Making the case: Investigating large scale human rights violations using information systems and data analysis*. Washington, DC: American Association for the Advancement of Science. http://shr.aaas.org/mtc/ (accessed September 24, 2003).

Banya, Kingsley, and Juliet Elu. 2001. The World Bank and financing higher education in sub-Saharan Africa. *Higher Education* 42: 1–34.

Barron, James. 2003. The Steinway with German accents. *New York Times*, August 27.

Baum, Rudy M. 2004. The open-access myth. *Chemical and Engineering News* 82(8). http://pubs.acs.org/email/cen/html/032804112410.html (accessed September 7, 2004).

Bazerman, Charles. 1988. *Shaping written knowledge: The genre and activity of the experimental article in science*. Madison: University of Wisconsin Press.

Benkler, Yochai. 1999. Free as the air to common use: First Amendment constraints on enclosure of the public domain. *New York University Law Review* 74(354): 354–446. http://www.nyu.edu/pages/lawreview/74/2/benkler.pdf (accessed September 27, 2003).

Benkler, Yochai. 2001. Property, commons, and the First Amendment: Towards a core common infrastructure. White Paper for the First Amendment Program, Brennan Center for Justice at New York University School of Law. http:// www.benkler.org/Pub.html (accessed October 3, 2003).

Bergstrom, Carl T., and Theodore C. Bergstrom. 2004. The costs and benefits of library site licenses to academic journals. *Proceedings of the National Academy of Sciences* 101(3): 897–902.

Bergstrom, Theodore C. 2001. Free labor for costly journals? *Journal of Economic Perspectives* 15(4): 183–198. http://www.econ.ucsb.edu/~tedb/Journals/ jeprevised.pdf (accessed September 27, 2003).

Bethesda Statement on Open Access Publishing. 2003. Meeting on Open Access Publishing, Howard Hughes Medical Institute, Chevy Chase, MD, April 11. http://www.earlham.edu/~peters/fos/bethesda.htm#summary (accessed October 6, 2003).

Bhattacharya, Ronica. 2003. U.S. secondary school outreach effort continues. *JSTORnews*, 2(2). http://www.jstor.org/news/2003.06/outreach.html (accessed October 3, 2003).

Blume, Martin. 2003. Re: Detecting plagiarism. *September '98 Forum.* American-Scientist-E-PRINT-Forum, July 23. http://www.ecs.soton.ac.uk/ ~harnad/Hypermail/Amsci/2925.html (accessed September 27, 2003).

Blumenstyk, Goldie. 2003. Universities collected $827-million in payments on inventions in 2001. *Chronicle of Higher Education,* May 22, p. A21.

Bot, Marjolein, Johan Burgemeester, and Hans Roes. 1998. The cost of publishing an electronic journal: A general model and a case study. *D-Lib Magazine* (November). http://www.dlib.org/dlib/november98/11roes.html (accessed September 27, 2003).

Bowen, G. William. 1995. JSTOR and the economics of scholarly communication. Paper presented at the Council on Library Resources conference, Washington, DC, October 4. http://www.mellon.org/jsesc.html (accessed September 27, 2003).

Boyle, James. 2003. The second enclosure movement and the construction of the public domain. *Law and Contemporary Problems* 66(33): 33–74. http:// www.law.duke.edu/pd/papers/boyle.pdf (accessed September 27, 2003).

Brabham, Edna Greene. 1997. Holocaust education: Legislation, practices, and literature for middle-school students. *Social Studies Teacher* 88: 139–142. http:// www.questia.com/PM.qst?action=openPageViewer&docId=95157961 (accessed September 27, 2003).

Brand, Amy. 2001. CrossRef turns one. *D-Lib Magazine* (May). http://www.dlib .org/dlib/may01/brand/05brand.html (accessed October 6, 2003).

Braun, Kim. 2003. The German academic publishers project—GAP. In *ELPUB 2003: From Information to Knowledge. Proceedings of the Seventh ICCC/IFIP International Conference on Electronic Publishing,* ed. S. M. de Souza Costa, J. A. Carvalho, A. A. Baptista, and A. C. Santos Morieira, 157–165. Guimarães, Portugal: Universidade do Minho.

Brody, Tim, Heinrich Stamerjohanns, François Vallières, Stevan Harnad, Yves Gingras, and Charles Oppenheim. 2004. The effect of open access on citation impact. Paper presented at National Policies on Open Access Provision for University Research Output, University of Southampton, February 19. http://opcit .eprints.org/feb19oa/brody-impact.pdf (accessed October 31, 2004).

Brown, M. Suzanne, Jana S. Edwards, and Jeneen Lasee-Willemssen. 1999. A new comparison of the Current Index to Journals in Education and the Education Index: A deep analysis of indexing. *Journal of Academic Librarianship* 25(3): 216–222.

Brown, Patrick O., Michael B. Eisen, and Harold E. Varmus. 2003. Why PloS became a publisher. *PloS Biology* 1(1): 1–2.

Brownlee, Shannon. 2003. The perils of prevention. *New York Times Magazine,* March 16, pp. 52–55.

Bruneau, William, and Donald C. Savage. 2002. *Counting out the scholars: How performance indicators undermine universities and colleges.* Toronto, ON: James Lorimer.

Budapest Open Access Initiative. 2002. New York: Budapest Open Access Initiative. http://www.soros.org/openaccess/read.shtml (accessed October 6, 2003).

Cameron, Robert D. 1997. A universal citation database as a catalyst for reform in scholarly communication. *First Monday* 2(4). http://www.firstmonday.dk/issues/issue2_4/cameron/ (accessed September 28, 2003).

Campbell, Eric G., Brian R. Clarridge, Manjusha Gokhale, Lauren Birenbaum, Stephen Hilgartner, Neil A. Holtzman, and David Blumenthal. 2002. Data withholding in academic genetics. *Journal of the American Medical Association* 287(4): 473–480.

Campion, Edward W., Kent R. Anderson, and Jeffrey M. Drazen. 2001. A new Web site and a new policy. *New England Journal of Medicine* 344: 1710.

Canagarajah, A. Suresh. 2002. *The geopolitics of academic writing*. Pittsburgh: University of Pittsburgh Press.

Caplan, Priscilla, and Stephanie Haas. 2004. Metadata rematrixed: Merging museum and library boundaries. *Library Hi Tech* 22(3): 263–269.

Cappella, Joseph N., and Kathleen Hall Jamieson. 1997. *Spiral of cynicism: The press and the public good*. New York: Oxford University Press.

Carlson, Scott. 2003. Logging in with ... Steven J. Bell: Has Google won? A librarian says students have more data than they know what to do with. *Chronicle of Higher Education*, January 23, p. A28.

Carlson, Scott. 2004. Cornell tires a new publishing model: Scholarship on demand. *Chronicle of Higher Education*, March 5, p. A29.

Casson, Lionel. 2001. *Libraries in the ancient world*. New Haven: Yale University Press.

Cavalier, Robert. 1990. *Plato for beginners*. New York: Writers and Readers.

Cetto, Ana María. 2000. Sharing scientific knowledge through publications: What do developing countries have to offer? In *World Conference on Science: Science for the Twenty-First Century; A New Commitment*, ed. Ana María Cetto, 148–150. London: Banson. http://unesdoc.unesco.org/images/0012/001207/120706e.pdf#120879 (accessed September 28, 2003).

Cetto, Ana María, and Octavio Alonso-Gamboa. 1998. Scientific and scholarly journals in Latin America and the Caribbean. In *Knowledge dissemination in Africa: The role of the scholarly journal*, ed. Philip G. Altbach and Damtew Teferra, 99–126. Chestnut Hill, MA: Bellagio.

Chan, Leslie. 2003. Open access in bioline international. Paper presented at ELPUB2003: From Information to Knowledge, Guimarães, Portugal, June 25–28.

Chomsky, Noam. 1997. *Media control: The spectacular achievements of propaganda*. New York: Seven Story.

Claude, Richard Pierre. 2002. *Science in the service of human rights*. Philadelphia: University of Pennsylvania Press.

Clymer, Adam. 2003. Government openness at issue as Bush holds on to records. *New York Times*, January 3.

Cohen, Joshua, and Joel Rogers. 2003. Power and reason. In *Deepening democracy: Institutional innovations in empowered participatory governance*, ed. Archon Funga and Erik Olin Wright, 237–255. New York: Verso.

The coming of copyright perpetuity. 2003. *New York Times*, January 16.

Cooper, Charles, Christopher Freeman, O. Gish, Stephen Hill, Geoffrey Oldman, and Hans Singer. 1971. Science in underdeveloped countries: World plan of action for the application of science and technology to development. *Minerva* 9: 101–121.

Cornell University Electronic Publishing Steering Committee. 1998. Electronic Publishing Steering Committee report on electronic publishing strategies for Cornell University. Ithaca, NY: Cornell University Electronic Publishing Steering Committee. October 20. http://www.library.cornell.edu/ulib/pubs/EPSCFinalReport1998.htm (accessed September 29, 2003).

Cox, June, and Laura Cox. 2003. *Scholarly publishing practice: The ALPSPS report on academic journal publishers' policies and practices in online publishing*. London: Association of Learned and Professional Society Publishers. http://www.alpsp.org/2004pdfs/SFpub210104.pdf (accessed September 28, 2003).

Creative Commons. 2005. *About*. San Francisco. http://creativecommons.org (accessed February 5, 2005).

Creative Research. 2002. *e-Democracy report of research findings*. London: Creative Research. http://www.edemocracy.gov.uk/downloads/Useful_Pointers.pdf (accessed October 6, 2003).

Crow, Raym. 2000. The case for institutional repositories: A SPARC position paper. Washington, DC: Scholarly Publishing and Academic Resources Coalition.

Dahdouh-Guebas, Farid, Jennifer Ahimbisibwe, Rita Van Moll, and Nico Koedam. 2003. Neo-colonial science by the most industrialised upon the least developed countries in peer-reviewed publishing. *Scientometrics* 56(3): 329–343.

D'Alessandro, Donna M., Clarence D. Kreiter, Susan L. Kinzer, and Michael W. Peterson. 2004. A randomized controlled trial of an information prescription for pediatric patient education on the Internet. *Archives of Pediatric and Adolescent Medicine* 158: 857–862.

Darch, Colin. 1998. The shrinking public domain and the unsustainable library. Paper presented at Electronic Library: Gateway to Information; Resource Sharing and User Services in the Electronic Library, Lund, Sweden, June 2–6. http://www.lub.lu.se/sida/papers/darch.html (accessed September 28, 2003).

David, Paul A. 2001. From keeping "nature's secrets" to the institutionalization of "open science." Working paper no. 01-006, Economics Department, Stanford University, Palo Alto, CA. http://www-econ.stanford.edu/faculty/workp/swp01006.pdf (accessed April 4, 2005).

Davis, Crispin. 2004. Testimony before Science and Technology Committee, House of Commons, March 1. Uncorrected transcript of oral evidence to be published as HC 399-i, House of Commons, Minutes of Evidence Taken before

Science and Technology Committee, "Scientific Publications." http://www
.publications.parliament.uk/pa/cm200304/cmselect/cmsctech/uc399-i/uc39902
.htm (accessed April 8, 2004).

de Lauretis, Teresa. 2003. Becoming inorganic. *Critical Inquiry* 29(4): 547–570.

del Castillo, Daniel. 2003a. Preparing to rebuild Iraq's universities. *Chronicle of Higher Education*, April 25, p. A42.

del Castillo, Daniel. 2003b. American colleges are offered grants to aid in revival of Iraqi higher education. *Chronicle of Higher Education*, June 2, p. A28.

Derrida, Jacques. 2001. The future of the profession or the unconditional university (Thanks to the "Humanities" what could take place tomorrow). In *Derrida downunder*, ed. Lawrence Simmons and Heather Worth, 233–247. Palmerston, New Zealand: Dunmore.

Derrida, Jacques. 2002. *Who's afraid of philosophy: Right to philosophy I.* Trans. Jan Plug. Stanford, CA: Stanford University Press.

Drake, Stillman. 1970. Learning and the printed book: The spread of science beyond the university. *Renaissance and Reformation* 6: 43–52.

Dyson, Freeman J. 2002. In praise of amateurs. *New York Review of Books*, 59(19): 4–8.

Eamon, William. 1990. From the secrets of nature to public knowledge. In *Reappraisals of the scientific revolution*, ed. David C. Lindberg and Robert S. Westman, 332–365. Cambridge: Cambridge University Press.

Edejer, Tessa Tan-Torres. 2000. Disseminating health information in developing countries: The role of the Internet. *British Medical Journal* 321: 797–800. http://bmj.bmjjournals.com/cgi/content/full/321/7264/797 (accessed September 29, 2003).

Egan, Timothy. 2002. Bill Gates views what he's sown in libraries. *New York Times*, November 6.

Eisenstein, Elizabeth L. 1979. *The printing press as an agent of change.* Cambridge: Cambridge University Press.

Eisermann, Falk. 2003. Mixing pop and politics. In *Incunabula and their readers: Printing, selling and using books of the fifteenth century*, ed. Kristian Jensen, 159–177. London: British Library.

e-Journal User Study. 2002. *Research findings: Second survey highlights.* Palo Alto, CA: Stanford University Libraries. http://ejust.stanford.edu/findings2/2SurveyHighlights.html (accessed September 28, 2003).

Ellis, Aytoun. 1956. *The penny universities: A history of the coffee-houses.* London: Secker and Warburg.

EPrints.org. 2005. Summary statistics so far: Self-archiving by journal. University of Southampton, Southampton, UK. http://romeo.eprints.org/stats.php (accessed February 1, 2005).

Epstein, Steven. 1996. *Impure science: AIDS, activism, and the politics of knowledge*. Berkeley and Los Angeles: University of California Press.

Erickson, Frederick. 2003. Arts, humanities, and sciences in educational research and social engineering in federal education policy. Paper presented to the American Educational Research Association conference, Chicago, April 23.

Etzkowitz, Henry, Andrew Webster, and Peter Healy, eds. 1998. *Capitalizing knowledge: New intersections of industry and academia*. Albany: State University of New York Press.

Everngam, Ray. 2004. Delayed free access: The experience at *Molecular Biology of the Cell*. Paper presented at the Society for Scholarly Publishing conference, Washington, DC. http://www.sspnet.org/files/public/Everngam.pdf (accessed April 4, 2005).

An experimental history of cold. 1664/1665. *Philosophical Transactions* 1(1): 8.

Ferris, Timothy. 2002. *Seeing in the dark: How backyard stargazers are probing deep space and guarding earth from interplanetary peril*. New York: Simon and Schuster.

Fischer, Frank. 2000. *Citizens, experts and the environment: The politics of local knowledge*. Durham, NC: Duke University Press.

Fisher, Janet H. 1999. Comparing electronic journals to print journals: Are there savings? In *Technology and scholarly communication: The institutional context*, ed. Richard Ekman and Richard E. Quandt, 95–101. Berkeley and Los Angeles: University of California Press.

Fishkin, James S. 1999. Deliberative polling as a model for ICANN membership. In *Representation in Cyberspace Study*. Cambridge, MA: Berkman Center for Internet & Society at Harvard Law School. http://cyber.law.harvard.edu/rcs/fish.html (accessed September 28, 2003).

Foray, Dominique. 2004. *The economics of knowledge*. Cambridge, MA: MIT Press.

Fox, Susannah, and Lee Rainie. 2000. *The online health care revolution: How the Web helps Americans take better care of themselves*. Washington, DC: Pew Internet and American Life Project. http://www.pewinternet.org/reports/toc.asp?Report=26 (accessed September 28, 2003).

Frankel, Mark S. 2002. *Seizing the moment: Scientists' authorship rights in the digital age; Report of a study by the American Association for the Advancement of Science, Washington, DC*. http://www.aaas.org/spp/sfrl/projects/epub/index.shtml (accessed October 6, 2003).

Freudenheim, Milt. 2000. New Web sites altering visits to patients. *New York Times*, May 30.

Fuchs, Ira. 2004. Needed: An "Educore" to aid publication. *Chronicle of Higher Education*, September 24, p. B19.

Gadd, Elizabeth, Charles Oppenheim, and Steve Probets. 2003. Journal copyright transfer agreements: Their effects on author self-archiving. In *ELPUB 2003: From Information to Knowledge. Proceedings of the Seventh ICCC/IFIP International Conference on Electronic Publishing*, ed. S. M. de Souza Costa, J. A. Carvalho, A. A. Baptista, A. C. Santos Morieira, 102. Guimarães, Portugal: Universidade do Minho.

Gallouj, Faïz. 2002. Knowledge-intensive business services: Processing knowledge and producing innovation. In *Productivity, innovation and knowledge in services: New economic and socio-economic approaches*, ed. Jean Gadrey and Faïz Gallouj, 256–284. Cheltenham, UK: Edward Elgar.

Galusky, Wyatt. 2003. Identifying with information: Citizen empowerment, the Internet, and the environmental anti-toxins movement. In *Cyberactivism: Online activism in theory and practice*, ed. Martha McCaughey and Michael D. Ayers, 185–205. New York: Routledge.

Gans, Herbert J. 2003. *Democracy and the news*. New York: Oxford University Press.

Garrido, Maria, and Alexander Halavais. 2003. Mapping networks of support for the Zapatista movement: Applying social-networks analysis to study contemporary social movements. In *Cyberactivism: Online activism in theory and practice*, ed. Martha McCaughey and Michael D. Ayers, 165–184. New York: Routledge.

Geiger, Roger L. 2004. *Knowledge and money: Research universities and the paradox of the marketplace*. Stanford, CA: Stanford University Press.

Gerhard, Kristin H., Trudi E. Jacobsen, and Susan G. Williamson. 1993. Indexing inadequacy and interdisciplinary journals: The case of women's studies. *College and Research Libraries* 54 (March): 125–135.

Gibbons, Michael, Camille Limoges, Helga Nowotny, Simon Schwartzman, Peter Scott, and Martin Trow. 1994. *The new production of knowledge: The dynamics of science and research in contemporary societies*. London: Sage.

Gibbs, W. Wayt. 1995. Information have-nots: A vicious circle isolates many third world scientists. *Scientific American* 272(5): B12–B14.

Gibbs, W. Wayt. 2003. Public not welcome—Libraries cut off access to the scientific literature. *Scientific American.com*, September 8. http://www.sciam.com/article.cfm?articleID=00061239-BAD6-1F58-905980A84189EEDF (accessed October 6, 2003).

Ginsparg, Paul. 2001. Creating a global knowledge network. Paper presented at Second Joint ICSU Press–UNESCO Expert Conference on Electronic Publishing in Science, Paris, February 19–23. http://arxiv.org/blurb/pg01unesco.html (accessed September 28, 2003).

Gitlin, Todd. 1980. *The whole world is watching: Mass media in the making and unmaking of the new left*. Berkeley and Los Angeles: University of California Press.

Gladwell, Malcolm. 2000. *The tipping point: How little things can make a big difference*. Boston: Little, Brown.

Gladwell, Malcolm. 2003. Making the grade. *New Yorker*, September 15, pp. 31, 34.

Glanz, James. 2001. Web archive opens a new realm of research. *New York Times*, May 1.

Glass, Gene. 2003. Education policy analysis archives activity. Paper presented at the annual meeting of the American Educational Research Association, Chicago, April 23.

Gleason, Bernard W. 2003. Open-source software fosters integration and stability. *Chronicle of Higher Education*, August 1, p. B13.

Glenn, David. 2003. European economists divorce Elsevier: *International Politics* finds new publisher. *Chronicle of Higher Education*, March 21, p. A18.

Golinski, Jan. 1988. The secret life of an alchemist. In *Let Newton be! A new perspective on his life and works*, ed. John Fauvel, Raymond Flood, Michael Shortland, and Robin Wilson, 147–167. New York: Oxford University Press.

Gorman, James. 2003. In virtual museums, an archive of the world. *New York Times*, January 12.

Grafton, Anthony. 1994. The footnote from de Thou to Ranke. *History and Theory* 33: 53–76.

Grisham, Dana L. 2002. "Recommended literature": A new children's literature resource. *Reading Online* 5(9). http://www.readingonline.org/editorial/edit_index.asp?HREF=may2002/index.html (accessed September 28, 2003).

Gross, Alan G., Joseph E. Harmon, and Michael Reidy. 2002. *Communicating science: The scientific article from the 17th century to the present*. Oxford: Oxford University Press.

Guédon, Jean-Claude. 2001. In Oldenburg's long shadow: Librarians, research scientists, publishers, and the control of scientific publishing. In *Creating the digital future: Proceedings of the 138th Annual Meeting of the Association of Research Libraries*. Washington, DC: Association of Research Libraries. http://www.arl.org/arl/proceedings/138/guedon.html (accessed September 29, 2003).

Guthrie, Kevin M. 1997. JSTOR: The development of a cost-driven, value-based pricing model. Paper presented at Scholarly Communication and Technology conference, Emory University, Atlanta, GA, April 25–27. http://www.arl.org/scomm/scat/guthries.html (accessed October 3, 2003).

Gutmann, Amy, and David Thompson. 1996. *Democracy and disagreement*. Cambridge, MA: Harvard University Press.

Haank, Derek. 2001. Is electronic publishing being used in the best interests of science? The publisher's view. In *Proceedings of the Second ICSU-UNESCO International Conference on Electronic Publishing in Science*. Paris: UNESCO. http://www.econ.ucsb.edu/~tedb/Journals/Haankspeech.doc (accessed September 28, 2003).

Haefeli, William. 2004. Cartoon. *New Yorker*, July 12, p. 83.

Hague, Barry N., and Brian D. Loader, eds. 1999. *Digital democracy: Discourse and decision making in the information age.* London: Routledge.

Hall, Marie Boas. 2002. *Henry Oldenburg: Shaping the Royal Society.* Oxford: Oxford University Press.

Hardt, Michael, and Antonio Negri. 2000. *Empire.* Cambridge, MA: Harvard University Press.

Hardy, Henry. 2002. Letter. *Times Literary Supplement*, March 29, p. 17.

Harnad, Stevan. 2003a. *The research impact cycle.* Paper presented at the Synergy Publishing Workshop, Simon Fraser University, Vancouver, October 15. http://www.ecs.soton.ac.uk/~harnad/Temp/self-archiving.htm (accessed October 6, 2003).

Harnad, Stevan. 2003b. Electronic preprints and postprints. In *Encyclopedia of library and information science.* New York: Marcel Dekker. http://www.ecs .soton.ac.uk/~harnad/Temp/eprints.htm (accessed September 28, 2003).

Harnad, Stevan. 2003c. On the need to take both roads to open access. Budapest Open Access Initiative forum archive, September 6. http://threader.ecs.soton.ac .uk/lists/boaiforum/130.html (accessed September 28, 2003).

Harnad, Stevan. 2003d. Re: How to compare research impact of toll- vs. open-access research. American-Scientist-Open-Access-Forum, September 8. http:// www.ecs.soton.ac.uk/~harnad/Hypermail/Amsci/3003.html (accessed October 6, 2003).

Harnad, Stevan. 2003e. On the deep disanalogy between text and software and between text and data insofar as free/open access is concerned. Re: Free access vs. open access. American-Scientist-Open-Access-Forum, August 16. http://www.ecs .soton.ac.uk/~harnad/Hypermail/Amsci/2967.html (accessed October 6, 2003).

Harnad, Stevan. 2004a. The UK report, press coverage, and the green and gold roads to open access. Liblicense-1, July 30. http://www.library.yale.edu/~llicense/ ListArchives/0407/msg00147.html (accessed February 1, 2005).

Harnad, Stevan. 2004b. The affordable-access (AA) problem and the open-access (OA) problem are not the same. Re: The green road to open access: A leveraged transition. American-Scientist-Open-Access-Forum, January 23. http://www.ecs .soton.ac.uk/~harnad/Hypermail/Amsci/3483.html (accessed August 10, 2004).

Harnad, Stevan. 2004c. Enrich impact measures through open access analysis, October 22. Rapid responses to: Kamran Abbasi, Let's dump impact factors, *British Medical Journal*, 329. http://bmj.bmjjournals.com/cgi/eletters/329/7471/ 0-h#80657 (accessed October 25, 2004).

Hartman, Geoffrey H., and Sanford Budick, eds. 1986. *Midrash and literature.* New Haven: Yale University Press.

Hawley, John B. 2003. The JCI's commitment to excellence—and free access. *Journal of Clinical Investigation* 112: 968–969.

Hawley, John B. 2004. JCI and open access. Paper presented at the Society for Scholarly Publishing conference, Washington, DC. http://www.sspnet.org/files/public/Hawley.pdf (accessed April 4, 2005).

Health InterNetwork Access to Research Initiative. 2003. *Scholarly Communication Report* 7(1): 11–12.

Heeks, Richard. 1999. *Reinventing government in the information age: International practices in IT enabled public sector reform.* London: Routledge.

Hill, Abraham. 1667. Inquiries for Guiny. *Philosophical Transactions* 2(25): 472.

Hitchcock, Steve. 2005. The effect of open access and downloads ("hits") on citation impact: A bibliography of studies. Open Citation Project. http://opcit.eprints.org/oacitation-biblio.html (accessed February 9, 2005).

Hitchcock, Steve, Donna Bergmark, Tim Brody, Christopher Gutteridge, Les Carr, Wendy Hall, Carl Lagoze, and Stevan Harnad. 2002. Open citation linking: The way forward. *D-Lib Magazine* 8(10). http://www.dlib.org/dlib/october02/hitchcock/10hitchcock.html (accessed September 28, 2003).

Holt, Jennifer, and Karen A. Schmidt. 1995. CARL-Uncover2 or Faxon Finder? A comparison of articles and journals in CARL-Uncover2 and Faxon Finder. *Library Resources & Technical Services* 39(3): 221–228.

Hunter, Michael. 1981. *Science and society in Restoration England.* Cambridge: Cambridge University Press.

IEEE. *See* Institute of Electrical and Electronics Engineers.

Institute of Electrical and Electronics Engineers. 2005. About the IEEE. New York. http://www.ieee.org/ (accessed February 5, 2005).

Integration of IDEAL with ScienceDirect. 2002. *Scholarly Communications Report* 6(6): 3.

Introduction. 1664/1665. *Philosophical Transactions* 1(1): 1.

ISI Web of Science to be enhanced. 2004. *Scholarly Communication Report* 8(2): 3.

Iyengar, Shanto. 1991. *Is anyone responsible? How television frames political issues.* Chicago: University of Chicago Press.

Jarvis, John. 2004. Testimony before Science and Technology Committee, House of Commons, March 1. Uncorrected transcript of oral evidence to be published as HC 399-i, House of Commons, Minutes of Evidence Taken before Science and Technology Committee, "Scientific Publications." http://www.publications.parliament.uk/pa/cm200304/cmselect/cmsctech/uc399-i/uc39902.htm (accessed April 8, 2004).

Jaygbay, Jacob. 1998. The politics of and prospects for African scholarly journals in the information age. In *Knowledge dissemination in Africa: The role of the scholarly journal,* ed. Philip G. Altbach and Damtew Teferra, 63–74. Chestnut Hill, MA: Bellagio.

Jefferson, Thomas. 1997. Letter of Thomas Jefferson to Edward Carrington, 1787. In *The Letters of Thomas Jefferson: 1743–1826*, ed. G. Welling. Groningen, The Netherlands: Humanities Computing. http://odur.let.rug.nl/~usa/P/tj3/writings/brf/jefl52.htm (accessed September 29, 2003).

Johns, Adrian. 1998. *The nature of the book: Print and knowledge in the making*. Chicago: University of Chicago Press.

Johns, Adrian. 2000. Miscellaneous methods: Authors, societies and journals in early modern England. *British Journal for the History of Science* 35: 159–186.

Junking science. 2004. *New York Times*, September 14.

Kamau, Nancy. 2001. Breaking information access barriers: The African Virtual Library initiative (AVL-I). Paper presented at The Web and Beyond: Harnessing the Potential of IT for Improving Health, Washington, DC, January 10. http://www.med.jhu.edu/ccp/ppt/2001/kamau/ (accessed September 29, 2003).

Kant, Immanuel. 1970. An answer to the question: What is enlightenment? In *Kant: Political writings*, ed. Hans Reiss, trans. H. B. Nisbett, 54–60. Cambridge: Cambridge University Press.

Keller, Michael. 2004. Letter to Dr. Elias A. Zerhouni, Director, National Institutes of Health, November 15. http://www-sul.stanford.edu/staff/pubs/MAK_to_Zerhouni_041115.pdf (accessed February 2, 2005).

Kemp, Simon. 2002. *Public goods and private wants: A psychological approach to government spending*. Cheltenham, UK: Elgar.

Kermode, Frank. 1986. The plain sense of things. In *Midrash and literature*, ed. Geoffrey H. Hartman and Sanford Budick, 179–193. New Haven: Yale University Press.

Keynes, John Maynard. 1947. Newton the man. In *Newton tercentenary celebrations*, ed. Royal Society, 27–34. Cambridge: Cambridge University Press.

King, Donald W., and Carol Tenopir. 1998. Economic cost models of scientific scholarly journals. Paper presented to the ICSU Press workshop, Keble College, Oxford, March 31–April 2. http://www.bodley.ox.ac.uk/icsu/ (accessed September 29, 2003).

Klevan, David G. 1997. Re: Holocaust lterature. H-High-S, H-Net Discussion Networks, September 10. http://h-net.msu.edu/cgi-bin/logbrowse.pl?trx=vx&list=h-high-s&month=9709&week=b&msg=tGTriGG4MV25xdKGJDjUKA&user=&pw= (accessed October 6, 2003).

Kling, Rob, Lisa Spector, and Geoff McKim. 2002. The guild model. *Journal of Electronic Publishing* 8(1). http://www.press.umich.edu/jep/08-01/kling.html (accessed September 29, 2003).

Klinger, Shula. 2001. "Are they talking yet?" Online discourse as political action in an education policy forum. Ph.D. diss., University of British Columbia, Vancouver.

Knight, Jonathan. 2004. Novartis goes public with DNA data in bid to tackle diabetes. *Nature* 431(1029), doi:10.1038/4311029b (accessed April 4, 2005).

Kolata, Gina. 2003. Hormone therapy, already found to have risks, is now said to lack benefits. *New York Times*, March 18.

Krasner, Jeffrey. 2004. Novartis to share diabetes research: Firm to fund Broad, Harvard, MIT work. *Boston Globe*, October 28.

Krikos, Linda A. 1994. Women's studies periodical indexes: An in-depth comparison. *Serials Review* (Summer): 64–75.

Kuhn, Thomas S. 1978. Newton's optical papers. In *Isaac Newton's papers and letters on natural philosophy and related documents*, ed. I. Bernard Cohen, 27–45. Cambridge, MA: Harvard University Press.

Kurtz, Michael J., Guenther Eichhorn, Alberto Accomazzi, Carolyn Grant, Markus Demleitner, Edwin Henneken, and Stephen S. Murray. 2004. The effect of use and access on citations. Unpublished paper, Harvard-Smithsonian Center for Astrophysics, Cambridge, MA. http://cfa-www.harvard.edu/~kurtz/IPM-abstract.html (accessed October 20, 2004).

Kurtz, Michael J., Guenther Eichhorn, Alberto Accomazzi, Carolyn Grant, Markus Demleitner, Stephen S. Murray. 2005. Worldwide use and impact of the NASA Astrophysics Data System Digital Library. *Journal of the American Society for Information Science and Technology* 56(1). Prepublication version: http://cfa-www.harvard.edu/~kurtz/jasist1.pdf (accessed October 20, 2004).

LaRose, Albert J. 1989. Inclusiveness of indexes and abstracts of interest to students of communication. *Reading Quarterly* 29(1): 29–35.

Larsen, Elena, and Lee Rainie. 2002. *The rise of the e-citizen: How people use government agencies' Web sites.* Washington, DC: Pew Internet and American Life Project. http://207.21.232.103/pdfs/PIP_Govt_Website_Rpt.pdf (accessed April 4, 2005).

Larson, Carolyn, and Linda Arret. 2001. Descriptive resource needs from the reference perspective. Unpublished paper, Library of Congress, Washington, DC. http://www.unicamp.br/bc/arret_paper.html (accessed September 29, 2003).

Lawrence, Steven. 2001. Online or invisible? *Nature* 411(6837): 521. http://www.neci.nec.com/~lawrence/papers/online-nature01/ (accessed September 29, 2003).

Lawrence, Steven, C. Lee Giles, and Kurt D. Bollacker. 1999. Digital libraries and autonomous citation indexing. *IEEE Computer* 32(6): 67–71. http://www.neci.nj.nec.com/homepages/lawrence/papers/aci-computer98/aci-computer99.html (accessed February 1, 2005).

Lerner, Josh, and Jean Tirole. 2000. The simple economics of open source. Working paper no. W7600, National Bureau of Economic Research, Cambridge, MA. http://papers.nber.org/papers/w7600 (accessed October 3, 2003).

Lessig, Lawrence. 2002. Free culture. Paper presented at Open Source Convention (OSCON) 2002, San Diego, July 22–26. http://www.oreillynet.com/pub/a/policy/2002/08/15/lessig.html (accessed September 29, 2003).

Lessig, Lawrence. 2004. *Free culture: How big media uses technology and the law to lock down culture and control creativity.* New York: Penguin.

Linn, Robert L. 2003. Performance standards: Utility for different uses of assessments. *Education Policy Analysis Archives* 11(31). http://epaa.asu.edu/epaa/v11n31/ (accessed July 8, 2004).

Longino, Helen. 2002. *The fate of knowledge.* Princeton: Princeton University Press.

Lorimer, Rowland, Adrienne Lindsay, and Géard Boismenu. 2003. Online publishing and Canadian social science and humanities journals: A financial and publishing survey and the SYNERGIES project. *Canadian Journal of Communication* 28(5): 1–44.

Lund University Libraries. 2004. *Directory of Open Access Journals.* Lund, Sweden: Lund University Libraries. http://www.doaj.org/ (accessed January 30, 2005).

Mabawonku, Iyabo. 2001. Providing information for capacity building: The role of an NGO library in Nigeria. *Information Development* 17(2): 100–106.

Machlup, Fritz. 1977. Publishing scholarly books and journals: Is it economically viable? *Journal of Political Economy* 85(1): 217–225.

Machlup, Fritz. 1984. *The economics of information and human capital.* Vol. 3, *Knowledge: Its creation, distribution, and economic significance.* Princeton: Princeton University Press.

Mahoney, Michael S. 1973. *The mathematical career of Pierre de Fermat (1601–1665).* Princeton: Princeton University Press.

Manmart, Lampang. 2001. Impact of Internet on schools of library and information science in Thailand. Paper presented at the 67th IFLA Council and General Conference, Boston, August 16–25.

Mansbridge, Jane. 1998. On the contested nature of the public good. In *Private action and the public good*, ed. Walter W. Powell and Elisabeth S. Clemens, 3–19. New Haven: Yale University Press.

McAfee, Noëlle. 2004. Public knowledge. *Philosophy and Social Criticism* 30(2): 139–157.

McCabe, Mark J. 1999. The impact of publisher mergers on journal prices: An update. *ARL Bimonthly Report* 207 (December). http://www.arl.org/newsltr/207/jrnlprices.html (accessed September 29, 2003).

McCabe, Mark J. 2002. Journal pricing and mergers: A portfolio approach. *American Economic Review* 92(1): 259–269.

McChesney, Robert W. 1999. *Rich media, poor democracy: Communication politics in dubious times.* Urbana: University of Illinois Press.

McGinn, Colin. 1999. The meaning and morality of *Lolita. Philosophical Forum* 30(1): 31–41.

McKiernan, Gerry. 2001. EJI(sm): A registry of innovative e-journal features, functionalities, and content. Ames: Iowa State University Library. http://www .public.iastate.edu/~CYBERSTACKS/EJI.htm (accessed September 29, 2003).

McLaughlin-Jenkins, Erin. 2003. Walking the low road: The pursuit of scientific knowledge in late Victorian working-class communities. *Public Understanding of Science* 12: 147–166.

McLuhan, Marshall. 1962. *The Gutenberg galaxy: The making of typographic man*. Toronto: University of Toronto Press.

McSherry, C. 2001. *Who owns academic work? Battling for control of intellectual property*. Cambridge, MA: Harvard University Press.

Meier, Barry. 2004. Major medical journals will require registration of trials. *New York Times*, September 9, p. C11.

Merger mania. 2003. *Scholarly Communication Reports* 7(5): 2.

Merton, Robert. 1968. Science and democratic social structure. In *Social theory and social structure*, 3rd ed., 604–615. New York: Free Press.

Merton, Robert. 1979. Foreword. In Eugene Garfield, *Citation index—Its theory and application in science, technology, and humanities*, v–ix. Philadelphia: ISI Press. http://www.garfield.library.upenn.edu/cifwd.html (accessed September 29, 2003).

Meyer, Mark L. 1998. To promote the progress of science and useful arts: The protection of and rights in scientific research. *IDEA: The Journal of Law and Technology* 39(1). http://www.idea.piercelaw.edu/articles/39/39_1/1.Meyer.pdf (accessed September 29, 2003).

Mialet, Hélène. 2003. Reading Hawking's presence: An interview with a self-effacing man. *Critical Inquiry* 29(4): 571–599.

Milstein, Sarah. 2002. New economy: Web-based peer-review programs are reducing turnaround time, postage bills and workload at many scholarly journals. *New York Times*, August 12.

Mirapul, Matthew. 2003. Far-flung artworks, side by side online. *New York Times*, May 22.

Monastersky, Richard. 2003. Paper on memory research forgot to give credit, critics complain. The Daily Report, *Chronicle of Higher Education*, January 22. http://chronicle.com/prm/daily/2003/01/2003012203n.htm (accessed February 12, 2005).

Morais, R. 2002. Double Dutch no longer. *Forbes.com*, November 11. http:// www.forbes.com/global/2002/1111/044.html (accessed September 29, 2003).

Murray, Elizabeth, Bernard Lo, Lance Pollack, Karen Donelan, Joe Catania, Ken Lee, Kinga Zapert, and Rachel Turner. 2003. The impact of health information on the Internet on health care and the physician-patient relationship: National U.S. survey among 1,050 U.S. physicians. *Journal of Medical Internet Research* 5(3): e17. http://www.jmir.org/2003/3/e17/ (accessed September 29, 2003).

Muthayan, Sal, and Florence Muinde. 2003. The Public Knowledge Project's open journal Systems: African perspectives from Kenya and South Africa. Paper presented at the International Symposium on Open Access and the Public Domain in Digital Data and Information for Science, NESCO, Paris.

Mutula, S. M. 2001. The IT environment in Kenya: Implications in public universities. *Library Hi Tech* 19(2): 155–166.

Nafisi, Azar. 2003. *Reading* Lolita *in Tehran*. New York: Random House.

Nagourney, Adam. 2001. For medical journals, a new world online. *New York Times*, March 20.

National Inquiry Services Centre. 2005. African research. Grahamstown, South Africa. http://www.nisc.co.za (accessed February 5, 2005).

National Institutes of Health. 2003. The health information prescription. Press release, United States National Library of Medicine, Bethesda, MD, March 18. http://www.nlm.nih.gov/news/press_releases/GAhealthRX03.html (accessed September 29, 2003).

Nelson, Richard R. 1959. The simple economics of basic scientific research. *Journal of Political Economy* 67(3): 297–306.

Newton, Isaac. 1671/1672. A letter of Mr. Isaac Newton, professor of the mathematicks in the university of Cambridge; containing his new theory of light and colors: sent by the author to the publisher from Cambridge, Feb. 6, 1671/72. *Philosophical Transactions* 6(80): 3075–3087.

Newton, Isaac. 1673. Mr. Newton's answer to the foregoing letter further explaining his theory of light and colors, and particularly that of whiteness; together with his continued hopes of perfecting telescopes by reflections rather than refractions. *Philosophical Transactions* 8(96): 6087–6092.

Newton, Isaac. 1959. *The correspondence of Isaac Newton*, Vol. 1, *1661–1675*, ed. H. W. Turnbull. Cambridge: Cambridge University Press.

NIH. *See* National Institutes of Health.

NISC. *See* National Inquiry Services Centre.

Nimmer, Melville B. 1970. Does copyright abridge the First Amendment guarantees of free speech and the press? *UCLA Law Review* 1180: 1181–1186.

Noll, Roger G. 1996. The economics of scholarly publications and the information superhighway. Brookings Discussion Papers in Domestic Economics no. 3, Brookings Institution, Washington, DC. http://www.brookingsinstitution.org/dybdocroot/views/papers/domestic/003.htm (accessed October 3, 2002).

Norris, Pippa. 2001. *Digital divide: Civic engagement, information poverty, and the Internet worldwide*. Cambridge: Cambridge University Press.

OCLC. *See* Online Computer Library Center.

Okamura, Kyoko, Judith Bernstein, and Anne T. Fidler. 2002. Assessing the quality of the infertility resources on the World Wide Web: Tools to guide clients through the maze of fact and fiction. *Journal of Midwifery and Women's Health* 47(4): 264–268.

Oldenburg, Henry. 1966. *The correspondence of Henry Oldenburg.* Vol. 2. Trans. and ed. A. Rupert Hall and Marie Boas Hall. Madison: University of Wisconsin Press.

Online Computer Library Center. 2002. How academic librarians can influence students' web-based information choices. OCLC White Paper on the information habits of college students. Dublin, OH: OCLC. http://www.mnstate.edu/schwartz/informationhabits.pdf (accessed October 3, 2003).

Open source in higher education: A sampling. 2004. *Chronicle of Higher Education*, September 24, p. B5.

Page, Benjamin I. 1996. *Who deliberates? Mass media in modern democracy.* Chicago: University of Chicago Press.

Parks, Robert P. 2001. The Faustian grip of academic publishing. Unpublished paper, Washington University, St. Louis. http://ideas.repec.org/p/wpa/wuwpmi/0202005.html (accessed September 29, 2003).

Patel, Jazshu, and Krishan Kumar. 2001. *Libraries and librarianship in India.* Westport, CT: Greenwood.

Persaud, Avinish. 2001. The knowledge gap. *Foreign Affairs* 80(2): 107–117.

Peterson, Melody. 2001. Medical journals to offer lower rates in poor nations. *New York Times*, July 9.

The *Philosophical Transactions* of two years, 1665 and 1666, beginning *March* 6, 1665, and ending with *February* 1666; abbreviated in an Alphabetical Table: And also afterwards digested into a more *natural method.* 1666. *Philosophical Transactions* 1(22): 399–406.

Pillow, Lisa. 1999. Scholarly African American studies journals: An evaluation of electronic indexing service coverage. *Serials Review* 25(4): 21–28.

Preface. 1682/1683. *Philosophical Transactions* 13(143): 2.

Quint, Barbara. 2004. Thomson ISI to track Web-based scholarship with NEC's CiteSeer. *Information Today*, March 1. http://www.infotoday.com/newsbreaks/nb040301-1.shtml (accessed October 19, 2004).

Raney, Rebecca Fairley. 2002. Bush signs e-government act. *New York Times*, December 18.

Rao, Siriginidi Subba. 2001. Networking libraries and information centres: Challenges in India. *Library Hi Tech* 19(2): 167–178.

Rauch, Alan. 2001. *Useful knowledge: The Victorians, morality, and the march of intellect.* Durham, NC: Duke University Press.

Raymond, Eric R. 2003. *The cathedral and the bazaar.* Unpublished manuscript. http://catb.org/~esr/writings/cathedral-bazaar/ (accessed September 29, 2003).

Reeves, Richard. 1998. *What the people know: Freedom and the press.* Cambridge, MA: Harvard University Press.

Reich, Victoria, and David S. H. Rosenthal. 2003. LOCKSS: Building permanent access for e-journals—Practical steps towards an affordable, cooperative, e-preservation, and e-archiving program. In *ELPUB 2003: From Information to Knowledge. Proceedings of the Seventh ICCC/IFIP International Conference on Electronic Publishing*, ed. S. M. de Souza Costa, J. A. Carvalho, A. A. Baptista, and A. C. Santos Morieira, 157–165. Guimarães, Portugal: Universidade do Minho.

Reichman, J. H., and Paul F. Uhlir. 2001. Promoting public good uses of scientific data: A contractually reconstructed commons for science and innovation. Paper presented at the Conference on the Public Domain, Duke University, Durham, NC, November 9–11. http://www.law.duke.edu/pd/papers/ReichmanandUhlir.pdf (accessed September 29, 2003).

A relation of an uncommon accident in two aged persons. 1666. *Philosophical Transactions* 1(20): 380–381.

Rogers, Theresa. 2001. Understanding in the absence of meaning: Coming of age narratives of the Holocaust. *Literacy Advocacy* 15(1): 23–37.

Romano, Michael S. 2002. Putting up a filter for the kids. *New York Times*, April 4.

Rose, Jonathan. 2003. *The intellectual life of the British working class*. New Haven: Yale University Press.

Rosen, Jonathan. 2000. *The Talmud and the Internet*. New York: Farr Giroux and Strauss.

Rosenberg, Diana B. 1997. *University libraries in Africa: A review of their current state and future potential*. 3 vols. London: International African Institute.

Rosenzweig, Roy. 2001. The road to Xanadu: Public and private pathways on the history Web. *Journal of American History* 88(2). http://chnm.gmu.edu/assets/historyessays/roadtoxanadu.html (accessed September 4, 2004).

Rowland, Fytton. 2002. The peer-review process. *Learned Publishing* 15(4): 247–258.

Rusin, David. 2002. The expected properties of dark lenses. *Astrophysical Journal* 572: 705–723.

Rusnock, Andrea. 1999. Correspondence networks and the Royal Society, 1700–1750. *British Journal for the History of Science* 32: 155–169.

Sabbatini, Renato. 2003. Open access in Brazil. Paper presented at ELPUB2003: From information to knowledge, Guimarães, Portugal, June 25–28.

Samuelson, Paul A. 1954. The pure theory of public expenditure. *Review of Economics and Statistics* 36: 387–389.

Sanders, L. 2003. Medicine's progress, one setback at a time. *New York Times Magazine*, March 16, pp. 29–31.

Santora, Marc. 2003. Scholars complain of feeling helpless as they see their campus destroyed. *New York Times*, May 19.

Schecter, Bruce. 2003. Telescopes of the world, unite! A cosmic database emerges. *New York Times*, May 20.

Schiller, Herbert I. 1996. *Information inequality: The deepening social crisis in America.* New York: Routledge.

Scholarly Publishing and Academic Resources Coalition. 2001. *Declaring independence.* Washington, DC: Scholarly Publishing and Academic Resources Coalition. http://www.arl.org/sparc/DI/Declaring_Independence.pdf (accessed January 11, 2005).

Scholarly Publishing and Academic Resources Coalition. 2004. Library and advocacy organizations praise call for free access to science. Press release, Washington, DC, March 16. http://www.arl.org/sparc/announce/031604.html (accessed January 11, 2005).

Schonfeld, Roger C., Donald W. King, Ann Okerson, and Eileen Gifford Fenton. 2004. Library periodicals expenses: Comparison of non-subscription costs of print and electronic formats on a life-cycle basis. *D-Lib Magazine* 10(1). http://www.dlib.org/dlib/january04/schonfeld/01schonfeld.html (accessed August 5, 2004).

Schulz, Renate A. 1998. Using young adult literature in content-based German instruction: Teaching the Holocaust. *Unterrichtspraxis/Teaching German* 31(2): 138–147.

Schwartz, John. 2003. With aid of amateurs, NASA builds mosaic of a disaster. *New York Times*, April 22.

Science and Technology Committee, House of Commons. 2004. *Scientific publications: Free for all?* London: Stationery Office.

Science journal to put research online. 2003. *New York Times*, October 17.

Secord, Anne. 1994. Science in the pub: Artisan botanists in early nineteenth century Lancashire. *History of Science* 32: 269–315.

Sen, Amartya. 1999. *Development as freedom.* New York: Anchor.

Shafack, Rosemary M., and Kiven Charles Wirsiy. 2002. *The universities of Cameroon.* Unpublished paper, University of Buea, Buea, Cameroon.

Shapin, Steven. 1996. *The scientific revolution.* Chicago: University of Chicago Press.

Singleton, Brent D. 2004. African bibliophiles: Books and libraries in medieval Timbuktu. *Libraries and Culture* 39(1): 1–12.

Smart, Pippa. 2003. Supporting indigenous published research: The African Journals Online (AJOL) case study. Paper presented at ELPUB2003: From information to knowledge, Guimarães, Portugal, June 25–28.

Smith, Marc A., and Peter Kollock, eds. 1999. *Communities in cyberspace.* London: Routledge.

Sommerville, John C. 1996. *The new revolution in England: Cultural dynamics of daily information.* New York: Oxford University Press.

Sorrells, Robert C., and Bruce K. Britton. 1998. What is the point? Tests of a quick and clean method for improving instructional texts. In *Learning from text across conceptual domains*, ed. Cynthia R. Hynd, 95–155. Mahwah, NJ: Erlbaum.

SPARC. *See* Scholarly Publishing and Academic Resources Center.

Sprat, Thomas. 1722. *The history of the Royal Society of London, for the improving of natural knowledge*. 3rd ed. London: J. Knapton.

SQW Ltd. 2003. *An economic analysis of scientific research publishing: A report commissioned by the Wellcome Trust*. London: Wellcome Trust. http://www.wellcome.ac.uk/assets/wtd003182.pdf (accessed January 11, 2005).

Stallman, Richard. 2001. Why "free software" is better than "open source." Free Software Foundation, Boston. http://www.gnu.org/philosophy/free-software-for-freedom.html (accessed January 17, 2005).

Stolberg, Sheryl G. 2001. Science, studies and motherhood. *New York Times*, April 22.

Strathern, Paul. 1996. *Kant in 90 minutes*. Chicago: Dee.

Suber, Peter. 2004a. Who should control access to research literature? *SPARC Open Access Newsletter*, no. 79. http://www.earlham.edu/~peters/fos/newsletter/11-02-04.htm (accessed November 1, 2004).

Suber, Peter. 2004b. The Credit Suisse report. *SPARC Open Access Newsletter*, no. 73. http://www.earlham.edu/~peters/fos/newsletter/05-03-04.htm (accessed August 1, 2004).

Suber, Peter. 2004c. University actions against high journal prices. *SPARC Open Access Newsletter*, no. 72. http://www.earlham.edu/~peters/fos/newsletter/04-02-04.htm (accessed April 1, 2004).

Suber, Peter. 2005a. Commens on the weakening of the NIH public-access policy. *SPARC Open Access Newsletter*, no. 82. http://www.earlham.edu/~peters/fos/newsletter/02-02-05.htm (accessed February 13, 2005).

Suber, Peter. 2005b. Google's gigantic library project. *SPARC Open Access Newsletter*, no. 81. http://www.earlham.edu/~peters/fos/newsletter/01-02-05.htm (accessed February 1, 2005).

Susman, Thomas M., and David J. Carter. 2003. *Publisher mergers: A consumer-based approach to antitrust analysis*. Washington, DC: Information Access Alliance. http://www.google.ca/search?q=cache:Trkj4DhBSeYJ:www.informationaccess.org/WhitePaperV2Final.pdf+Publisher+mergers:+A+consumer-based+approach+to+antitrust+analysis&hl=en&ie=UTF-8 (accessed September 29, 2003).

Swan, Alma P. 2005. Self-archiving: It's an author thing. Paper presented at the Southampton Workshop on Institutional Open Access Repositories, University of Southampton, Southampton, UK. http://www.eprints.org/jan2005/ppts/swan.ppt (accessed April 4, 2005).

Swan, Alma P., and Sheridan N. Brown. 1999. What authors want: Report of the ALPSP Research Study on the Motivations and Concerns of Contributors to Learned Journals. *Learned Publishing* 12: 170–172.

Swan, Alma P., and Sheridan N. Brown. 2004. *JISC/OSI Journal Authors Survey*. Truro, UK: Key Perspectives. http://www.jisc.ac.uk/uploaded_documents/ JISCOAreport1.pdf (accessed August 20, 2004).

Tamber, Pritpal S. 2000. Is scholarly publishing becoming a monopoly? *BMC News and Views* 1(1). http://www.biomedcentral.com/1471-8219/1/1#B4 (accessed September 29, 2003).

Teferra, Damtew. 1998. The significance of information technology for African scholarly journals. In *Knowledge dissemination in Africa: The role of scholarly journals*, ed. Philip G. Altbach and Damtew Teferra, 39–62. Chestnut Hill, MA: Bellagio.

Tenopir, Carol. 2003. *Use and users of electronic library resources: An overview and analysis of recent research studies*. With Brenda Hitchcock and Ashley Pillow. Washington, DC: Council on Library and Information Resources. http://www.clir.org/pubs/reports/pub120/pub120.pdf (accessed October 5, 2003).

Tenopir, Carol. 2004. Online scholarly journals: How many? *Library Journal* 129(2): 32. http://www.libraryjournal.com/article/CA374956 (accessed February 1, 2005).

Tenopir, Carol, and Donald W. King. 2001. Lessons for the future of journals. *Nature* 413(672–674), doi:10.1038/35099602 (accessed September 29, 2003).

Testa, James. 1998. The ISI database: The journal selection process. Unpublished paper, Institute for Scientific Information, Philadelphia, March. http://cs.nju.edu .cn/~gchen/isi/help/HowToSelectJournals.html (accessed September 29, 2003).

Thapa, Neelam, K. C. Sahoo, and B. P. Srivastava. 2001. E-publishing: Beginning of a new era on e-journals. In *Digital asset management: Proceedings of the National Conference on Recent Advances in Information Technology*, ed. Harish Chandra and S. Venkadesan, 69–74. Chennai, India.

Thompson, Nicholas. 2002. May the source be with you. *Washington Monthly* (July/August). http://www.washingtonmonthly.com/features/2001/0207 .thompson.html (accessed September 29, 2003).

To the Royal Society. 1665. *Philosophical Transactions* 1.

Tracz, Vitek. 2004. Testimony before Science and Technology Committee, House of Commons, March 8. Uncorrected transcript of oral evidence to be published as HC 399-ii, House of Commons, Minutes of Evidence Taken before Science and Technology Committee, "Scientific Publications." http://www.publications.parliament.uk/pa/cm200304/cmselect/cmsctech/uc399- ii/uc39902.htm (accessed April 8, 2004).

Trosow, Samuel E. 2003. Copyright protection for federally funded research: Necessary incentive or double subsidy? Unpublished paper, University of

Western Ontario. http://publish.uwo.ca/~strosow/Sabo_Bill_Paper.pdf (accessed September 29, 2003).

2003 in context. 2003. *Nature* 426(755): 748–757.

Unauthorized access to e-journal. 2002. *Scholarly Communication Report* 6(12): 16.

UNESCO, IFS, OECD, and WEIP. *See* United Nations Educational, Scientific, and Cultural Organization, Institute for Statistics, Organization for Economic Cooperation and Development, and World Education Indicators Program.

Union of Concerned Scientists. 2004. *Scientific integrity in policymaking: An investigation into the Bush administration's misuse of science.* Cambridge, MA: Union of Concerned Scientists.

United Nations Development Program. 1999. *Human development report 1999.* New York: United Nations Development Program and Oxford University Press.

United Nations Development Program. 2002. Wireless link gives Bangladesh agriculture students faster Internet access. Press release, New York, January 4. http://www.undp.org/dpa/frontpagearchive/2003/january/21jan03/index.html (accessed September 29, 2003).

United Nations Educational, Scientific, and Cultural Organization, Institute for Statistics, Organization for Economic Cooperation and Development, and World Education Indicators Program. 2002. *Financing education—Investments and returns: Analysis of the world education indicators, 2002 edition. Executive summary.* Paris: UNESCO Publishing and OECD Publications. http://www.oecd.org/dataoecd/27/8/2494749.pdf (accessed February 5, 2005).

University of British Columbia Library. 2003. *User results survey.* Vancouver: University of British Columbia.

Van de Sompel, Herbert, and Oren Beit-Arie. 2001. Open linking in the scholarly information environment using the OpenURL framework. *D-Lib Magazine* 7(3). http://www.dlib.org/dlib/march01/vandesompel/03vandesompel.html (accessed October 6, 2003).

Van de Sompel, Herbert, and Carl Lagoze. 2002. Notes from the interoperability front: A progress report on the Open Archives Initiative. In *Proceedings of the Sixth European Conference on Digital Libraries,* ed. Maristella Agnosti and Constantiano Thanos, 144–157. Rome: Springer. http://www.openarchives.org/documents/ecdl-oai.pdf (accessed October 6, 2003).

van Orsdel, Lee, and Kathleen Born. 2003. Big chill on the big deal? *Library Journal,* April 15. http://libraryjournal.reviewsnews.com/index.asp?layout=article&articleId=CA289187&display=searchResults&stt=001&text=big+chill (accessed September 29, 2003).

Varmus, Harold. 1999. *PubMed Central: An NIH-operated site for electronic distribution of life sciences research reports.* Washington, DC: National Institute of Health. http://www.nih.gov/about/director/pubmedcentral/pubmedcentral.htm (accessed September 29, 2003).

Varmus, Harold. 2004. Testimony before Science and Technology Committee, House of Commons, March 8. Uncorrected transcript of oral evidence to be published as HC 399-ii, House of Commons, Minutes of Evidence Taken before Science and Technology Committee, "Scientific Publications." http://www.publications.parliament.uk/pa/cm200304/cmselect/cmsctech/uc399-ii/uc39902.htm (accessed April 8, 2004).

Verba, Sidney. 2003. A letter from Sidney Verba. Harvard University Library, Cambridge, MA, December 9. http://hul.harvard.edu/letter040101.html (accessed April 1, 2004).

Vine, Rita. 2001. Real people don't do boolean: How to teach end users to find high quality information on the Internet. *Information Outlook* 5(3): 16–23.

Walker, Thomas J. 2001. Authors willing to pay for instant Web access. *Nature* 411(6837): 521–522. http://www.nature.com/nature/debates/e-access/Articles/walker.html (accessed September 29, 2003).

Washington D.C. principles for free access to science: A statement from not-for-profit publishers. 2004. Washington, DC, March 16. http://www.dcprinciples.org/statement.htm (accessed April 4, 2004).

Waters, Donald J. 2004. Building on success, forging new ground: The question of sustainability. *First Monday* 9(5). http://firstmonday.org/issues/issue9_5/waters/index.html (accessed August 7, 2004).

Weber, Max. 1930. *The Protestant ethic and the spirit of capitalism.* London: Unwin University.

Weber, Steven. 2000. Political economy of open sources software. Working paper no. 140, Berkeley Roundtable on the International Economy, Berkeley, CA. http://www.ciaonet.org/wps/wes02/ (accessed October 4, 2003).

Weiss, Peter. 2004. Borders in cyberspace. *Geospatial Today* (March–April), 24–41.

Weitzman, Jonathan B. 2003. Sabo bill sparks copyright controversy. *Open Access Now,* August 25. http://www.biomedcentral.com/openaccess/archive/?page=features&issue=3 (accessed October 6, 2003).

Wilhelm, Anthony G. 2000. *Democracy in a digital age: Challenges to political life in cyberspace.* New York: Routledge.

Williams, Gaye. 2002. Librarians and working families: Bridging the information divide. *Library Trends* 51(1): 78–84.

Willinsky, John. 1994. *Empire of words: The reign of the OED.* Princeton, NJ: Princeton University Press.

Willinsky, John. 1998. *Learning to divide the world: Education at empire's end.* Minneapolis: University of Minnesota Press.

Willinsky, John. 1999. *Technologies of knowing: A proposal for the human sciences.* Boston: Beacon.

Willinsky, John. 2001. Extending the prospects of evidence-based education. *IN>>SIGHT* 1(1): 23–41.

Willinsky, John. 2003a. Scholarly associations and the economic viability of open access publishing. *Journal of Digital Information* 4(2). http://jodi.ecs.soton .ac.uk/Articles/v04/i02/Willinsky/ (accessed February 3, 2005).

Willinsky, John. 2003b. Policymakers' use of online academic research. *Education Policy Analysis Archives* 11(2). http://epaa.asu.edu/epaa/v11n2/ (accessed October 6, 2003).

Willinsky, John. 2004. As open access is public access, can journals help policymakers read research? *Canadian Journal of Communication* 29(3–4): 381–394.

Willinsky, John, and Wolfson, Larry. 2001. The indexing of scholarly journals: A tipping point for publishing reform? *Journal of Electronic Publishing* 7(2). http:// www.press.umich.edu/jep/07-02/willinsky.html (accessed February 8, 2005).

Wilson, Steven M. 1999. Impact of the Internet on primary care staff in Glasgow. *Journal of Medical Internet Research* 1(2). http://www.jmir.org/1999/2/e7/ (accessed September 29, 2003).

Winchester, Simon. 1998. *The professor and the madman: A tale of murder, insanity, and the making of the* Oxford English Dictionary. New York: HarperCollins.

Wineburg, Sam. 2001. *From historical thinking and other unnatural acts: Charting the future of teaching the past.* Philadelphia: Temple University Press.

Wineburg, Sam. 2003. Teaching the mind good habits. *Chronicle of Higher Education*, April 11, p. B20.

Woolf, Virginia. 1925. *The common reader.* London: Hogarth.

World Bank. 2000. *World development report 1999/2000.* Oxford: Oxford University Press. http://www.worldbank.org/wdr/2000/fullreport.html (accessed September 29, 2003).

Young, Jeffrey R. 1997. HighWire press transforms the publication of scientific journals. *Chronicle of Higher Education*, May 16, p. A21.

Young, Jeffrey R. 2004. Universities offer homegrown course software. *Chronicle of Higher Education*, July 23, p. A27.

Young, Mark, Martha Kyrillidou, and Julia Blixrud. 2003. *ARL Supplementary Statistics, 2000–01.* Washington, DC: Association of Research Libraries. http:// www.arl.org/stats/sup/index.html (accessed October 6, 2004).

Zeleza, Paul Tiyambe. 1996. Manufacturing and consuming knowledge: African libraries and publishing. *Development in Practice* 6(4): 293–303.

Zeleza, Paul Tiyambe. 1998. The challenges of editing scholarly journals in Africa. In *Knowledge dissemination in Africa: The role of scholarly journals*, ed. Philip G. Altbach and Damtew Teferra, 13–38. Chestnut Hill, MA: Bellagio.

Zielinski, Chris. 2000. Documenting the divide in global health information—and doing something about it. Unpublished paper, Information Waystations and Staging Posts, Petersfield, Hants, UK. http://www.iwsp.org/Documenting_the _divide.htm (accessed September 29, 2003).

Index

AAS. *See* American Astronomical Society
Abbasi, Kamran, 22n11
Abrahamson, John, 116
"Academic exception" principle, 46
Academic freedom, 45
Academic publishing. *See* Scholarly publishing
Academics, vanity factor, 21–23
Access to Global Online Research in Agriculture (AGORA), 102, 102n9
Access principle. *See also* Human rights
  decline in, 25
  defined, 5, 28–29, xii
  in developing countries, 98, 106–107, 109–110
  early history of, 5
  expectations of faculty, 21
  Oldenburg, Henry, 5, 56, 177
  online publishing, 78–79
  right to know, 6, 143, 146
Accomazzi, Alberto, 23
Acosta-Cazares, Benjamin, 107n12
Adebowale, Sulaiman, 103
Adeya, Catherine Nyaki, 96n2, 97, 106n11
Africa Journals Online (AJOL), 104
African Information Society Initiative, 96n2
African Periodicals Exhibit Catalogue, 103

African Virtual University (AVU), 101, 101n7
AGORA. *See* Access to Global Online Research in Agriculture
Ahimbisibwe, Jennifer, 107n12
AIDS activists, 119–120
AJOL. *See* Africa Journals Online
Alexander, Cynthia J., 128n1
Alexander, Patricia A., 158, 158n5, 159, 159n6, 161, 165
Alliance for Taxpayer Access, 2, 2n1
Alonso-Gamboa, Octavio, 105
ALPSP. *See* Association of Learned and Professional Society Publishers
American Association for the Advancement of Science, 9, 39, 78
American Astronomical Society (AAS), 57–58, 61
American Psychological Association (APA), 55
Anderson, Deborah Lines, 16n4
Anderson, Kent R., 23n12, 118
Angell, Marcia, 117n5
Antelman, Kristin, 211n1
APA. *See* American Psychological Association
Archive. *See also* E-print archives, open access
  advantages for authors, 49
  arXiv.org E-Print Archive, 24, 59, 63, 70, 175, 212t
  bias, self-selection, 23–24
  cooperative, 227–232

Archive (cont.)
Education Policy Analysis Archives,
    29–30, 50, 215
E-print, 48
growth of, 53
institutional, 33
JSTOR, 81–85, 82n1–3, 89, 230–
    232
mandate to create, 53n19, 54
NASA Astrophysics Archive, 175,
    179, 233, 234t
nonprofit, 81–85, 89
open access, 26, 150, 175, 227–232
Open Archives Initiative (OAI), 73
open source solutions, 71n2
Project Gutenberg, 15n3
Research Papers in Economics
    (RePEc), 139
security systems, 81, 83, 84
self-archiving, 48, 54, 59n3, 72, 78,
    212t
surplus capacity, 83, 86, 88, 92
truth, access to, 148
Aristotle, 6–7, 7n3
ARL. *See* Association of Research
    Libraries
Aronson, Barbara, 94, 101, 102
Arret, Linda, 183
ARTstor, 82, 82n4, 124–125, 230
Arunachalam, Subbiah, 98n4, 108n14
ArXiv.org E-Print Archive
automated repository, 70
database, open access, 24, 59, 122,
    175
e-print self-archive, 59n3, 63, 212t
Association of Learned and
    Professional Society Publishers
    (ALPSP), 24
Association of Research Libraries
    (ARL), 18, 18n7, 24, 44, 64, 85
Associations
American Association for the
    Advancement of Science, 9, 39,
    78
American Psychological Association
    (APA), 55

Association of Learned and
    Professional Society Publishers
    (ALPSP), 24
Association of Research Libraries
    (ARL), 18, 18n7, 24, 44, 64, 85
budgets, scholarly publication, 217–
    219
journals, revenue from, 55, 60–62
membership model, 57, 58, 60–61
open access, delayed, 63
publishing, historical, 55–56
publishing, new paradigm, 56–58,
    65
publishing cooperative, 64–65
revenue, open access model, 61–62,
    65
scholarly, 19, 64–65, 218t
transition to, digital publishing, 59–
    60, 64
Astronomical Journal, 58n2
Astrophysical Journal, 179, 180n6
Ausubel, David, 158n5
Author fee open access
BioMed Central, 78, 212t, 214
economic model, 212t, 214
Florida Entomologist, 214
Nucleic Acids Research, 77–78
Oxford University Press, 76–77, 100
PLoS Biology, 1, 6, 27, 214
PLoS Medicine, 214
Springer Open Choice, 4–5, 214
AVU. *See* African Virtual University
Aykroyd, Dan, 58

Bachrach, Steven, 52n17
Bagdikian, Ben H., 134
Ball, Patrick, 145
Banya, Kingsley, 95, 95n1
Barron, James, 76
Baum, Rudy M, 7, 8
Bazerman, Charles, 199n15, 202n18
Beit-Arie, Oren, 157n4
Bell, Stephen J., 178
Belushi, John, 58
Benkler, Yochai, 40–41, 40n2, 42,
    51–52, 51n14, 52n16

Bergstrom, Carl T., 20n9
Bergstrom, Theodore C., 19, 20n9
Bernstein, Judith, 114, 165n12
Berry, Steven, 52n17
Bethesda Statement on Open Access
    Publishing, 27n14, 213t
Bhattacharya, Ronica, 88
Bibliographic information, 78, 213t,
    216, 233, 234t
Bioline International, 103
Biological Abstracts, 174
BioMed Central, 78, 87, 212t, 214
Birenbaum, Lauren, 36n18
Black, Justice Hugo, 51
Blackwell Publishing, 100, 154,
    219n2
Blixrud, Julia, 173n1
Blume, Martin, 43n7, 52n17
Blumenstyk, Goldie, 46n9
Blumenthal, David, 36n18
Boismenu, Gérard, 229t
Bollacker, Kurt, 182n8
Books, scholarly, 15–16, 47
Born, Kathleen, 26
Bot, Marjolein, 70
Boulin, Janet, 76–77
Bowen, William G., 82, 82n1
Boyle, James, 40, 40n2
Boyle, Robert, 198n13
Brabham, Edna Greene, 167
Brand, Amy, 157
Brandeis, Justice Louis, 41, 41n4
Braun, Kim, 216
Britton, Bruce K., 158n5
Brody, Tim, 23n12
Brown, M. Suzanne, 234n1
Brown, Patrick O., 1, 27n14, 36n19,
    190n2
Brown, Sheridan N., 52
Brownlee, Shannon, 114, 115
Bruneau, William, 22n11
Budapest Open Access Initiative,
    27n14, 213t
Budick, Sanford, 162n8
Burgemeester, Johan, 70
Bush, George W., 140n12

Cameron, Robert D., 184n9
Campbell, Eric G., 36n18
Campion, Edward W., 118
Canadian Centre for Studies in
    Publishing, xiv
Canagarajah, A. Suresh, 105–108
Caplan, Priscilla, 124n8
Cappella, Joseph N., 134n6
Carlson, Scott, 178
Carrington, Edward, 133
Carter, David J., 79
Catania, Joe, 114
Cavalier, Robert, 152
Centre for Evidence-Based Policy,
    138, 138n9, 140n12
Cetto, Ana Maria, 105, 181
Chan, Leslie, 103
Chemical Abstracts, 173, 174
Cherrington, Alan D., 117
Chomsky, Noam, 134n6
Citation counts, 23–24, 44, 49
Citation index
    Citebase, 181
    CiteSeer.IST, 181, 216, 233, 234t
    ISI Web of Science, 18, 44, 50, 173,
        179–182
    rankings, 185
Citebase, 181
CiteSeer.IST, 181, 216, 233, 234t
Clarridge, Brian R, 36n18
Claude, Richard Pierre, 143–146, 151
ClinicalTrials.gov, 116–117
Clymer, Adam, 128n1
Cohen, Joshua, 136n8
"Coming of Copyright Perpetuity,"
    47n10
Commercial publishing, 6, 13
Commercial serial index
    Biological Abstracts, 174
    Chemical Abstracts, 173, 174
    Education Index, 234t
    ISI Web of Science, 18, 44, 50, 173,
        179–182, 234t
    Journal of Economic Abstracts, 174
    Physics Abstracts, 173
Cooper, Charles, 94

Cooperative open access
  archive, 227–232
  economic model, 84–92, 213t, 216,
    227–232
  German Academic Publishers, 213t,
    216
  subscription fees, 228
Copyright
  "academic exception," 46
  author/editor/publisher versus, 43–45
  author versus public, 41
  "Coming of Copyright Perpetuity,"
    47n10
  concessions, for developing
    countries, 48
  Copyright Act (U.S.), 40
  Copyright Term Extensions Act
    (1998), 46–47
  Digital Millennium Copyright Act,
    40n2
  e-print archive, 39, 48
  European Database Protection
    Directive, 40n2
  freedom of speech versus, 42
  intellectual property rights, 41
  moral claim versus, 47
  ownership contradiction, 43–48
  ownership transfer, 47
  patents, academic, 46, 46n9
  plagiarism versus, 43, 43n7
  profitability protection and, 47
  Public Access to Science Act, 3n2
  public interests versus, 42, 49
  public versus private rights, 39–40,
    42, 52n17
  publication rights versus, 47
  publisher's rights, protecting, 47
  redundant publication and, 59–60,
    59n3
  research results and, 42–43, 46n8
  revisions to, proposed, 40–41
  rights, first-publication, 47
  royalties, 49
  scholarly books, 47
  temporal limits of, 45, 46, 47n11,
    49, 49n12
  transfer of, 44–45
  U.S. Copyright Act, 45
  work-made-for-hire and, 44–45
Copyright Term Extensions Act
  (1998), 46–47
Core Metalist of Open Access EPrint
  Archives, 29, 29n15
Corporate publishers
  American Association for the
    Advancement of Science, 9, 39, 78
  Blackwell Publishing, 100, 154,
    219n2
  Chemical and Engineering News, 7
  Harcourt, Inc., 18n6
  HighWire Press, 2–3, 70, 86, 156n3,
    175, 175n4
  journals, expansion of, 19
  Nature Publishing Group, 1
  News Corp., 51
  Oxford University Press, 76–77, 100
  Public Library of Science (PLoS), 8,
    21–22
  Reed Elsevier, 4, 28, 71, 154, 216,
    233, 234t
  reputable journals, 21
  The Scientist, 1
  Springer Verlag, 4–5, 100, 154, 214
  Stanford University Press, 3
  subscription pricing, journals, 22
  Time Warner, 51
  Wall Street Journal, 1
  Wiley Europe, 8
Cox, John, 213n2
Cox, June, 14
Cox, Laura, 14, 213n2
Crampton, Margaret, 103
Creative Commons, 40
Critical point, 16–17
Cronenberg, David, 150–151
Crow, Raym, 71n2, 85

Dahdouh-Guebas, Farid, 107n12
D'Alessandro, Donna M., 115n4
Darch, Colin, 94
David, Paul A., 195
Davis, Crispin, 71

de Lauretis, Teresa, 151
Delayed open access
  economic model, 212t, 215
  Molecular Biology of the Cell, 63
  National Council of Teachers of
    English, 63
  New England Journal of Medicine,
    6, 63, 117–118, 215
  NIH-funded research, 3
  PubMed Central, 2, 3, 115, 156n3,
    175n4
del Castillo, Daniel, 33, 33n16
Demleitner, Markus, 23
Democratic divide, 127
Derrida, Jacques, 143, 147–151,
  152n5, 153
Developing countries
  access principle, 98, 106–107, 109–
    110
  Addis Ababa University (Ethiopia),
    94
  Africa, 95, 96n2, 97–105
  Africa Journals Online (AJOL), 104
  African Information Society
    Initiative, 96n2
  *African Periodicals Exhibit
    Catalogue*, 103
  Bioline International, 103
  copyright concession, by publishers,
    48
  Global Information for Africa, 103
  Global Information Infrastructure
    Commission, 96n2
  India, 96, 98nn3–4, 99
  Indian National Scientific
    Documentation Center, 94
  indicators, educational, 95
  infrastructure of, technical, 96–97
  International Network for the
    Availability of Scientific
    Publications, 100
  journal collections, 93–94
  journal subscriptions, cancellation of,
    99
  knowledge output of, 95
  Latin America, 105

New England Journal of Medicine,
  117–118
  online journal management, 108
  open access, 25, 78
  publishing, challenges for, 106–108,
    107n12
  research capacity of, 94, 98
  Scientific Electronic Library Online,
    105
  Southern Hemisphere countries, 94
  Sri Lanka, 105–106
  university faculty of, 97
  World Bank High Education Project,
    96n2
  World Health Organization (WHO),
    94, 101
Digital divide, 111–112, 112n1, 127
Digital Millennium Copyright Act,
  40n2
Digital Opportunity Taskforce, 96n2
Directory of Open Access Journals,
  26, 29, 175
Donelan, Karen, 114
Doss, M. Jinandra, 108n14
Douglas, Mary, 137
Drake, Stillman, 192
Drazen, Jeffrey M., 118
Dspace, institutional repository, 71,
  89, 150n4, 214
Dual-mode open access
  economic model, 212t, 215
  HighWire Press, 2–3
  Journal of Postgraduate Medicine,
    212t, 215
  journals, online editions, 14
  K. E. M. Hospital (Mumbai), 215
  Science Update, 5
  Seth G. S. Medical College (Mumbai),
    215
Dublin CoreMetadata Initiative, 241,
  242t. *See also* Metadata
Duncan, Dan, 186–187
Dyson, Freeman J., 122, 122n7

Eamon, William, 195
EBSCO, search engine, 100, 173

Edejer, Tessa Tan-Torres, 111
Educational indicators, 95
Education Policy Analysis Archives, x,
    29–30, 50, 215
Education Research Information
    Clearinghouse. *See* ERIC
Edwards, Jana S., 234n1
Eichhorn, Guenther, 23
eIFL.net (Electronic Information for
    Libraries), 100n5
Eisen, Michael B., 1, 27n14, 36n19,
    190n2
Eisenstein, Elizabeth, 189, 189n1,
    191, 193
Eisermann, Falk, 193n6
e-journal, 70
E-Journal User Study, 65
Electronic Information for Libraries.
    See eIFL.net
Electronic Publishing Trust for
    Development (EPT), 100n5
Ellis, Aytoun, 30
Elsevier. *See* Reed Elsevier
Elu, Juliet, 95, 95n1
e-mail, 26
e-print archives, open access. *See also*
    Archive
  arXiv.org, 24, 59, 59n3, 63, 70, 122,
    175, 212t
  citation counts, 23–24
  copyright, 39, 48
  Core Metalist of Open Access EPrint
    Archives, 29
  Dspace, institutional repository, 71,
    89, 150n4, 214
  economic model, 71, 213–214
  growth of, 35
  Reed Elsevier, 4, 28, 78, 154, 216, 233
  ScienceDirect, 28, 71, 78, 213t, 216,
    234t
  Springer Verlag, 4–5, 100, 154
EPrints.org software, 53n19, 71n2,
    72, 89
Epstein, Steven, 119, 120
EPT. *See* Electronic Publishing Trust
    for Development

ERIC (Education Research Informa-
    tion Clearinghouse), 216, 233,
    234t
Erickson, Frederick, 140n12
Etzkowitz, Henry, 46n9
European Database Protection
    Directive, 40n2
Everngam, Ray, 63

Fee-restricted access, 42. *See also*
    Subscriptions
Fenton, Eileen Gifford, 82n1
Fernandez, Irene, 144
Ferris, Timothy, 121–122, 122n7
Fidler, Anne T., 114, 165n12
First Monday (journal), 6, 47n11,
    212t
Fischer, Frank, 119
Fisher, Janet H., 70
Fishkin, James S., 131
Florida Entomologist (journal), 214
For-profit publishing, 8
Foray, Dominique, 36
Forrest, Christopher, 135–136
Fowler, Alexander, 52n17
Fox, Susannah, 113, 114
Frank, Anne, 168
Frankel, Mark S., 9, 39, 46n8, 78,
    90n11
Franklin, Benjamin, 85
Freedom House, 145
Freeman, Christopher, 94
Freudenheim, Milt, 114
Fuchs, Ira, 91

Gadd, Elizabeth, 48, 213n2
Gallouj, Faïz, 84n6
Galusky, Wyatt, 146
Gans, Herbert J., 134
Garrido, Maria, 128n1
Gates, Bill, 111n1, 150n3
Geiger, Roger L., 14
Genbank, 36, 36n19
Gerhard, Kristin H., 234n1
German Academic Publishers, 213t,
    216

Gibbons, Michael, 17
Gibbs, W. Wayt, 94, 153
Giles, C. Lee, 182n8
Gingras, Yves, 23n12
Ginsparg, Paul, 52n17, 70
Gish, O., 94
Gitlin, Todd, 134n6
Gladwell, Malcolm, x, xi
Glanz, James, 70
Glass, Gene, 29–30, 69–70, 76
Gleason, N., 73n4
Glenn, David, 219n2
Global Information for Africa, 103
Global Information Infrastructure
    Commission, 96n2
Gogol, Nikolay Vasilyevich, 121
Gokhale, Manjusha, 36n18
Golinski, Jan, 198n13
Google Print, 16
Google Scholar search engine, 178
Google search engine, 177–178
Gorman, James, 123
Gova, Alnoor, 183, 233
Grafton, Anthony, 155n2
Grant, Carolyn, 23
Gray, Horace, 42
Grisham, Dana L., 167
Gross, Alan G., 203n19
Guèdon, Jean-Claude, 193n5
Gutenberg, Johannes, 189
Guthrie, Kevin M., 81, 82, 83, 84,
    230
Gutmann, Amy, 130–131, 131n3,
    132, 133n5

Haank, Derek, 78
Haas, Stephanie, 124n8
Hague, Barry N., 128n1
Halavais, Alexander, 128n1
Hall, Marie Boas, 195
HaNasi, Rabbi Judah, 162
Hardt, Michael, 108, 109n15
Hardy, Henry, 47
Harmon, Joseph E., 203n19
Harnad, Stevan
    citations, open access, 23n12

e-print archives, open access, 214
open access, impact measures, 182n8
open access, research impact, 22
open access versus open source, 72
self-archiving, cost containment, 90
self-archiving, e-print archives, 48
self-archiving, by faculty, 53, 54
self-archiving, open access, 78
self-archiving, open access journals,
    214, 214n3
Harrington, Mark, 119–120
Hartman, Geoffrey H., 162n8
Harvard University Library, 25
Haslanger, Sally, 150n3
Hawking, Stephen, 151
Hawley, John B., 61–62, 62n5
Health Inter-Network Access to
    Research Initiative (HINARI), x,
    101–102, 102n8, 215
Healy, Peter, 46n9
Heeks, Richard, 128n1
Hefeli, William, 111
Heller, Stephen, 52n17
Henneken, Edwin, 23
Hevelius, Johannes, 196n9
HighWire Press, 2–3, 70, 86, 156n3,
    175, 175n4
Hilgartner, Stephen, 36n18
Hill, John, 203
Hill, Stephen, 94, 193
HINARI. *See* Health Inter-Network
    Access to Research Initiative
Hitchcock, Steve, 23, 49, 53, 182n8
Holt, Jennifer, 234n1
Holtzman, Neil A., 36n18
Home page open access, 211–213,
    212t
Hooke, Robert, 200
Hooks, M., 177
House of Commons Science and
    Technology Committee (U.K.), 3, 8
Human rights. *See also* Claude,
    Richard Pierre; Derrida, Jacques;
    Kant, Immanuel
    academic freedom, unconditional,
    147

Human rights (cont.)
access, equitable, 146
access to humanities, 147, 153n6
access to information, 145, 146
access to knowledge, 143, 146
access to philosophy, 143, 147, 148, 150, 151
access to science, 144, 146
access to training, 148
access to truth, 148
autodidactism and education, 151
circulation of research and scholarship, 143, 146, 147
cloning and biotechnology, 151
freedom of speech, 51
impediments to, 144, 145
Internet and, 145
open access and, 22, 145, 150, 205
right to know, 117, 125, 138, 143, 146, 151
scholarly dimension of, 143, 152–153
Tenagantia, women's group, 144, 145n1
Hunter, Michael, 197, 197n11
Husmann, Werner, 75
Huygens, Christiaan, 198, 200, 201n17

IEEE. *See* Institute of Electrical and Electronics Engineers
INASP. *See* International Network for the Availability of Scientific Publications
Indexing. *See also* Metadata; Pay-per-view access
citation index
Citebase, 181
CiteSeer.IST, 181, 216, 233, 234t
rankings, 185
commercial serial index
Biological Abstracts, 174
Chemical Abstracts, 173, 174
Education Index, 234t
ISI Web of Science, 18, 44, 50, 173, 179–182, 234t
Journal of Economic Abstracts, 174
Physics Abstracts, 174
EBSCO search engine, 100, 173
economic model, 213t, 216
educational journals, 235t, 236t
Global Information for Africa, 103
Google Scholar, 178
Google search engine, 177–178
indexers, professional, 186–187
indexes, fragmented, 183
indexing, historical, 176–177
OAIster, 175, 184, 216, 241
open access index
ERIC, 173, 175, 216, 233, 234t
NASA Astrophysics Archive, 175, 179, 179n5, 233, 234t
PubMed, 115, 173, 175, 216, 233, 234t
overlap and gaps in, 179, 183–188, 233–240, 234–239t
PKP Harvester, 184–185
publisher portal index
HighWire, 233, 234t
Journals@Ovid, 234t
ScienceDirect, 71, 78, 175, 213t, 216, 234t
Reed Elsevier, 4, 28, 78, 154, 216, 233
science indexers, service comparison, 239t
science journals, top, 237t
searching documents, 125–126
serial aggregator index, 234t
serial literature, 233–240
Ingenta, 57
Institute of Electrical and Electronics Engineers (IEEE), 55, 62n5, 175
Institute of Physics journals, 215
Institutional repositories, 35
Intellectual property rights, 41
Internal Revenue Service Form 990, 217n1, 218t
International Network for the Availability of Scientific Publications (INASP), 78, 100, 100n5, 101, 216

Internet
  access, on-line open, 25–26, 145
  African Information Society
    Initiative, 96n2
  digital divide, 111–112, 112n1, 127
  Digital Opportunity Taskforce, 96n2
  free press and, 145
  freedom, 145
  Global Information Infrastructure
    Commission, 96n2
  human rights and, 145
  Pew Internet and American Life
    Project, 113
  public access to, 113–117
  scholarly publishing and, 35
  subsidized publishing on, 8
  United Nations Development
    Program, 96n2
  World Bank Group's Global
    Development Learning Network
    Project, 96n2
ISI Web of Science, 18, 44, 50, 173,
  179–182, 234t
Islamic fundamentalism, 31–33
Iyengar, Shanto, 134n6

Jacobsen, Trudy E., 234n1
Jamieson, Kathleen Hall, 134n6
Jarvis, John, 8
Jaygbay, Jacob, 103
Jefferson, Thomas, 133, 134
Jetton, Tamara L., 158, 158n5, 159,
  165
Johns, Adrian, 191n4, 194
Johnson, Samuel, 169
Journal of Clinical Investigation, 61–
  62
Journal of Economic Abstracts, 174
Journal of Postgraduate Medicine,
  212t, 215
Journal publishing. *See also* Online
    journals
  access to journals, 13–20, 150
  bundling of titles, 17, 24–25, 24n13,
    57
  commercial, 6

  copyright ownership transfer, 47
  cost reduction of, 64, 64n7
  e-print, transition to, 10, 15, 56
  growth of, 35, 54
  journals, dual mode open access, 14
  journals, numbers of, 14
  libraries, licensing arrangements, 17
  online, advantages of, 14–15
  open access, 26, 27, 35, 36–37, 150
JSTOR
  international fee structure, 83n5
  open access, 81–85, 82n1–3, 230–
    232
  Secondary Schools Pilot Project, 88–
    89

Kahle, Brewster, 15n3
Kamau, Nancy, ix, 101
Kant, Immanuel, 121, 149–150, 152
Keller, Michael, 2–3
K. E. M. Hospital (Mumbai), 215
Kemp, Simon, 89n8
Kenya Medical Research Institute
    (KEMRI), ix, x, xi
Kermode, Frank, 163
Kestner, Neil, 52n17
Keynes, John Maynard, 198n13
King, Donald W., 56, 70, 71, 82n1,
  230
Kinzer, Susan L., 115n4
Klevan, David G., 168
Kling, Rob, 59, 70
Klinger, Shula, 129
Knight, Jonathan, 117
Knowledge circulation
  cognitive failure and, 34
  as common property, 42
  distant education, 149
  Education Policy Analysis Archives,
    29–30, 50, 215
  evidence-based approach, 138,
    138n9, 140n12
  human rights and, 143, 146, 147
  open access and, 33–34, 131–133,
    147, 196, 202–207
  politics and, 131–133

Knowledge circulation (cont.)
  public value of research, 120–123
  scholarship, 131–133, 147, 152–
    153, 196, 202–207
Knowledge industries, 9
Kolata, Gina, 115
Kollock, Peter, 72
Krasner, Jeffrey, 117
Krauss, Lisa, 23n12
Kreiter, Clarence D., 115n4
Krikos, Linda A., 234n1
Kuhn, Thomas S., 199n15, 200,
    201n16, 202n18
Kulikowich, Jonna, 159, 165
Kumar, Krishan, 99, 174n2
Kurtz, Michael J., 23, 179n3
Kyrillidou, Martha, 173n1

Lagoze, Carl, 242n1
Lancet (journal), 212t, 215
LaRose, Albert, 234n1
Larsen, Carolyn, 183
Larsen, Elena, 113n3
Lasee-Willemssen, Jeneen, 234n1
LaTeX, 44
Lawrence, Steven, 182n8
Lee, Ken, 114
Lerner, Josh, 72n3
Lessig, Lawrence, 40, 40n2, 49
Libraries
  Addis Ababa University Library, 94
  Agricultural Sciences University
    (Bangalore), 99
  Arizona State University Library, x
  Association of Research Libraries
    (ARL), 18, 18n7, 24, 44, 64–65,
    85
  Bangladesh Agricultural University
    Library, 96, 174, 175, 176
  Cornell University Library, 25
  Delhi University Library, 99
  Harvard University Library, 25
  Library of Congress Library, 103
  licensing arrangements, 17
  Lund University Libraries, 26, 29
  New York Public Library, 16

  online journals, 15, 108
  Oxford University Library, 16
  Public Library of Science (PLoS), 8,
    21–22
  Scientific Electronic Library Online,
    105, 105n10
  Simon Fraser University Library, xiv
  Stanford University Library, 3
  subscription fees, cancellation of, 7–
    8, 35
  University of Bangalore Library,
    174–176
  University of British Columbia
    Education Library, 24, 173, 175,
    176, 233, 234, 235t, 238
  University of California Library,
    15n5, 25
  University of Chicago Library, 179
  University of Illinois Library, 104
  U.S. National Library of Medicine,
    97, 113, 238
Limoges, Camille, 17
Lindsay, Adrienne, 229t
Linn, Robert, x, xi
Linus, Francis, 200
Listservs, 26
Lo, Bernard, 114
Loader, Brian D., 128n1
Lobel, Anita, 167
Locke, John, 198n13
LOCKSS (Lots of Copies Keep Stuff
    Safe), 74, 74n6, 77, 86
Longino, Helen, 34–35, 34n17
Lorimer, Rowland, 229t
Lots of Copies Keep Stuff Safe. *See*
    LOCKSS
Lund University Libraries, 26, 29

Mabawonku, Iyabo, 99–100
MacColl, Ewan, 120, 121
Machlup, Fritz, 9, 56n1, 66
Mahoney, Michael S., 42
Manmarat, Lampang, 96
Mansbridge, Jane, 10–11, 11n4
Mason, David, 113n2
McAfee, Noëlle J., 132

McCabe, Mark, 18n6, 20nn9–10, 79
McChesney, Robert W., 134n6
McGinn, Colin, 32
McKiernan, Gerry, 156n3
McKim, Geoff, 59, 70
McLaughlin-Jenkins, Erin, 120
McLuhan, Marshall, 189n1
McSherry, C., 42, 43, 46, 46n9
MedlinePlus, 115
Meier, Barry, 116
Mellon Foundation, Andrew W., 81–82, 85, 91, 232
Merton, Robert, 41
Metadata. *See also* Indexing; OAIster
  defined, 241
  Dublin CoreMetadata Initiative, 241, 242t
  Open Archives Initiative (OAI), 73, 175, 184–185, 214, 243
  Open Journal Systems, 243
  Public Knowledge Project, 243
  standard for, 184
  vocabulary, controlled, 186
Meyer, Mark L., 46n8
Mialet, Hélène, 151
Milstein, Sarah, 75, 75n7
Mirapul, Matthew, 123
Moffat, Anne, 52n17
Molecular Biology of the Cell (journal), 63
Monastersky, Richard, 43n7
Morais, R., 78
Moray, Robert, 200
Muinde, Florence, 100
Murray, Elizabeth, 114
Murry, Stephen S., 23
Muthayan, Saloshini, 100
Mutula, S. M., 100

Nafisi, Azar, 31–33
Nagourney, Adam, 102
NASA Astrophysics Archive, 175, 179, 179n5, 233, 234t
National Council of Teachers of English, 63

National Federation of Science Abstracting and Indexing Services, 186
National Institutes of Health (NIH), 2, 3
Natriello, Gary J., 50, 50n13
Nature (journal), 1, 2, 5–6
Negri, Antonio, 108, 109n15
Nelson, Richard R., 42
New England Journal of Medicine, 6, 63, 117–118, 215
Newton, Isaac, 190, 197–201, 198n12, 205
NIH. *See* National Institutes of Health
Nimmer, Melville B., 42
No Child Left Behind Act, x, 139, 139n11
Noll, Roger G., 20n9
Norris, Pippa, 127
Nowotny, Helga, 17
Nucleic Acids Research (journal), 77–78

OAI (Open Archives Initiative), 73, 175, 241, 243
OAIster, 175, 184, 216, 241
Odlyzko, Andrew, 52n17
Okamura, Kyoko, 114, 165n12
O'Keefe, Lori, 23n12
Okerson, Ann, 52n17, 82n1
Oldenburg, Henry
  access principle, 5, 56, 177
  Royal Society Secretary, 193–202, 193n5, 196n9, 205
Oldman, Geoffrey, 94
Online journals
  access to, 13–20
  advantages of, 14–15
  Africa Journals Online, 104
  Brazil, open access policy, 29
  Directory of Open Access Journals, 26
  e-print, transition to, 10
  EPrints.org software, 72
  Internet access, 48
  LaTeX, 44

Online journals (cont.)
library access to, 15, 108
management software, 71n2, 73–78, 108
operational costs, 69–79
pay-per-view access, 48
plagiarism versus copyright, 43
PloS Biology, 27
pricing of journals, 6, 7, 17, 19, 35, 37
profitability, protecting, 47
public money and, 66
redundant access to, 59–60
reputable, 21
rights, first-publication, 47
"serials crisis," 18
subscription fees, 19, 26, 58n2
tools, context driven, 136, 164–170
Online management system. *See* Open Journal Systems (OJS)
Online publishing. *See* Publishing online
Open access, 85. *See also* Knowledge circulation; *individual types/flavors*
advantages of, 8–9, 49
archive, 26
arXiv.org E-Print Archive, 24, 59, 63, 70, 175, 212t
author fee, 76–78, 212t, 214
author interests, 49–51, 54
Bethesda Statement on Open Access Publishing, 27n14, 213t
Budapest Open Access Initiative, 27n14, 213t
citation counts, 22–23
cooperative, 84–92, 213t, 216, 227–232
critical point, economics of, 16–17
defined, 27n14
delayed, 49–50, 63, 212t, 215
in developing countries, 25, 28
Directory of Open Access Journals, 26
dual-mode, 2–3, 5, 14, 212t, 215
economics of, 16–17, 221–225
educational interest, 9

e-mail, 26
e-print archive, 27, 53, 212t, 213–214
flavors of, 28, 212–213t
freedom of speech, 51
history of, 30–31
home page, 26, 53, 211–213, 212t
human rights and, 22
indexing, 28, 213t, 216
Islamic fundamentalism versus, 31–33
knowledge circulation and, 33–34, 131–133, 147, 196, 202–207
by listservs, 26
objections to, 7–9, 31
partial, 212t, 215
pay-per-view access, 26, 39
per capita, 78, 105, 212t, 215–216
public access, 111
public interests, 9, 54
publishing, for-profit, 8
research impact and, 22
restrictive licensing agreement versus, 79
royalty-free publishing, 22
subsidized, 3, 6, 212t, 214–215
universities, role of, 10
Web sites, 26
Open Access Education E-journal List, 236t
Open access index
ERIC, 173, 175, 216, 233, 234t
NASA Astrophysics Archive, 175, 179, 179n5, 233, 234t
PubMed, 115, 173, 175, 216, 233, 234t
Open Archives Initiative. *See* OAI
OpenCourseWare, 149–150, 150n3
Open Citation Project, 29
Open government information policies, 35
Open Journal Systems (OJS)
features, 75–76, 221–225, 222–223t
metadata, 243
operating costs, 73

overview, xiv
reading tools, 164–170
Open Knowledge Initiative, 149–150
Open source biology, 36
Open source content management software
  DSpace Federation, 71, 89, 150n4, 214
  EPrints.org software, 53n19, 71n2, 72, 89
  for higher education, 91
  journal publishing, 71n2, 73–78, 73n4
  online publishing, 71n2, 89
  Open Journal Systems, 73, 75–76, 164–170, 221–225, 243
Oppenheim, Charles, 23n12, 48, 213n2
Oxford University Press, 76–77, 100
Oyelaran-Oyeyinka, Banji, 96n2, 97, 106n11

Page, Benjamin I., 134n6
Paintal, Autar S., 94
Pal, Leslie A., 128n1
Pardies, Gaston, 200
Parks, Robert P., 53n18
Partial open access
  economic model, 212t, 215
  Institute of Physics journals, 215
  Lancet, 212t, 215
Patel, Jazshu, 99, 174n2
Patents, 46
Pay-per-view access. *See also* Indexing
  Bioline International, 103
  IEEE (engineering), 55, 62n5, 175
  Ingenta, 57, 175
  journals, 48, 138
  PubMed, 39
  "Penny universities," 30
Per capita (open access)
  economic model, 212t, 215–216
  Health InterNetwork Access to Research Initiative (HINARI), 78, 215

International Network for the Availability of Scientific Publications, 78, 216
Scientific Electronic Library Online, 105
Persaud, Avinish, 94
Peterson, Melody, 102
Peterson, Michael W., 107n12, 115n4
Pew Internet and American Life Project, 113, 113n3
Physics Abstracts, 173
Pillow, Lisa, 234n1
PKP Harvester, xiv, 184–185
PLoS Biology (journal), 1, 6, 27, 214
PLoS Medicine (journal), 214
Politics
  democratic divide, 127
  digital democracy, 124–125
  "information class," 137
  Internet, as information medium, 124
  knowledge circulation, 131–133
  No Child Left Behind Act, 139, 139n11, 141
  open access, 111, 130–131, 142
  propaganda, 124
  public access to research, 120–126, 131–136
  Public Knowledge Policy Forum, 128–130
  transparency, 124
Pollack, Lance, 114
Private rights, 39–40
Probets, Steve, 48, 213n2
Public access
  AIDS activists, 119–120
  Centre for Evidence-Based Policy, 138, 138n9, 140n12
  ClinicalTrials.gov, 116–117
  digital divide, 111–112
  environmental groups, 119
  genetic data, 117
  health issues, Internet search, 114–117
  information class, 137
  Internet, 112–116, 112n1

Public access (cont.)
  MedlinePlus, 115
  open access, 111, 142
  Pew Internet and American Life
    Project, 113
  Public Access to Science Act, 3n2
  public good, 66–67, 130–138
  to research, 120–126, 131–136
  U.S. National Library of Medicine
    Web site, 113
  Web Resources for Social Workers,
    138
Public Access to Science Act, 3n2
Public education, 9
Public good
  dangers of, 10–11
  disagreements over, 11n4
  economic definition, 9
  online publishing and, 138
  open access and, 157
  public access, 66–67, 130–138
  right to know, equitable access to,
    146
  scholarly publishing, role of, 11
Public Knowledge Policy Forum, 128–
  130
Public Knowledge Project, xiv, 73,
  164, 243. *See also* Open Journal
  Systems (OJS)
Public Library of Science (PLoS), 8,
  21–22
Public rights, 39–41
Publisher portal index
  HighWire, 233, 234t
  Journals@Ovid, 234t
  ScienceDirect, 71, 78, 173, 213t,
    216, 234t
Publishing history
  access principle, 5, 56, 177
  copyright, protecting profitability,
    47
  ideas, circulation of, 33–34, 131–
    133, 147, 196, 202–207
  Internet, 191
  journals, 193–196
  landmark study of, 189

Newton, Isaac, 190, 197–201,
  198n12, 205
noncorporate publishing, 191, 191n3
Oldenburg, Henry, 193–202, 193n5,
  196n9, 205
print to digital, 190n2, 191
printing press, 192
public exchange, 197–202, 201n16,
  202n18
rights, first-publication, 47
Royal Society of London, 197–199,
  201–205
scholarship, 190–191, 205–206
self-archiving mandate, 54
work-made-for-hire, 44–46
Publishing online
  access principle, 78–79
  advantages of, 14–15, 75–76
  for developing countries, 108
  EPrints.org. software, 72
  licensing agreements, restrictive, 79
  LOCKSS (Lots of Copies Keep Stuff
    Safe), 74, 74n6, 77
  open access, dual-mode, 14
  open access, journals, 36–37
  Open Journal Systems (OJS), 73, 75–
    76, 164–170, 221–225, 243
  operational costs, 69–79
  public good and, 138
  software, management, 71n2, 73–78,
    89
  software, self-archiving, 72
  subscription costs, 26
PubMed, 156n3, 175n4
  abstracts, 115n4
  indexing, open access, 156n3, 216
  open access, 2, 115
  pay-per-view access, 39

Quint, Barbara, 240

Rainie, Lee, 113, 113n3, 114
Raney, Rebecca Fairley, 128n1
Rao, Siriginidi Subba, 96
Rauch, Alan, 111, 113n2
Raymond, Eric R., 72n3

Reading online
  benefits of, 155–157, 155n1,
    156n3
  environment, reading, 157–158
  habits, reading, 160–161
  knowledge base, missing, 161–164
  motivation, personal, 158–160
  Open Journal Systems, 164–170
  tools, reading, 164–170
Reed Elsevier
  indexing, open access, 4, 28, 154,
    216
  ScienceDirect, 71, 78, 213t, 233,
    234t
Reeves, Richard, 134
Reich, Victoria, 74n6
Reichman, J. H., 66
Reidy, Michael, 203n19
Research Papers in Economics
  (RePEc), 139
Right to be known, 6, 7n3, 108–109,
    109n15
Right to know
  access principle, 6, 143, 146
  AIDS research in Africa, 146
  approach, evidence-based, 138,
    138n9, 140n12
  Aristotle and, 7–8
  benefits of, 144
  Bhopal environmental issue, 146,
    146n2
  equitable access, public good, 146
  new technology and, 8
  open universities and, 31
  public expectation, 117, 125, 151
Rights. *See* Human rights
Roes, Hans, 70
Rogers, Joel, 136n8
Rogers, Theresa, 167, 168
Romano, Michael S., 51n15
Roosevelt, Eleanor, 145
Rose, Jonathan, 30, 120–121, 137
Rosen, Jonathan, 162n9
Rosenberg, Diana B., 94, 102, 103
Rosenthal, David S. H., 74n6
Rosenzweig, Roy, 122n7, 153n6

Ross, W. D., 7n3
Rowland, Fytton, 225n1
Royal Society of London, 55
Royalty-free publishing, 22
Rusin, David, 58, 59, 178–180
Rusnock, Andrea, 196–197n10

Sabbatini, Renato, 29
Sack, John, 23n12
Sahoo, K. C., 14
Said, Edward, 178
Sakai Project, 73
Samuelson, Paul A., 89
Sanders, L., 115
Santora, Marc, 33
Sathyanarayana, N. V., 174
Savage, Donald C., 22n11
Schecter, Bruce, 122
Schiller, Herbert I., 134n6
Schmidt, Karen A., 234n1
Scholarly associations, 19, 64–65,
    218t
Scholarly publishing
  benefits, academic, 6
  books, scholarly, 15–16
  budgets, 217–219
  citation scores, 22
  impasse to, 18–19
  Internet and, 35
  knowledge circulation, 33–34, 131–
    133, 147, 196, 202–207
  mergers, effects of, 18
  open access, 190–191, 205–206
  publication budgets, scholarly, 217–
    219
  public good, role of, 11
  rights, first publication, 47
  royalty-free, 22
  vanity factor, 21–24
Scholarly Publishing and Academic
  Coalition, 76n8
Scholarly Publishing and Academic
  Resources Centre (SPARC), 90,
    191n4
Schonfeld, Roger C., 82n1
Schulz, Renate A., 167

Schwartz, John, 122n6
Schwartzman, Simon, 17
Science Commons, 40
Science Update Web site, 5
ScienceDirect, 71, 78, 216, 233, 234t
 indexing, open access, 28, 213t, 216
Scientific Electronic Library Online,
 105, 105n10
Scott, Peter, 17
Secondary Schools Pilot Project, 88
Secord, Anne, 120
Security systems, 84
Segal, Eliezer, 162n9
Self-archiving
 arXiv.org E-Print Archive, 59n3, 63,
 72, 212t
 concession, publishers', 48, 54
 ScienceDirect, 78
Self-selection bias, 23–24
Sen, Amartya, 98, 98nn3–4, 99
Serial aggregator index, 234t
Seth G. S. Medical College, 215
Shafack, Rosemary M., 112n1
Shain, Steve, 197
Shaping, Steven, 202
Singer, Hans, 94
Singleton, Brent D., 93
Smart, Pippa, 48, 73, 100, 101n6, 104
Smith, Marc A., 72
Sommerville, John C., 194
Social Sciences and Humanities
 Research Council of Canada Aid
 to Research Journals, 228n1
Soros Foundation, 100n5
Sorrells, Robert C., 158n5
SPARC. *See* Scholarly Publishing and
 Academic Resources Centre
Spector, Lisa, 59, 70
Spirer, Herbert F., 145
Spirer, Louise, 145
Sprat, Thomas, 197
Springer Verlag, 4–5, 100, 154, 214
SQW Ltd., 18n7, 24n13
Srivastava, B. P, 14
Stallman, Richard, 73n5
Stamerjohanns, Heinrich, 23n12

Stolberg, Sheryl G., 136
Strathern, Paul, 152
Suber, Peter, xiii, 3, 17, 25
Subscriptions
 Astronomical Journal, 58n2
 average, 19–20
 bundling of titles, 17, 24–25, 24n13,
 57
 cancellation of, 7–8, 35
 cooperative, 228
 corporate journals, 22
 inflation versus, 17
 JSTOR international fee structure,
 83n5
 licensing agreements, restrictive, 79
 open access, risk of, 61
 protests against, 24
 publishing costs and, 61–62
 quality versus, 20
 subscription rebuilding, cost of, 44
Subsidized open access
 The Alliance for Taxpayers Access,
 2n1
 economic model, 212t, 214–215
 Education Policy Analysis Archives,
 29–30, 50, 215
 First Monday, 6, 47n11, 212t
 House of Commons Science and
 Technology Committee, 3
 Public Library of Science (PLoS), 8
Surplus capacity, 83, 86, 88, 92
Susman, Thomas, 79
Sutton, Michael M. D., 139n10
Swaminathan, M. S., 98n4
Swan, Alma P., 20n9, 52, 53, 63

Tamber, Pritpal S., 18n6
Tartaglia, Niccolò, 192
Teachers College Record, 50, 50n13
"Teacher's exception" principle, 46
Teferra, Damtew, 97
Tenagantia, 144
Tenopir, Carol, 14, 14n2, 56, 70, 71,
 156n3, 170, 230
Testa, James, 180–181
Thapa, Neelam, 14